LAST BOAT FROM BORDEAUX

For Molly & Mike,
With fond memories of our barge trips on "Napoleon" and "Nenuphar" in 1999 + 2001 and looking forward to future ones.

July 5, 2001

Francis de Marneffe, arriving in England from France, June 1940.

LAST BOAT FROM BORDEAUX

War Memoirs of Francis de Marneffe

Coolidge Hill Press
Cambridge, Massachusetts

Copyright 2001 by Francis de Marneffe
All rights reserved. No part of this book may be transmitted in any form
by any means without permission in writing from the publisher.

Designed by Jill Shaffer
Printed in the United States of America
First Printing, April 2001

ISBN 0-9709515-0-7

Coolidge Hill Press
126 Coolidge Hill
Cambridge, MA 02138

For my children:

Peter, Daphne, and Colette.

With all my love and pride
and admiration for who you are
and what you have accomplished.

And also for my grandchildren:

Sophia, Elias, Alexander, Delia, Shane,
Nicholas, Francesca, and Caroline.

With all my love and hope that
you will meet life's challenges with
courage, determination, and confidence,
whatever the circumstances.

TABLE OF CONTENTS

List of Illustrations ix

Acknowledgments xi

Preface xiii

CHAPTER I My Early Years 1

CHAPTER II The Phony War 21
September 1, 1939–May 10, 1940

CHAPTER III The German Attack 27
Brussels: May 10–15, 1940

CHAPTER IV Escape from Belgium 37
May 15–June 23, 1940

CHAPTER V The English Schoolboy 91
June 1940–January 1943

CHAPTER VI My Service in the Royal Air Force 119
January 19, 1943–October 1, 1945

CHAPTER VII Medical School 151
October 1945–July 1950

CHAPTER VIII Postgraduate Training 163
July 1950–January 1953

Postscript 175

APPENDIX A How My Family Learned about My Travels in France and Arrival in England 179

APPENDIX B Robert's 1940 Journey 185

APPENDIX C My Family's Life under German Occupation, 1940–44 187

APPENDIX D The Belgian Government's Dilemma: Loyalty to King or Country? 199

About the Author 205

LIST OF ILLUSTRATIONS

Arriving in England from France, June 1940 . . . . . . frontispiece

My mother's family, Manor House, Wardington, England, circa 1890 xvi

Sir Hilgrove Turner 2

The Manor House, Wardington, 1994 3

My mother in the *Illustrated London News,* circa 1912 4

My father as a Belgian Army colonel, in 1932, age 58 6

My mother in 1932, age 50 9

Three weeks old, at the Boat Club, May 1924 10

In a single scull, age 10 11

My brother Robert, age 12½ 13

The author, age 4½ 14

My sister Pauline, age 9½ 15

Figure 1. Map of my journey from Brussels to England, May-June 1940 39

Figure 2. Pass issued in Blaringhem, France 44

Figure 3. Railway voucher from Belgian Consulate, Rouen 51

Figure 4. Receipt for bicycle to be sold, Rouen 54

Figure 5. Pass from Monsieur Gutt, Poitiers 76

Figure 6. British boarding pass for SS *Mariva,* Bordeaux 82

Nut Tree Cottage, Bloxham, Banbury, Oxfordshire 92

Arriving in England, June 1940 93
The English Schoolboy 97
Aunt Cary Schuster, age 90 104
With Etienne Gutt, Bloxham, 1942 109
Figure 7. Letter of January 18, 1943 from M. Gutt 113
Figure 8. Letter of January 26, 1943 from M. Gutt 116
Formation flying, Canada, 1944 129
British Military Cemetery, St. Manvieux, near Caen (France) 131
François Gutt's grave 132
Pilot officer in the Royal Air Force, September 1944 134
Informal RAF photo, Bloxham, Spring 1945 142
HRH Princess Elizabeth presenting Wyfold Cup to the King's College Crew, Henley Royal Regatta, 1946 153
The Thames Rowing Club Grand Challenge Cup Crew, Henley, 1947 157
My parents at Bloxham, 1946 159
My parents in Brussels, in the late 1940s 160
The de Marneffe family coat of arms 177

ACKNOWLEDGMENTS

THIS IS THE PLACE to acknowledge the contributions of many people to the book.

But since there would have been no memoir had I not lived to "tell the tale," I want first of all to recognize my parents, who prepared me to cope with the dramatic events recorded herein.

It was thanks to the kindness of many people—some of them named in the text, others whose names I never knew—that I eventually arrived in England. I owe a special debt of gratitude to the Gutt family, without whose help I probably would not have reached England.

It is obvious from the text that I also owe undying thanks to my English family, and especially my Aunts Dorothy and Katherine, for taking care of me during the war.

With respect to these memoirs specifically, I always thought that someday I would write them. I was encouraged in this by the comments of the many people who seemed interested in my story.

My wife Bobbie was the greatest source of encouragement and she also helped with her advice and suggestions, as well as being the faithful reader of the manuscript. Over the past thirty years, she must have heard this story hundreds of times, yet she always encouraged me to tell it again.

A strong motivation for writing this memoir was the feeling that I had not adequately informed my children about my early life. I hope this account will in some way make up for that omission.

Since I do not know how to type, I was very dependent on people who did (and would): Dale Swett, whom I first met at McLean Hospital, typed several chapters, and I am deeply grateful to her, especially since she transcribed what I dictated onto a tape and saved me from having to try and write legibly.

Laurin Holmes, also formerly from McLean, typed a number of the appendices.

Additionally, I thank my friend Rob Trowbridge of Yankee Publishing Inc. in Dublin, New Hampshire, through whom I found Benjamin Watson, who edited this manuscript. Under his expert eye and hand it began to take on the appearance of a book. He was meticulous in many ways, and particularly in questioning the correct spellings of strange towns and words. I learned a lot from him during this first writing attempt, and it has been fun working with him.

Through Ben I found the help of Jill Shaffer for the design of the pages and the cover, and the scanning and placement of the photos.

I also want to acknowledge the contribution of countless, marvelous people who showed an interest in my origins in Belgium, my adventure in France on the way to England, and my life in England. Depending on the circumstances, I gave them a short or longer (sometimes too long) version of the story. Sometimes they asked me if I had written all of this down. Well, now I have.

One such person was my friend Kim Prince, who one evening in August 1999, over dinner in Dublin, New Hampshire, wanted to hear my story. As I wrapped up my probably too long tale with the statement that I was lucky to have caught the last boat from Bordeaux, he said, "That's it! That is the title of your book." And so it is.

Thank you to one and all.

PREFACE

DECADES HAVE PASSED since the German Army invaded Belgium on May 10, 1940. Yet for me, a 16-year-old boy living in Brussels with my family at the time, that momentous event and what followed are indelibly imprinted on my memory. I have led a very full life, but very few events, have had the impact on me, my personality and life which those cataclysmic months in 1940 had. I was suddenly plunged from the security and safety of family life into the chaos of a bigger world and had to fend for myself in order to survive.

I have always thought that leaving my family and home on May 15, 1940 on my bicycle, journeying through Belgium and France, pursued by the German Army, and eventually arriving in England on June 20 was the most dramatic and in some respects most interesting period of my life. It is not surprising, therefore, that in subsequent years when someone asked me about myself it was always with enthusiasm, mixed with pride (sometimes hidden under a cloak of shyness) that I would recount my "escape story" as it came to be called by my children.

My children, in fact, are one of the main reasons for writing this book. From time to time during their lives they have asked about my earlier years and escape from Belgium, and I feel I have short-changed them—that I have not always recounted those events as fully to them as I have to others. Therefore, they have been somewhat less informed about their father's doings in 1940 than others have, and I have decided to remedy this by writing this memoir.

Another reason is that when I retired as General Director of McLean Hospital in 1987, I decided to write for the hospital's archives several chapters on various aspects of McLean and my directorship. Often my friends and colleagues thought of me as a survivor of many professional crises. Reflecting upon these professional experiences I realized that my will and ability to survive was developed at a very early age, and these qualities proved of inestimable value in my escape from Belgium.

Yet another reason is that I have reached a point in my life where there is a certain inner peace, and I have come to terms with myself more than before. I think I am better able now to view my life journey with some perspective. For some years now, I have been savoring the anticipation of looking back on those weeks when I was 16 and wondering whether I would feel differently than I did then, and also wanting to review those events in the context of my later experiences.

I have been encouraged by my wife Bobbie to write this memoir. She has been telling me for years that "you know so much and you had so much experience that you really ought to write." I have never quite believed her, whether out of laziness or humility, I am not sure. But on this occasion her encouragement as well as the other reasons mentioned above, have finally prompted me to put pen to paper.

As a child I had from time to time kept a diary, but this was a sporadic exercise usually confined to recounting my travels or my vacations. However, on May 10, 1940, I started keeping my "war diary" on a daily basis. In it, I wrote what had happened during the day, whom I was with, and even something of my feelings. Since after the first four days of war I was on my own, my family having stayed behind in Brussels, I was also keeping a diary as a means of eventually (after the war) conveying to my parents, my brother and sister what had happened to me. Later still, when I was in the Royal Air Force, I thought of my diary as a means of communicating with them in the event of my death.

Writing in my diary was often done at moments when I was alone and feeling lonely, and recounting the events and feelings of the moment provided a necessary catharsis and a tonic for my spirits. I have used my diary to refresh my memory and to recapture some of the events and moods of those times.

After I completed the main task of writing "my story," I realized that my children, who were the main audience for this effort, as I have said, as well as interested friends might be interested in a broader focus—the family context in which I grew up and even the family history, genealogy, and anecdotes which have contributed to our sense of who we are and where we came from. Therefore, I have expanded my comments about various family members, some of them long dead but important in the family history and myths, and also have included considerable background material in the Appendices.

My mother's family at the Manor House, Wardington, near Banbury, Oxfordshire, circa 1890.
BACK ROW: *My grandmother, Magdalene Loveday; Edward, eldest son; my grandfather, George Loveday*
MIDDLE ROW: *Arthur, Clement, Francis*
FRONT ROW: *Katherine, Pauline, Esther (my mother), Laura, Cecilia, Dorothy*

CHAPTER I

MY EARLY YEARS

I WAS BORN IN Brussels, Belgium at 103 Avenue Louise on May 7, 1924—a date which was to have a great deal of significance sixteen years later. My brother, Robert, had been born in 1919 and my sister Pauline in 1921. My father Armand, born in 1874, was a physician who had made his career in the Belgian Army Medical Corps and was, at the time of my birth, the director of the Military Hospital in Brussels with the rank of colonel. In spite of a family lineage that went back to 1103 and an aristocratic name, his origins were humble.[1] My grandfather, who lived to be 93, and who died in 1930, had been an employee of the Borough of Schaerbeek, a suburb of Brussels. My father did not often talk about his childhood and his family, but I think his was not a very happy childhood. He was very bright, a hard worker and a successful student, and by joining the army as a young man he ensured his medical education at government expense. By all accounts, he had a very successful army career, retiring in 1933 with the rank of major general.

My mother, Esther, was English by birth, one of ten children born to George and Magdalene (Turner)[2] Loveday at Wardington, near Banbury

---

[1] One of our earliest ancestors, Guillaume de Marneffe, went on the Second Crusade.

In 1925, on the occasion of the silver wedding anniversary of the King and Queen, a book was published in French, *The Belgian Blood & H.M. Albert I, King of the Belgians, Genealogical Study on the Belgian Ancestry of its King* and our family name can be found among many others. (See the de Marneffe family's coat of arms on page 177.)

[2] My great-great-grandfather, Tomkyns Hilgrove Turner (1764–1843) had a distinguished career in the British Army and at the Courts of George III, George IV, and William IV. In Egypt in 1801 as a Colonel in the Guards he was assigned the task of taking possession of the Rosetta Stone from the defeated French, who were reluctant to surrender it as required by the Treaty of Capitulation. He did so and escorted it to England on the frigate

in Oxfordshire in 1882. In contrast to my father's youth, my mother seemed to have had a very happy, almost idyllic life, and I remember her stories and reminiscences of life at the Manor House in Wardington playing with her many brothers and sisters. They belonged to the landed gentry, but Grandpapa, who died in 1907, was a dreamer and a poor manager of money, though well respected as a retired Proctor of Doctors Commons. He had legal training and served as a Justice of the Peace for many years. I only know him from family photographs as a rather stern-looking individual with a beard sitting with his family on the steps in front of the Manor House.

Sir Hilgrove Turner

The contrast between the life my mother had as a young girl and the life she led in Belgium always puzzled me. It was traditional in her family for the children to go abroad for their education; thus as I have always understood it she went to school at Les Peupliers in Vilvorde near Brussels and eventually returned as a teacher. When she graduated from Les Peupliers, which was a secondary school, she got two scholarships: one to the Brussels Conservatory of Music (she was apparently a very talented pianist) and one to the Royal Institute of Massage and Gymnastics in Stockholm (Sweden). She chose the latter and spent several years in Sweden, and when she graduated from the institute she returned to Les Peupliers as gymnastics teacher.

Sometime around 1908 she and my father must have met and found a similarity of professional interests. They were both athletic and did a good

---

Egyptienne. Knighted in 1815, General Sir Hilgrove Turner served as Lieutenant Governor of Jersey and from 1825–1832 as the Governor of the Bermuda Islands. He then was appointed groom of the bedchamber to William IV (as he had been previously to George IV). Upon the king's death in 1837, he returned to Jersey where he died in 1843. (From *Sir Hilgrove Turner—1764–1843—Soldier and Courtier under the Georges* by Arthur F. Loveday [my uncle], Alkham Press, 1964.)

Manor House, Wardington, near Banbury, Oxfordshire. Birthplace of my mother and her siblings, as it looked in 1994. Now the residence of Lord & Lady Wardington.

deal of sports. In many ways, my parents were ahead of their time in Belgium in their emphasis on sports, gymnastics, and encouraging initiative. Before World War I, my mother rode a motorcycle, and this was considered so unusual that a British magazine published her photograph. I suppose it was her relationship with my father which led her to remain in Belgium as well as her employment, though it is not clear to me whether their relationship continued throughout this period. I believe it did most of the time, but I remember vaguely hearing that at some point my mother had returned to Sweden to visit friends because of her disappointment that her relationship with my father seemed to be leading nowhere. In his younger years my father had a reputation as a dandy who always dressed very elegantly, and he was considered a very eligible bachelor.

The First World War began on August 4, 1914. At the time my father was in the Belgian Army and my mother was working in Brussels. In the initial part of the war my father served as a medical officer in one of the regiments at the front. He served with great distinction, receiving several citations and decorations. Eventually, because of his organizational skills,

A sportswoman in Belgium.—Miss E. Loveday.

Sport for ladies in Belgium is little known, and Miss E. Loveday, who has for some years resided in Brussels, is by way of being a pioneer for her sex in that health-giving field. As a high diver she has no lady rival in the Belgian capital, and is, perhaps, the only lady single sculler in the country, while, as well as skating a good deal, she creates something of a stir by riding a 4 cyl. F.N. motor-cycle

My mother was a most remarkable woman, ahead of her times, as noted in this photo and caption published in the Illustrated London News *circa 1912, when she was 30.*

he was appointed as the director of the Anglo-Belgian Military Hospital in Bon Secours near Rouen, France, where he could apply his special skills in rehabilitation. My mother, too, had exciting and dangerous war experiences. She continued to live and work as an Englishwoman in Brussels under the German occupation for many months. But she also crossed the German lines on several occasions, at tremendous risk, on her bicycle, sometime to convey messages to various people, but also to visit my father at his regiment. In the early 1930s she finally succumbed to the urgings of her sisters in England and wrote the story of her war adventures—a copy of which I have always treasured and which I have also given to each one of my children. She eventually joined my father at the hospital in Bon Secours, where, for the rest of the war, she applied her remedial skills in massage, physiotherapy, and gymnastics to the rehabilitation of the most severely wounded patients. My father received permission in the last few months of the war to leave the directorship of the hospital and rejoin his regiment as the final big offensive began, which eventually resulted in the German defeat in November 1918.

My parents were professional partners, colleagues as well as lovers. They were married in London on May 22, 1918 towards the end of the war. Their wedding day almost ended in tragedy. They had gone to a swimming pool in London and were practicing diving, a sport in which they both excelled and were nearly of championship caliber. Thinking that the depth of the water was marked in yards, if not in meters, my father dove and hit his head on the bottom of the pool. The depth, of course, had been marked in feet. Twenty years later, diving from a bridge in Belgium into the canal at Lanklaer in the Campine, he did exactly the same thing. He was lucky to have survived both accidents. At Lanklaer it was fortunate he did not pass out and drown. I remember he had a large flap of skin detached from his scalp which had to be sutured at a doctor's office.

When the war ended in 1918, my parents settled in Brussels at 103 Avenue Louise, where we children were born. In addition to working at the Military Hospital in Brussels, my father did some private practice in physiotherapy, medical massage, and gymnastics, and my mother of course was the expert in this field. In 1929 we moved to Number 497 on the avenue. Avenue Louise was probably the "best" address in Brussels. It was a wide, divided avenue with horse chestnut trees on both sides, and a central grassy area adorned by statues and flower beds. There was a path for bicycles and one for horses. Our house, at the corner of the Rue Emile Claus, was two blocks from the entrance of the Bois de la Cambre, famous for its beautiful trees, bridle paths, small restaurants, and playgrounds. In the middle of it was a small lake with a restaurant on an island at its center, reached by a small hand-operated ferry. Beyond the Bois lay the extensive Forêt de Soignes.

Our house was a typical five-story brick building: rather narrow, but very deep and with very high ceilings. From the front hall a door led into the basement, where the extensive kitchens, which extended to the back of the house were located. A wide stairway of white marble led to the mezzanine (entre-sol) floor, which was the professional level, with a waiting room for my parents' clients in the front end and a large room beyond filled with instruments and appliances necessary for massage, medical rehabilitation, physiotherapy, electrotherapy, etc.

On the next level were located my father's study, with a balcony overlooking the avenue in the front, our dining room, and the "games" room, where the children kept their toys and played. The level above this was the bedroom level: my brother's, my parents', mine, and a guest room, which was initially my sister's. The top floor consisted of my sister's room and an attic for storage. At the back of the house there was a one-car, two-story garage beyond a small yard.

My father's career was in the Belgian Army Medical Corps. Here he is as a Colonel, aged 58 in 1932 before his retirement as a general, with his World War I medals and one civilian medal awarded by the King for rescuing, with my mother, a drowning couple who fell off a pleasure boat on the Meuse in the Ardennes.

Because both my parents worked full-time professionally for most of my years in Belgium, we had a number of servants—usually a cook and two maids. Until 1933, when my father retired from the army, he had an orderly who came to the house every day and did various chores such as washing our car and servicing our bicycles. My parents did not own our house—it was leased—and periodically we thought we might have to move, but in fact they occupied it until the late 1940s, after the end of the war.

A building they did own was the gymnasium located about two miles from our house. Here, Swedish gymnastic classes were given three evenings a week, at first by my mother, but eventually by a graduate of the school my parents had founded. I began gym classes at the age of three and continued for the next thirteen years, until I left home. No doubt the rigorous gymnastics training I and my siblings participated in has been responsible for our athletic successes in later life.

A dumbwaiter connected the kitchen in the basement with the dining room on the third floor. Lunch was the main meal of the day and was served between 12:00 and 2:00 P.M., at which time we had to be back in school. A maid stood by the dumbwaiter and placed the dishes next to my mother, who served each of us.

The evening meal was much less formal. I often had supper alone or with Tante Jeanne, my father's maiden sister, because my parents were still at their gym class when I had returned home from mine. As I thought of my parents in later years, they seemed a strange combination in some respects. My father was stern, autocratic, opinionated, restless, and somewhat lacking in sensitivity, yet also action-oriented and a first-rate planner and administrator. Honesty, integrity, self-reliance, and independence were the virtues he favored.[3] For some peculiar reason he seemed to place a higher premium on physical fitness and prowess than on the development of the intellect. To me he conveyed the idea that school was less important than the gym or athletics. Therefore, getting by with a minimum exertion at school was my objective. He did not encourage learning particularly. Somehow, I developed the strange idea that real learning would begin when I went to university at the age of 18 and that, until then, coasting by on one's innate intelligence and developing one's athletic prowess was more important. This emphasis on physical training seemed to be based on the idea that one's body should be developed while growing, whereas one's brain could develop later! It was also a surprising notion coming from him because he was widely read, attended many lectures with my mother, and encouraged our intellectual development through many family travels and visits to museums. I think he was rather

[3] A striking example of his integrity is this following event. He and my mother were teachers at a gymnastics and massage school. He had failed one of the students in her final exam, but was asked by the director to reverse his decision and pass her because she was the daughter of a Board Member. He refused and instead resigned from the school, taking three-quarters of the faculty with him to found a new school, the École Medicale de Massage et de Gymnastique, which was still in existence until recently.

selfish and self-centered: the family did what he decreed we would do. There was no living room in the house; *his* study was where the family gathered at odd moments. Feelings did not seem very important to him. I did not feel a great deal of warmth emanating from him. Yet, as the years went by, I recognized that, under his rather gruff exterior, my father was a very emotional and sentimental man—on Mother's Day, for instance, a tear would come to his eyes as he read a poem from the newspaper.

In retrospect I think that, in spite of my father's great achievements in the sporting, professional, and military worlds, there lurked within him a great sense of inadequacy and insecurity. He seemed to have few friends that I could see. An occasional person or couple would flit in and out of our lives for a brief period of time, but they were not his social, intellectual, or professional peers. He had no appreciation of music. The moment the news program ended on the radio and music began again he switched it off, sometimes quoting King Leopold II of the Belgians, who once said that "music is the most expensive way of making noise." At school I got no encouragement to study history or drawing or music. Yet he claimed to be an intellectual.

It seems that, for my father, life was a constant struggle to avoid being corrupted, overly influenced, or controlled by other people. As a result, he cut himself off from others. I have never solved this puzzle about him because as a young man I think he was gregarious, enjoyed social life and playing cards. He did, however, in later years enjoy going to restaurants and the theater, and he was in some ways interested in the arts, to the extent that he went to many museums and took us with him. He also had a good sense of humor, which his three children inherited. He used to cut out jokes from the weekly *Pourquoit Pas?* and paste them in a scrapbook, which I read from time to time. I can still remember some of the jokes.

I think my father was in some ways and at times an unhappy man. I remember an occasion in the 1930s when he was quite depressed and crying. My mother worried he might harm himself and she took a revolver away from him. As a retired army officer he had two revolvers, one of which he kept in the glove compartment of his car. Another story I heard was that, when my mother and father had been sculling on the canal before World War I, Belgian peasants took a dim view of a woman doing sport and they tried to drop heavy stones on the boat as my parents were sculling under a bridge. From then on, for a while, my father took his revolver in the boat and fired it a few times in the air, threatening the peasants as they prepared to attack them. It is still a mystery to me why my father was so depressed at that time. It was never, to my knowledge talked about in the family. Was it related to his financial situation, to his retirement from the army a few years previously, to his work, or to his relationship to his family? I do not know.

Although totally areligious, my father took us to visit many churches, but wholly from the standpoint of looking at the art. And yet he was also a compassionate man. I remember that, during the Depression in the thirties he decided to have all his paperback books bound in hardcover in order to give work to a man who was an intelligent, unemployed professional.

A formal photo of my mother, age 50, in 1932, wearing her World War I medals and one civilian medal awarded by the King for rescuing, with my father, a drowning couple who fell off a pleasure boat on the Meuse in the Ardennes.

Mother, on the other hand, was a rather gentle soul. Although a successful professional, she had a certain softness, generosity, humility, and sensitivity. I think of her as an idealist with compassion and tenderness towards the underdog. I think she thought of herself as a bit naive, not quite as smart in the ways of the world as she should have been—an image of herself which my father tended to encourage and believe in. I think she was rather sad and wistful.

Years later I talked to my brother about my parents in my attempt to understand this rather improbable couple. It seemed to us that at some point my mother had surrendered her individuality and her personality; that she had decided that in order to be married to my father she would have to suppress many aspects of her personality and simply let him run the show. I wondered how someone who loved to draw and who had won a scholarship to the conservatory as a talented pianist, could put up with someone who in some ways denigrated art and music.

Both my parents were devoted to their children. They strongly believed that most of our childhood should be spent together as a family. Therefore our leisure time was always considered family time. As far back as I can remember, Thursday afternoon (which was a half-day holiday at school), Saturday afternoon, and most of Sunday were spent at the Boat Club on the Canal de Willebroeck. In fact I have a photograph taken of me when I was three weeks old lying on the grass at the club in the shade of one of the boats. Our whole social life seemed to be centered on the Boat Club. I learned to swim when I was five and a half, and I began to row in a single sculling boat on the canal when I was six. We played basketball and tennis, and went kayaking and swimming—all at the Boat Club. Our whole life was very physical. I used to envy other children: they seemed to play together and see each other outside of school, but not us.

My life at the Boat Club began very early, 3 weeks old, Brussels, May 1924.

We went to the Boat Club three times a week in all weather—here I am, age 10, sculling on the canal in Brussels.

We were made to feel that *their* parents did not care as much as ours did because *they* did not do things with their children all the time. Because Robert had at one time joined the Boy Scouts and Pauline the Girl Scouts, and had not liked it, I was discouraged from joining the Scouts, even though I wanted to.

My parents were very possessive and protective and believed firmly that we were *lucky* to have parents who spent so much of their time with their children rather than being like so many other children whose parents did not arrange an interesting life for them and who therefore had nothing else to do but to be with their friends. I believe they were well-meaning and that in some ways they were ahead of their times. They believed very firmly in the principle of a healthy mind in a healthy body, and they knew that Belgium was a rather backwards country as far as physical exercise and sports were concerned.

What I missed most in my childhood were friends. But I must not be too harsh in judging my parents, for they gave me much. They inculcated in us firm principles of honesty and integrity, of work, professional achievement, and even—though I used to complain of the weekly routine of going to the Boat Club—my lifelong devotion to physical fitness, exercise, rowing, and swimming derive directly from them. The successful careers of their three children is clear evidence that they did many things right! My mother particularly was quite self-sacrificing. She was often quite willing to put herself at great discomfort in order to make life better for both her husband and her children.

They were both very liberal in their political views and supported liberal causes. *Le Peuple*, the Socialist newspaper, was daily reading fare, along with *Le Soir*, the national newspaper. Politically, we were brought up to be anti-fascists, supporting Ethiopia against Italy, the Loyalists in Spain against General Franco, etc. We were also brought up totally without religion. None of us was baptized, even though my father had been baptized as a Catholic and my mother in the Church of England. While they preached tolerance for other political and religious beliefs, the net result of the family conversation was that the Roman Catholic Church and the Catholic Party in Belgium had done some pretty bad things, and that Belgian democracy and freedom were not quite safe in their hands. The glaring exception was in the middle thirties when the Catholic Prime Minister Paul van Zeeland defeated Leon Degrelle the Fascist (Rexist) leader in an election. My parents were Freemasons, quite actively so, and I found their devotion to it (when I learned something about their secret society) rather puzzling at the time. It seemed to me strangely at odds with some of their other attitudes, and I felt that they were as religious in their anti-clericalism as religious people are in the pursuit of their religion. At the time I espoused their views, but as the years went by I think I missed the lack of religious upbringing. It was symptomatic of our rootlessness. We did not belong to any group except the Boat Club. Compared to many people's parents mine were extremely successful, yet as I grew up I always felt inferior. I did not do well at school, and avoiding having to repeat grades or having to repeat exams in the summer seemed the only goal. I did not feel that intellectual pursuits were encouraged and we did not have friends. Birthdays were celebrated "en famille," but with no birthday party with friends of one's own age.

The thirties were hard on our family from the financial point of view. My father had lent money to his wartime military cook to start a hotel at St. Idesbald on the coast. The man went bankrupt and absconded with some of the furnishings. To recoup his losses, in self-defense my father bought the hotel at auction. In the early years it was a financial drain, and so was the drop in the stock market, and he sold much of what he had. But it turned out to have been a good financial investment after all after the war.

My brother Robert, at 12½, May 1932.

As a child, I was a gentle, sensitive person. From my mother I inherited a sympathy for the underdog. When I was quite young I joined the Society for the Prevention of Cruelty to Animals and read their magazine for many years. Later was added to this a great compassion and sympathy during the Spanish Civil War for the Spanish refugees and especially the children. I sold pencils and calendars for the benefit of the Spanish children who were refugees in Belgium. I had a feeling that my father was somewhat cynical about such activities. He was quick to feel taken advantage of and seemed to think that to avoid being made a fool of was of paramount importance. I think he thought that my mother was an easy mark for manipulators who played on her sentimentality towards the deprived. Yet he was very dependent upon my mother, though he never quite admitted it.

As I look back on my life, I can see that I was quite lonely as a child, and did not feel that I quite fit in anywhere. I kept much of what I felt inside; I noticed a lot, but was afraid of expressing it much of the time. My father was to me a rather frightening and forbidding person. He expected obedience and did not like us to argue or disagree with him. My brother was more daring than I was, and he used to have intense arguments with my father. He had the guts to stand up to my father and occasionally was punished for it. I did not stand up to him until after the war, and I often used my mother as a go-between, a mediator on whom I relied to try and get the best deal for me possible. And she did this quite often. I think I traded on my being the youngest child and felt that as such I had a special relationship to her. Before the age of five I remember treasuring the moments at home when my brother and sister were already attending school. I wished my mother were at home more often, but unfortunately she was engaged in her professional life and English nannies took care of me as they had Robert and Pauline. We were brought up bilingually in French and in English, and I used to pride myself on being able to speak English. Only later did I realize that my English was not as perfect as I had thought. We attended state schools, that is, public schools, in the American sense of the word. I went to primary school in St. Gilles, a borough of Brussels, and to secondary school in Uccle. I did not like school, and I don't think any of my classmates did, either. I was amazed when, years later, my children were attending Shady Hill School in Cambridge, Massachusetts, to note their enthusiasm and eagerness to be in school. This was, for me, a completely new experience: imagine, a child liking school!

Francis de Marneffe, age 4½.

Because of my closeness in age to my older sister, I had a closer relationship to her than I did to my brother. But we all got on well with each other. We spent a great deal of time together, since most of our activities were done as a whole family. Because my brother was a few years older, during vacations he went to England more often than my sister and I did, and that left Pauline and me to do things together. My brother was a very responsible individual who, from a young age, developed great technical skills. In later years he became an outstanding orthopedic surgeon and professor at the University of Brussels. He was warm and friendly and caring and took responsibility for his younger siblings, although there were not too many opportunities to do that since my parents fulfilled that role to the greatest extent. I think I felt closer to Pauline, partly because of the closeness in age, but also because we shared more activities together. Not only did we go on vacations together, with or without our parents, but also some of the sporting activities were done together. My parents believed that it was important for us to learn how to box and, therefore, even though Pauline was a girl, she used to take lessons in boxing—that is, before puberty—and she and I would have boxing bouts under the supervision of our boxing coach, Mr. Alexander.

My sister Pauline, age 9½, January 1931.

From a very young age, I thought I would become a doctor. Like everyone else I had gone through the stages of wanting to be a policeman or a fireman, but deep down I knew it would be medicine in the end, probably because of the strong impression my father made on me, and also because it seemed inevitable that Robert and Pauline's destinies would also be in the medical profession.

But for many years I also had fantasies of escaping the limits and rigidities of my existence. I was very conscious that beyond the confines of Belgium there was a big world where many interesting things were going on. I did not take much pride in being Belgian or in Belgian history. I was very much aware that half of me was English, with a long tradition and history one could be proud of. Sometimes I even resented that my mother had not married an Englishman, thereby depriving me of my

English birthright! I read widely in British history, including accounts of some of the naval and military battles England had won. In my early teens I remember discussing with my mother what possibilities there might be of my joining the Royal Navy and, when that proved impossible, my attention turned, however briefly, towards the French Navy. Adventure seemed to have an irresistible appeal for me. Nowadays I would tend to think of it in retrospect as an escape from the loneliness and sadness of my youth.

My parents arranged interesting vacations for us. Almost every year we went somewhere different. Every summer we went to the beach for two or three weeks at St. Idesbald at the hotel that my father eventually bought. Often we also went to England for two or three weeks to visit some of our relatives. Robert usually went to stay with my mother's eldest sister—actually a half sister—Aunt Cary Schuster, at Yeldall in Berkshire. And later on he stayed at her house called Bulwell, also in Berkshire: sometimes Pauline and I would go also. Other times we were traveling around in Belgium. Pauline sometimes went to visit a first cousin, Meg, in Somerset. Pauline and I went, two years running, to a camp in England, and then in the late thirties, when my Aunts Dorothy and Katherine had moved from London, we went to Nut Tree Cottage at Bloxham, near Banbury in Oxfordshire. And there we played, swam, worked on a farm and rode horses. In looking at the diary I kept of my vacations, when I was in grade school: in 1933, when I was nine, Robert, Pauline, and I went with Mother to England—Robert going to Yeldall and my sister and I going to camp at the Dunlops. For that Christmas we went to Elsenborn in the eastern part of Belgium and went skiing. Then in 1937, when I was 13 the whole family went bicycling for two weeks in the Grand Duchy of Luxembourg and at Christmas of '37 we went skiing in Austria. At Christmas of 1938 we went skiing in Switzerland and at Easter 1938 the family went bicycling in Holland, staying in youth hostels. At Easter of 1939 we went to visit the Chateaux de la Loire in France.

But I remember clearly that, during my vacations in England, I always felt that something was missing. I felt very acutely (and perhaps excessively) that my parents were making a great financial sacrifice to make it possible for us to go on these trips, and this interfered with my enjoyment.

At the end of every day, I would ask myself if I had enjoyed myself as much as I should and seldom answered yes. Then I would count the days remaining of the vacation, hoping that I could make up for it during the balance of the days! Returning home I often felt that my vacation had been a disappointment. These feelings were particularly strong when I was in England and that is why when, years later, I arrived in England during the war it was such a relief and I loved it. Because then I could say to myself that I was there because of the war and it was an open-ended thing, and that therefore the oppressive burden of having to have a good time was lifted off my shoulders. Some of the vacations in England were spent with my parents. Once we spent two weeks living in a converted railway carriage near Coltishall in Norfolk. The trips were planned meticulously by my father with maps and guidebooks galore. Little was left to chance—a tendency which, for better or for worse, I seem to have inherited. My father was very knowledgeable about architecture and where the various artworks were located. Yet he did not succeed in inspiring in me the same interests, at least at that time and for many years afterwards. On the way to the beach, which would normally take two, three, or four hours at the most, he would make a whole-day affair of it, stopping at every museum and every church on the way. At the time I found it incredibly boring. I was much more interested in looking around at other people than at listening to my father's monotonous reading from the Baedecker or other guidebooks. He loved to read *the description* of what we were looking at. I was more interested in the history and the development of what we were looking at and the people who had been involved in it. But that he left out. I can't begin to count the number of museums across Europe we visited, in which my main objective was to find a comfortable bench in the middle of the display room. I was bored and tired. It was only many years later, when I married Bobbie, that I learned the enjoyment of looking at works of art and trying to understand them in the context of the culture in which they were created.

"The War" loomed very large in my childhood. With great frequency my parents' conversation would be loaded with references to "The War," that is, the First World War. I remember wondering why they were still living so much in the past. Reference to the war had a frightening, ominous ring to it, and of course some of my childhood reading involved stories and histories about the war. The hated Germans and the Kaiser; the brave English, French, and Belgian troops; American generosity; the death and destruction. This last was very vivid to us because, on our way to the beach every year on our annual vacation, we visited some of the scenes of the battles and the towns which had been destroyed and were now rebuilt: Ypres, Dixmude, Nieuport, La Panne, etc. Thinking now about those years, what is most surprising is the change in my perspective about time. When I think that more than sixty years have passed since war came to Belgium for the second time in 1940, and how fresh and recent are my recollections of those events, it is hardly surprising that my parents and their friends should have still been so preoccupied about their recollections of the war, and its aftermath a mere decade after 1918, when the war ended.

War was something very real to me, not just something I read about in books, but something my parents had lived and still talked about, and the evidence of which was everywhere around me as I moved around Belgium and France.

From a very young age I was interested in the world around me: in politics, the government, international affairs, and history. I remember reading the almanacs published by *Le Soir*, the national daily newspaper, which contained the dates and events of the previous year, obituaries, significant events, and so on. I think this interest must have started even before I was ten years of age. I remember reading about the skirmishes between the Japanese and the Chinese; the Lindbergh kidnapping; the purge trials in the USSR; and the election of Adolf Hitler as Chancellor of Germany in 1933, when I was only nine. The death of King Albert I in a climbing accident in 1934 is very vivid in my mind, as is also the death in 1935 of Queen Astrid. I read voraciously about all kinds of current events, but what I think galvanized me into more serious and consistent reading was the reoccupation of the Rhineland by the German Army on March 7, 1936. On the day it happened, I remember being at the dinner table and my father saying, with heavy foreboding, "I think we shall have another World War within ten years." This was a shattering, electrifying statement. Since the time I was born there had been talk about the Great War, the "war to end all wars": the importance of collective security, the

League of Nations, the appalling results of the war. Germany was supposed to have been defeated and disarmed, and the Allies were supposedly the victors, and yet here was my father predicting another war with Germany! From then on I followed the zigzags of international affairs in great detail and with great zest. I read two newspapers a day as well as magazines and books. Somehow I needed to know and find out why war was going to come. The prospect of war was both frightening and fascinating. Yet the horror of what war might be like was not real to me. The opportunities for adventure, for heroism—these were the real things. I became a serious student of the League of Nations and followed closely the Abyssinian War and the Spanish Civil War. Each year brought new evidence of the German danger. We could not yet believe, however, how helpless the democracies were going to be.

The Anschluss, the annexation of Austria by Germany, was an ominous sign in 1938. Then the pressure began on Czechoslovakia: Heinlein, the Sudetenland. We, Pauline and I, were in England that summer of 1938, staying at Bloxham with Aunts Dorothy and Katherine. War seemed very close. There was something unreal about the whole episode. I was afraid of war, yes—but also excited and fascinated by the possibility of adventure, that something would happen in my life to relieve the monotony, the dullness of everyday life. When I went back to Brussels and the crisis was continuing, the Belgian Army was mobilized, and I remember going about a mile away from our house to the Belgian Army barracks to watch and absorb the atmosphere of crisis and mobilization that was taking place. But then the crisis passed, with Neville Chamberlain, the British prime minister, going to Munich and meeting Edouard Daladier (the French prime minister), Hitler, and Mussolini and averting war as a result of the Munich Agreement. "Peace with honor?" The relief at having escaped a disaster was offset by the sense that an ally, Czechoslovakia, had been betrayed and sold down the river. Perhaps there was also a certain disappointment at being deprived of the adventure of war.

Then a new year, 1939, began and on the Ides of March, March 15, the German Army occupied the whole of Czechoslovakia. At last Hitler was seen by everyone for what he was—an insatiable, ruthless aggressor, determined to take over Europe. Belatedly England and France signed a mutual defense treaty with Poland. Germany wanted Danzig and started its propaganda war of intimidation.

Again in the summer of 1939 we went to England. A school friend of mine, Jacques Piraux, went to Bloxham with me, and Pauline went to visit Meg in Somerset. Robert visited Aunt Cary for the tenth year in a row. Did we realize then that the world would never be the same again after that summer? I don't remember. I know we had a sense of moving inexorably towards war. The "miracle" of Munich could not be repeated again. England and France had positioned themselves, figuratively speaking, across the path of Germany. Would Germany hold back? Would the USSR make a difference? On August 23, 1939 we had our answer: Hitler and Stalin had signed a non-aggression pact. Unbelievable!

On September 1, the German Army invaded Poland. On September 3, England and France declared war on Germany. The die was cast.

CHAPTER II

THE PHONY WAR
September 1, 1939 – May 10, 1940

IN THE LAST FEW DAYS of peace, events moved at a rapid pace. There was a great deal of international activity: messages were sent by President Roosevelt to many countries; the Pope spoke from the Vatican; all hoped that the European powers could avert war. Even though Poland was invaded at dawn on September 1, 1939, and the British and French governments were committed to helping Poland, there was a puzzling delay in the British and French declarations of war. Subsequently we learned that the delay was on the French side, and that is why the British declaration of war on Germany was made several hours before the French.

The 3rd of September was a Sunday and, as usual, we went to the Boat Club. I remember standing next to a radio at eleven o'clock that morning and listening to the doleful voice of Neville Chamberlain, the British prime minister. He announced that, since no reply had been received to the British ultimatum requiring the Germans to stop fighting in Poland, a state of war now existed between Great Britain and Germany.

The words "phony war" have been applied to the next several months of the war because this was indeed a relatively quiet time, at least in Western Europe. There were, however, many events that occurred during this period which gradually prepared us for the tragedies and carnage of the future. Poland, of course, bore the brunt of it: invaded and bombed, not only by the Germans, but also from the east by the Russian Army. On September 4 the ship *Athenia*, a passenger ship having 1,400 people on board, including 350 Americans and Canadians, was torpedoed by a German submarine. Most of the passengers were saved, except for those actually killed by the explosion. Although there were some raids by the Royal Air Force on Germany (most of them actually dropping propaganda pamphlets), and the war in Poland continued for a few weeks before the Poles were defeated, on the whole there was something unreal about this period, because after the total occupation of Poland things quieted down. One couldn't help wondering what was going to happen next, and when and if the real war would start. The Belgian Army had indeed been mobilized to some extent, but not completely. My life continued pretty much as before: I continued to go to school, and we still went to the Boat Club three times a week. During this time I used to go sculling in a double scull with Etienne Gutt, the son of the Belgian finance minister. He was a little younger than I, but we enjoyed each other's company, and my friendship with him and his family turned out to be a godsend in later years.

My friendship with Etienne began in 1938 as a result of my brother Robert sculling with his brother, François, in a crew of the Brussels University Boat Club. They had entered some regattas, and Madame Gutt thought sculling would be good also for her youngest son, Etienne. His father, Camille Gutt, was a very distinguished man who was born in 1884; he was a lawyer as well as a specialist in political science. He had been a journalist earlier in his career, and had served as chief of staff until 1925 to George Theunis, a former prime minister. He then became minister of finance of Belgium from 1934 to 1935 and again in 1939. He did not belong to a political party and he was described as a "technician," that is, an expert in financial matters as opposed to a politician. My relationship with the Gutt family would later become crucial to my future, as will be seen in these memoirs.

I followed the developments of the war very closely at this time, identified with the British cause, read voraciously everything I could lay my hands on, and followed very closely the movements of the German Army in Poland. I also kept a diary, not so much reflecting what I myself was doing as listing the highlights of world events and also sticking in news articles from the newspapers.

We were reassured by the fact that Winston Churchill had, on the first day of the war, been reappointed First Lord of the Admiralty—the same job he had had in the First World War. We were great admirers of Winston Churchill because we saw him as a man of remarkable vision, who had read correctly the intentions and ambitions of Hitler's Germany. He had been pleading for years for Britain and the Allies to rearm and prepare themselves for war. He believed that only if the Allies were strong and determined was there any possibility of dissuading Hitler from embarking upon another World War.

Much of the war activity during this period took place at sea. In December the German pocket battleship *Graf Spee* was cornered by British ships and took refuge in Montevideo in the River Plate off the coast of Uruguay in South America. Eventually, after being told by the Uruguayan authorities that he had to leave, Captain Langsdorf, the captain of the *Graf Spee*, sailed out of the port and scuttled his ship, going down with her himself. A German submarine found it possible to enter the British naval base of Scapa Flow in Scotland and sink a British capital ship, the *Royal Oak*. Also during this period, a British naval ship entered Norwegian territorial waters and boarded the *Altmark*, a German ship that contained 300 British sailors who were prisoners of war; there was a big hullabaloo about this because supposedly the British had violated Norwegian territorial waters to achieve this rescue. The British response was that Norwegian neutrality had already been violated by the German ship.

The naval war touched our family very personally because my first cousin, John Loveday, the son of Aunt Lilias and my Uncle Francis Loveday (after whom I was named, and who had died as a result of World War I), was an officer in the Royal Navy and was lost at sea. In January, my mother had tried to find out what ship John was serving on, and she had received a letter from Aunt Lilias saying that he was serving on the destroyer "HMS_______________." The name of the destroyer had been cut out by the British censors before the letter left England. On the 24th of January 1940, we read in the Belgian newspaper under a headline that the British Admiralty had announced that HMS *Exmouth* had been lost at sea with all hands, presumably hit either by a mine or a torpedo. We learned subsequently that this was indeed the ship on which John had been serving as navigating officer. Thus, John Loveday was the first casualty in our family and the first of four first cousins to be killed during the war. I had only met John once in my life, and that was the previous summer when I had visited him at his mother's house in Bampton in Oxfordshire and we had played tennis.

John's father, Francis Loveday, had been a regular army officer in the Royal Artillery, who had served in the Boxer Rebellion (China), in South Africa during the Boer War, and had served with distinction during the First World War as a colonel. He had received a DSO (Distinguished Service Order) for having moved his artillery battery into a position that nobody thought possible. He suffered a great deal in World War I and died as a result of the war in the influenza epidemic. His death, as a war casualty, was nevertheless recognized, because his name appears on the Menin Gate at Ypres in Belgium; we visited this monument a number of times in the thirties on our way to the Belgian coast.

We knew John's sisters better than we knew him because Aunt Lilias had come to stay with us in Brussels with her mother, Mrs. Dallas (her husband's family had been involved in the foundation of Dallas in Texas), in the early thirties for her health, in order to receive some treatment from my mother. At that time John's youngest sister, Penelope, had also stayed with us, and we had gone skiing at Elsenborn in the eastern part of Belgium in 1933. Subsequently, I also got to know Elizabeth, who lived in Birmingham and with whom I stayed later on in the war when I was beginning to study medicine.

During these months, although life was proceeding at home pretty routinely, there were nevertheless a number of scares when we believed that the invasion of Belgium was imminent. On one occasion a German plane was forced to land on Belgian territory, and when the pilot and his companion, a German colonel, were searched, a map was found indicating a route for the potential invasion of Belgium by the German Army. At the time it was thought to have been a hoax for the purpose of misleading the Belgian High Command, but, in point of fact, it turned out to be the exact route which the Germans subsequently used. I enjoyed feeling that I had some special insight into the activities of the Belgian government as a result of my rowing with Etienne Gutt. Oftentimes when we were sculling on the canal we would talk about politics, and I would get a glimpse of what was going on in the government. Although Etienne never really divulged any secrets, I did feel that I got rather a fuller story than what I read in the newspapers.

After the defeat of Poland when things were relatively quiet, Germany attempted to convince Britain and France to give up the war, but they refused and the war continued.

During the winter of 1939–40, another event complicated the war picture. The Soviet Union invaded Finland in order to extend its buffer zone beyond the Baltic States of Latvia, Estonia, and Lithuania. To everybody's surprise the Finns managed to hold off the Russians to a large extent, and they became the big heroes of the day. There was, in the West, a tremendous outpouring of sympathy and support for the Finnish Army, under the command of Marshal Mannerheim. We were deeply moved by the pictures of the Finnish Army, in white garb on skis, very successfully for a while defending their country and inflicting very heavy casualties on the Soviet forces. Everybody had considered the Soviets extremely powerful, and the sight of a small country like Finland being able to withstand the onslaught was very surprising. In Belgium, we collected medical supplies and provided other support for the Finns. It wasn't clear how the invasion of Finland by the Soviets related to the war with Germany, but eventually the Finns did have to make peace with the Russians and ceded a certain amount of territory.

I continued to be very much of an Anglophile, identifying very much with the British cause, and I wanted to involve myself and do something for Britain. I contacted the British embassy in Brussels and obtained propaganda pamphlets, which I distributed to my friends, also surreptitiously leaving them in various places. As a result of these efforts, I received from the embassy as a gift a book entitled *Failure of a Mission*, written by Sir Neville Henderson, the British ambassador in Berlin from 1937 to 1939.

Sometime during the spring of 1940, a very serious episode took place in which some British bombers flying from Germany back to their bases in England had by mistake dropped some bombs on Belgian territory—not hurting anyone, but, nevertheless, violating Belgian neutrality. We were afraid that this error might somehow precipitate some German reaction that would lead to an attack on Belgium.

On April 9, 1940 the German Army invaded Denmark and Norway. The Danish government decided that it could not resist the German attack and therefore stayed in place and allowed itself to be overrun, with King Christian of Denmark remaining at his post in Copenhagen. In Norway, however, the story was different: the Norwegian Army, Air Force, and Navy fought off the Germans, and the British and French sent an expeditionary force to Norway to assist the Norwegians in fighting the Germans. Once again, during this whole period I followed in great detail the battles that were raging in the north. We wondered whether this new German adventure would absorb their attention sufficiently long for us to be spared war in Belgium, but that was not to be. On the 10th of May 1940, at dawn, Germany invaded Luxembourg, the Netherlands, and Belgium. The "phony war" was over. Thus began my really great adventure at the age of 16 and three days.

CHAPTER III

THE GERMAN ATTACK

Brussels: May 10 – 15, 1940

MAY 10, 1940. War began for me today when, dreaming of galloping horses, I was suddenly woken up by gunfire. It was half past five. I looked out of my bedroom window and saw further up the street antiaircraft guns firing into the air. Suddenly the whole house was shaken as if by an earthquake. My parents, brother, sister, and I rushed to the front of the house. Standing on the balcony of the third floor, we saw smoke coming up from the street. One of us said, "It must be a plane," yet somewhere in our minds at that point came the realization that war had at last come to Belgium. With this realization came both fear and relief: fear at what it might mean for our survival; relief that "the second shoe had dropped" and that the long period of waiting was over. For a dreadful moment, however, we worried that the bombing—for that is what we concluded it was—was being done by a British plane as had happened a few weeks before by mistake.

We dressed quickly and rushed out on our bicycles towards the area where we had seen the smoke. A dead person was lying in the street, and many windows of the houses in the neighborhood were broken. We looked for "the plane" but none was found. We concluded therefore that the smoke was either the result of an antiaircraft gun or a German bomb. While we were out, the air raid alarm sounded for the second time and, frightened, we rushed back home.

We listened on the radio to the BBC news program, which announced that Belgium, the Netherlands, and the Grand Duchy of Luxembourg had been invaded by the German Army and that the Netherlands and Belgium had appealed to their British and French allies for military help. A short while later, at 7:20 A.M., we listened to the Belgian radio news and the announcer appealed for calm and courage and announced that military personnel should, as rapidly as possible, return to their units. It was also made clear that the civilian population should prepare itself for civil defense. Trucks and cars with trailers were beginning to fill the streets, and it seemed as if the exodus of the Belgian population had begun. It was announced that schools were closed until further notice and, at half past eight, the National Radio announced the general mobilization of the army and that martial law had been declared. At 9:00 A.M. the third air raid alert was sounded, and we went into the basement of our house, where we assumed that from now on we would be spending much of our time, especially at night. We expected Robert, who was by then 21 and a medical student, to be shortly called into the army. He had already heard from some of his friends that they were to go and join the army at the recruiting center for the Army Medical Corps. We mostly spent the morning listening to the radio and the repeated air raid alerts. At 2:00 P.M. Robert received his calling-up papers and he was ordered to go to Ghent to the Center of Instruction of the Army Medical Corps.

During the afternoon we also spent some time in preparing the basement for sleeping and in sticking pieces of paper on the windows in order to avoid their being shattered by the blast of bombs. From now on it would be our air raid shelter. Throughout the day the weather was beautiful and the sun was shining practically all the time. Later that afternoon, at approximately half past four, the first British troops came through Brussels. The population was enthusiastic and applauded and cheered them. One block away from our house on the Avenue Louise they were passing in a constant stream. Later that evening we drove Robert to the South Station where many of his friends, also called up into the army, had gathered. On the road to the South Station we met a lot of British troops, and they seemed to be very happy and were joyously received by the Belgian population.

In the course of this eventful day, my parents and I had a number of conversations about what the family was going to do in view of the German invasion. For many years it had been understood that, in the event of war, Pauline and I would go to England and be looked after by my mother's sisters at Bloxham, Aunt Dorothy and Aunt Katherine. It was assumed that Robert would be called up into the army, as indeed he was. In the past two years when, on many occasions, it looked as if war would begin, there had been repeated discussions of these plans. Pauline and I would go to Bloxham. I would go as a day student to Bloxham School, and Pauline would go to Tudor Hall, a girls' school located between Bloxham and Banbury. This expectation was reassuring and I looked forward to the adventure, but now I was shocked and disappointed by the sudden change in my father's plans for us. He had decided unilaterally—without discussion with Pauline or with me—that we would not be sent to England. He explained that, based on his experiences in the First World War, he was worried that if he and mother were to leave our house, it would increase the chances of it being vandalized, occupied, or even partially destroyed by the occupying troops. He said he would much prefer to remain in Brussels, even if it meant dying in the rubble of his own home. He also decided that it was better for the whole family to stay together. My reaction to his decision, which I did not express, was that it was all very well for him to decide to stay in Brussels, but that it was not really in the best interests of Pauline and of me.

Today was indeed a very traumatic day, not only because of the invasion of the country, but also because it forced me to reexamine my image of my parents and my relationship to them. I had always pictured my father as a man very much in control, knowing what to do and able to cope. Yet today he revealed himself as a person who does not seem to know what the next steps should be in order to ensure the protection and survival of his family. That was indeed a shock and a great disappointment.

[I realize now, with the hindsight of more than sixty years, that perhaps I was expecting too much of him and was perhaps unduly harsh in my judgment. Probably he genuinely believed he was acting in our best interest, but my realization on this day catapulted me into assuming from then on much more responsibility for myself, something which I did increasingly over the next several weeks.]

Saturday, May 11. We all had a rather restless night sleeping on mattresses in the basement of our house. We woke up to the wonderful news that Winston Churchill had succeeded Neville Chamberlain as British prime minister. Throughout the day British troops poured into Brussels, and in front of our house on the Avenue Louise there were lots of army trucks filled with troops. In the afternoon, as was our custom on the weekends, we went to the Boat Club, and on the way we encountered two huge bomb craters, probably meant for the airfield a mile or two away. I went double sculling with Etienne Gutt, and while we were out on the canal nothing very special occurred. We saw a number of planes in the air, but strangely enough, even though there were more military targets in the immediate vicinity of where we were rowing, there seemed to be less military activity here than around our house, where there were no military targets. On the way back from the Boat Club, we were not able to go through the center of Brussels, where the royal palace and the ministries are—presumably for security reasons.

On reaching home, Pauline and I continued to stick strips of paper on the windows of the basement, where we are sleeping at night. Before we went to bed, we went for a walk and across the street we talked to many British soldiers. They told us that they had left England in September 1939 and that they had left their base in France at two o'clock that afternoon and had arrived at about half past four. Brussels was the first large city they had visited since leaving England, and they were finding the Belgians very friendly. They felt Belgium is much cleaner and greener than what they were used to in France. Because of the blackout we went to bed at 9:00 P.M., since we didn't yet have appropriate covering for the windows when the lights are on. Once again, we went to bed to the sound of an air raid siren.

Sunday, May 12. This second night of the war we all slept better. I suppose we were getting accustomed to sleeping in the basement on simple mattresses. I received a telephone call from Jacques Piraux, my best friend, who had spent the last summer vacation with me at Bloxham in England. He told me that he and his mother had gone to visit his grandmother in the country for a few days, and that upon their return their bus had been machine-gunned by a German plane and his mother had been killed sitting next to him. I felt very sad for him and realized how the war would have a very personal impact.

After this telephone call we left for the Boat Club and, during lunch, we heard an intense bombardment of Brussels. In the sky we saw two German planes being fired upon by antiaircraft batteries. Suddenly one of the German planes began to dive towards the antiaircraft battery and we heard very clearly the sound of machine guns mixed with the antiaircraft fire. A few seconds later we saw only one plane, and we hoped that one of the German planes had been shot down. Later in the afternoon, after we had returned home, we listened to a speech on the radio by Monsieur Pierlot, the Belgian prime minister, giving a report on the war situation. He seemed to report honestly our losses to date, but said that they were not as severe as they had been in the First World War. He also explained why one of the bridges across the Meuse River had not been blown up, thus allowing the German Army to come through at a very critical point at the front. Armored columns of the German Army had managed to take Tongres in the eastern part of the country. The Germans are obviously advancing rapidly and getting closer to Brussels. It was also reported that hundreds of German paratroopers had been dropped over Belgium, some in civilian clothes, and some reported to be particularly close to Brussels. [Little did I anticipate that, a few years later, I would spend a week in England in the same house as Monsieur Pierlot.]

Monday, May 13. Today we went by car to visit Robert at Ghent. He was pleased to see us and has everything he needs. In order to reach Ghent we had to use a very circuitous route covering about 175 kilometers instead of half that distance, which is the usual route. On the way we encountered many British and French troop convoys. We were happy, however, that the sky was cloudy and low, since this diminished the opportunities for German planes to bomb the road. After we arrived in Ghent we finally managed to track down which army barracks Robert was located in. We were not going to be allowed to visit him very long and, since he was going to be permitted out later that evening between 6:00 and 9:00 P.M., we went for lunch at a pastry shop. We wandered around the old city of Ghent when, unfortunately, the sky cleared and very soon the air raid alarm sounded. We took refuge in the doorway of a building for a few minutes and then started walking again, but at that point a second alarm sounded. As six o'clock was approaching, we walked towards Robert's barracks. We began walking around the town with him when one more air raid alarm sounded, and again we placed ourselves in the entrance of a building. When the all-clear siren sounded, we had supper with Robert and his two friends, Andre Duprez and Jacques Henri. While we were peacefully having our meal, all of a sudden, again, the air raid alarm sounded, and the most deafening sound occurred in the street just outside the café where we were eating. It sounded like a mixture of machine-gun fire and antiaircraft cannons. We were terrified and flattened ourselves against the wall. According to an individual who had stayed in the street, it was two German Messerschmidts, which had flown over the street but apparently had not fired. This was the most frightening experience since the beginning of the war on Friday. At that point, my father decided that we should return to Brussels as rapidly as possible, and this we did.

My father, who is usually a very careful and relatively slow driver, drove carefully but extremely fast on our return. Twice aircraft flew over the road but did not machine-gun or bomb us. Since we did not know the nationality of the planes, we stopped the car and took shelter, but after the second time, my father decided not to stop the car anymore and drove as fast as he could back to Brussels. At Alost, a town between Ghent and Brussels, the whole area surrounding the bridge which crossed the canal was destroyed. Many, many houses were completely destroyed down to the level of the basements. A few yards from the bridge we saw a huge bomb crater. This was the worst devastation we had seen so far. We were very pleased, however, that the bridge had been spared, so that we were able to cross the canal and finally able to return home. According to the news on the radio, supposedly the allies were victoriously resisting on all fronts, and it was claimed that, since the invasion of Belgium and the Netherlands, 400 German planes had been shot down. [We wanted to believe all this good news at the time, but later realized that much of it was wishful thinking designed to keep up the morale of the population.]

Tuesday, May 14. According to the radio the German Army has reached the Meuse at Liege and at least 2,000 German tanks were in action. Papa today went to the headquarters of the Belgian Army Medical Corps to see whether he could be useful in some way. He learned there that the Army Medical Corps had been evacuated to the Belgian coast and, because the Medical Corps is part of the Ministry of Defense, we concluded that the government had probably already left Brussels. Shortly after this, however, my friend Etienne Gutt telephoned me to find out if we were going to the Boat Club that afternoon to go sculling. We were not going because we had some shopping to do, but since I had him on the phone I asked him whether, in fact, the government had left Brussels. He told me that, although the archives of the government had already left Brussels, the government itself was still very much in town. Later on in the day we went to pick up gas masks, which were being issued to the civilian population, and we went food shopping at the market. On our return, Pauline and I continued to stick strips of paper on the windows in the basement, in our continuing effort at protecting ourselves in the event of a bomb exploding near our house. At 6:00 P.M. we turned on the radio to listen to the news, and it was announced by the Ministry of Defense that the government had ordered boys and men between the ages of 16 and 35 to leave their homes and to congregate in two Belgian towns—Ypres and Roulers—in order to be taken into the Army Reserves. The purpose of this order was to avoid what had happened in the First World War, when boys who were 16 in 1914 were 20½ by the end of the war, and thus could have been serving in the army for several years, were it not for the fact that they were under German occupation. The government was assuming that at some point the front would be stabilized, as it had been in World War I, with a significant portion of either France or Belgium remaining free and not occupied by the Germans.

This radio announcement came on the one hand as a tremendous shock, and yet, on the other hand, I heard it with relief. After all, I was not going to be stuck in Brussels during the war, but I was going to be able to get out and lead an adventurous life. It seemed to me that, after my family's decision that Pauline and I would not go to England, the government had taken a hand in the matter. Since I was today 16 and seven days old (how lucky I felt not to have been born a few weeks later!) I would be taken over by the army and would have an opportunity of doing something worthwhile in this war. I suppose I must have been sad at the prospect of leaving home, but I don't think that I really allowed myself to feel the full implications of this announcement. I was proud of the opportunity of serving my country and at the chance of making my way in life, while at the same time somewhat regretful at leaving home. My father was a stickler for details, and I am quite sure that if I had not already been 16 at the time this order was given he would not have permitted me to leave, and I don't think I would have dared disregard his decision. When I informed my father of the radio order, which I don't think he had heard, and that I would have to leave he said, no, that I should not leave until I had received from the army a written order, just as Robert had received one. Once again, I felt that my hopes of leaving for an adventurous life in response to the government order were to be dashed.

Wednesday, May 15. It was announced in London this day that the Dutch Army has surrendered because the Commander-in-Chief of the Army had concluded that further resistance was pointless. After the news, Papa and I went to do some shopping and then Pauline, Suzanne (her friend), and I went for a bicycle tour in the wood. During this trip I decided to visit Andre Chiliade, a school friend of mine who lived nearby. When I arrived at his house, I learned from his parents, who were in tears, that he had left that morning at 3:00 A.M. for Ypres, one of the towns where males between 16 and 35 were supposed to congregate. His parents were surprised that I had not already left home. I asked whether he had received a written order to leave. He hadn't, and they said that there were no such written orders, and that one was expected to respond to the radio announcement. Since the initial radio announcement the order had been repeated many times with additional details; namely, that it was recommended that all young men leave on bicycle with a blanket and enough food for 48 hours, with the implication that, at the end of this period, they would be taken over by the army and looked after by the government. As I bicycled back to my house, all I could feel was a sense of tremendous excitement that a major adventure in my life was about to begin.

In retrospect, I was very insensitive to the way in which my parents and, in particular, my mother must have been feeling. I remember when I got back home, rushing into the house and yelling at my mother,

"Mommy, I have to leave," and her response, saying, "Oh, no, not really," and my explaining that, yes, indeed that was the order, and that I had to go. I remember a look of sadness on her face and feeling that I was inflicting pain upon her. At the same time, I was being very glad that I was going to leave, that I was going to escape the occupation of Belgium. I felt I was going to be free, that the whole world was opening before me, and that I was perhaps after all going to have an opportunity of serving the cause of freedom, the Allies, and my country. She tried to put a good face on it and she said, "Well, now you will be able to have your heart's desire and you will be able to camp out-of-doors after all." This was a reference to the fact that I had been bothering her for years to let me go camping on my own or with friends under a canvas tent. I was allowed to go camping when I was part of a formal camp, as I was in England once or twice in my earlier years. Also, my mother had been quite a good sport when, in my younger years, she had permitted me to set up a tent outside the hotel at the coast, and she had even spent the night in the tent with me (when she had a more comfortable bed in the hotel!) in order to keep me company, since my parents would not allow me to camp by myself. It had always been my parents' decision that I would have to be older before I could sleep under canvas alone. Now, before reaching the age that had been set for me to be permitted to do so, the government had stepped in and I was being ordered to leave, hence my mother's comment: that now perhaps I would have my heart's desire and do what I had wanted to do all along, that is, sleep under canvas. But there was a bittersweet tone in her voice as she said this.

My father, too, was distressed, but he finally accepted that I had to leave. We then spent some time packing a rucksack and making sure that my bicycle was in good order, which it usually was because my father took very good care of it, since we went to school everyday by bicycle. I selected the clothes that I would wear and take with me. In the weeks that followed, I wished I had selected rather better. We were brought up to be rather frugal, and, since the assumption was that within 48 hours the army would take me over and look after me, I had selected the oldest clothes I owned with the expectation that I would be discarding them in two days with the greatest ease and the least guilt.

Before I left my father spoke to me rather awkwardly and gave me some parting advice. He surprised me somewhat because he warned me against the evils of smoking and of drinking, and even (though I didn't quite understand what he was saying) about certain kinds of women, who might take advantage of an innocent young man! He had the best of intentions and he was trying to protect me. He gave me 500 Belgian francs, which even in those days was remarkably little money. But again, his reason was that within 48 hours the government was supposed to take me over and meet all my needs. Five hundred francs was more money than I had ever had in my life before, and so by this measure it may have seemed a considerable amount of money, but it is hard for me now to translate what the value of that money was then in current terms.

We had lunch as usual. After lunch everybody—that is, Mommy, Papa, and Pauline—helped me to prepare my luggage and, after the last recommendations and goodbyes were made, I left at 1:55 P.M. I felt very happy at the dawn of this great adventure, which would lead me to who knows where. And yet in the midst of this excitement there was a certain regret at leaving—a sadness at leaving my parents and thinking that I would be separated from them for . . . I didn't know how long, but certainly for many months. It was certain that I would be separated from them by the two armies, the Allies and the enemy, because it seemed certain at that point that Brussels would, very shortly, be occupied by the German Army. I was not aware of any fear, although the future was unknown. What I was most aware of was excitement and anticipation at this forthcoming adventure. One chapter of my life was closing and a new one was beginning, but even that is an afterthought; I don't think I looked upon these events philosophically at the time. Would I have felt differently had I known it would be five years before I saw my family again? I wonder, but I do not know.

CHAPTER IV

ESCAPE FROM BELGIUM

May 15 – June 23, 1940

As I bicycled away from my house along the Rue Emile-Claus, I waved to my family, who were standing on the sidewalk. This was the road that, ever since I was 5½ years old, I had taken every morning and afternoon as I left the house on my bicycle to go to school. It was a ritual that Mommy would stand at an upper window of the house and wave to us until we disappeared from view around the corner of the Chaussée de Waterloo. And so it was on this occasion, too. I bicycled and turned around constantly and waved and waved and waved until I turned the corner and they disappeared from my view.

I bicycled all afternoon, leaving the city of Brussels through the Chaussée de Waterloo, heading towards Ghent. I went through Alost, the same town we had gone through a few days earlier after seeing Robert. Alost had been bombed by the German Air Force fifteen minutes before I arrived and part of the town was burning. The roads were crowded with refugees, all going in the same direction, west and south, away from the German advance. As I left Alost, I found myself bicycling next to a man whom I asked for the time. He very pleasantly gave me the information and we began to talk to one another. He did not speak much French, so I tried to speak to him in my very imperfect Flemish. We somehow managed to maintain a conversation, and he asked me quite unexpectedly whether I would care to spend the night at his house. I promptly accepted his offer. We continued to bicycle together until Melle, where we had to leave the main road on orders from the military authorities. At that very moment, an enemy squadron appeared in the sky and we threw ourselves in a ditch lining the road. While we were lying in this ditch, my newfound companion described how he had escaped death a few days before. A bomb had fallen within a few yards of his body, but fortunately the bomb did not explode. After lying in the ditch for a while we no longer heard the noise of guns, and we got back on our bicycles and resumed our journey. A few miles further down the road, another air raid alarm sounded, and once again we stretched ourselves out in a ditch, which was completely dry so we did not get wet.

The summer of 1940 was remarkably dry, which had both its advantages and disadvantages. The advantage was that the millions of refugees who were in Western Europe, bicycling or walking along the roads to escape the German invasion, were able to travel and sleep in fields, out-of-doors, without the additional discomfort of the rain. On the other hand, the disadvantage was that the rivers and the canals, which have traditionally been obstacles in the way of invading armies in Belgium, were very dry and proved no hindrance to the tanks and cars of the advancing enemy. In retrospect, however, it is quite clear that a few more feet of water in the rivers would not have really impeded the German armies for very long, and it would not have made any difference to the outcome of the battle in the West.

Just as we were about to resume our journey, my companion discovered that his bicycle chain had left its wheel, and for a while I had to pull him to get away as quickly as possible from the railroad bridge under which we were taking shelter at the time. A railroad bridge was not a particularly safe place to pause given the frequent bombing of bridges by the German Air Force! A quarter of an hour later, we arrived in Ghent, where we visited his mother-in-law. She gave us a cup of coffee and a piece of cake. After that we went through the town and, as we arrived at the city hall, another air raid alarm sounded and we quickly returned to his mother-in-law's house for safety.

Later I inquired at the city hall where I was supposed to go, remembering that I was to be under the orders of the Belgian Army. I was told that I should go into France and that when I reached French soil I would be given more instructions. At that time I still had the illusion that there was a Belgian governmental organization which would look after me. I was naive

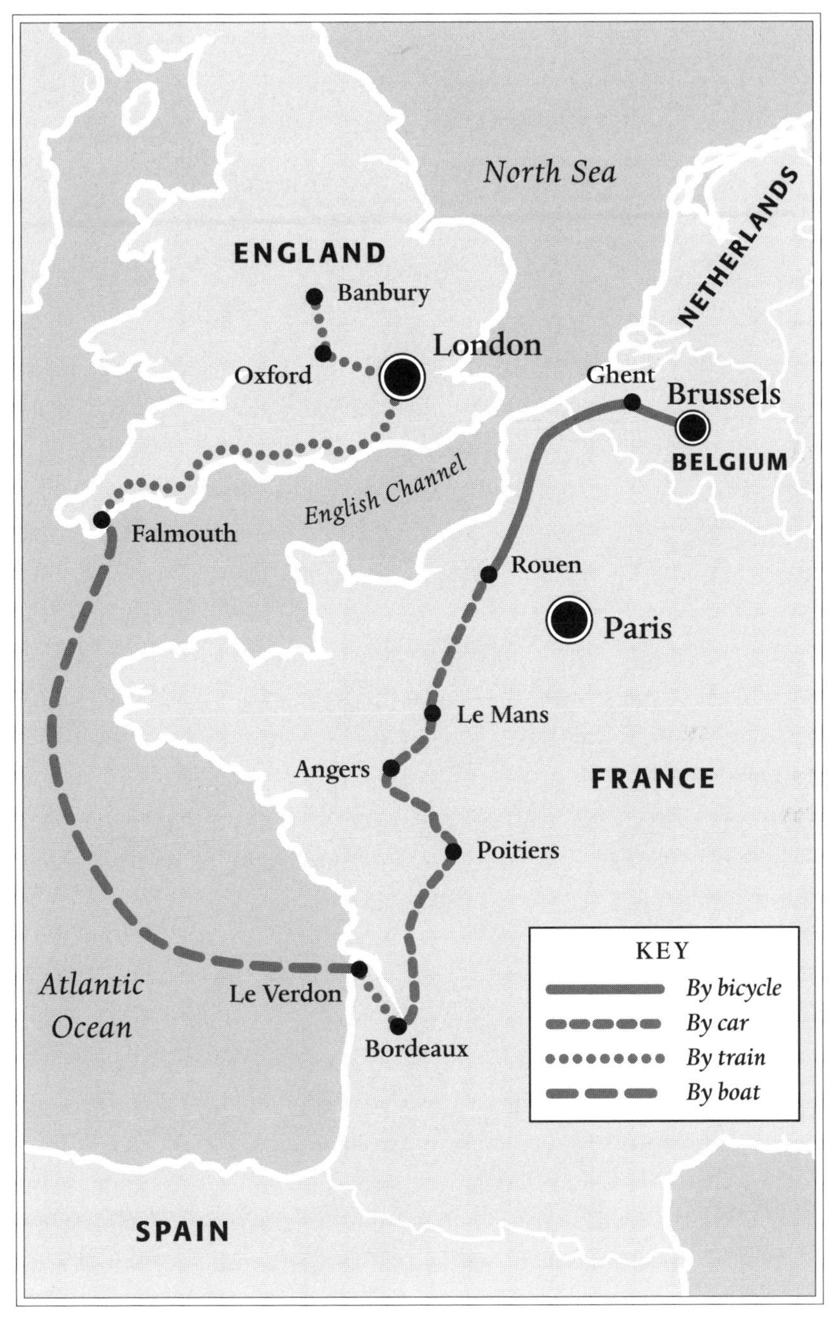

Figure 1. My journey from Brussels, Belgium, to Bordeaux in France and on to England, May–June 1940.

enough to ask the police chief whether, by leaving tomorrow for Roulers, I would arrive in time before the others had already left for France! My question was based on the notion that there was in fact an organized plan for the mobilization of young men between the ages of 16 and 35 and that I would be part of a group, a body of recruits looked after by the army. As I was to discover later, there was nothing of the sort. Had the Germans not advanced as rapidly as they did, the government might have been able to implement its plans. But as it turned out the only thing it could do was to urge us to keep moving south until a front was stabilized.

Later that afternoon, after more bicycling, my companion and I arrived at his house. His name was Louis Baes and he lived at Eleventh of Novembre Street in Mariakerke, a town just beyond Ghent. My companion and his wife lived in a very humble, extremely clean and neat house, and they were very generous and pleasant to me. They put a sofa at my disposal in their living room, and this was the first of many times that the blanket I had taken with me as ordered came in very handy. After arranging my "living quarters" for the night, I examined my map and went over the route I would follow tomorrow. It turned out that there were only 45 kilometers between Ghent and Roulers. After this, Louis and his wife kindly invited me to join them and his mother-in-law for supper. At 9:00 P.M. I went to sleep, knowing that tomorrow would be a long day and that I would have to start early. Earlier in the day I had sent a postcard to my parents, and wondered now if they would receive it.

Thursday, May 16. I left Ghent at six o'clock in the morning after thanking my hosts. I bicycled alongside the railroad station, which had suffered some bomb damage during the night. The severe bombing had kept me awake for part of the night and was very frightening. I went through Deynze, and then I had to make a detour going through Vive St. Eloi because the other road through Thiel was filled with troops and impassable. Along the road there were thousands of refugees using almost any method of transportation. It was pathetic to see so many people who had put all their belongings on carts drawn by horses, by mules, sometimes even by donkeys—the whole of their worldly belongings piled one on top of the other with a mattress or two on top of the load for protection.

Sometimes their dogs walked along the road with them. Cats perched on top of the mattresses; canaries in cages were tied to the side of the carts. Some people were driving trucks or cars, others motorcycles and bicycles. As their journey continued many of them ran out of gasoline and, since they were not permitted to slow down the traffic while they were looking for gasoline, the cars were often simply pushed into the fields by the side of the road. Heaven only knows what happened to the owners and how they continued their journey. This mass of humanity, of which I was a part, kept going west and south, in the opposite direction from which the Allied armies coming from France—French and British troops—were moving in. The armies were traveling as fast as they possibly could in order to meet the Germans as far north and east as possible. This mass of refugees was a tremendous obstacle to the movement of the Allied armies, although again, in retrospect, it is doubtful that it made any difference to the outcome of the battles. There were eventually two million Belgians, one-quarter of the Belgian population, who traveled as refugees to France in 1940.

Returning to my own personal story, I arrived in Roulers at ten o'clock in the morning and I went where I was told to go. When I got there I was told to come back later, so I went and had lunch and after an hour and a half came back. I was informed that I should continue beyond Roulers and go to Ypres. It began to dawn on me that this whole effort of trying to mobilize males between the ages of 16 and 35 was very poorly organized. For some reason, which I do not now remember, I had on that day a vague hope of running into my brother Robert, but I didn't find him. I arrived in Ypres and met two 18-year-old young men who also were supposed to go to Ypres. Again, I sent a postcard to my parents from Ypres. I ate a few slices of bread and butter and again enquired where I was supposed to go. There was a large belfry in the main square of the town: I remembered this square very well from having gone through it many times with my parents, because Ypres was one of the towns we used to visit on our way to the coast on vacation. It was an important town in World War I, a place where much fighting occurred, and over the years we had visited it many times and had seen, as the years went by, its rebuilding following the war destruction. I was told that the compulsory route to follow was toward Rouen, in France, and that we should proceed into France through the Flanders border towns of Poperinge, Abeele, and Cassel. It was here, in Ypres, that I lost all hope of finding Robert in the immediate future and also where I began to feel that there was no overall direction to this so-called mobilization of young men.

I left Ypres with the two young men mentioned earlier. We went through Poperinge and on to Abeele, where we actually crossed the frontier into France without any difficulty. After going along the frontier for several miles, we arrived in Steenvoorde, and, at a crossroads, we were informed by soldiers that we must not to go to Cassel but Hazebrouck instead. When we arrived in Hazebrouck, we were told to go to a receiving center located nearby in Blaringhem where we would have to register and obtain official documents permitting us to travel in France. In retrospect, this is the moment—although I don't think I quite realized it at the time—that I began to reassess my situation. I was probably beginning to feel the effects of having left home the previous day: a sense of loneliness and uncertainty. This feeling was compounded by the fact that I had not been able to trace Robert (although why I expected to do so is a mystery to me in retrospect). Also, I had left Belgium and was now in France, and I did not know France particularly well, although our countries shared a common language. It was very upsetting to discover that there was no effective organization in place to take care of us young males who had been ordered to leave our homes. The 48-hour supply of food we were told to take with us in the original order was running out. It was also discouraging to be told at our every destination, "Keep moving. Go to the next town, and the next one, and the next one! . . ." Thus, within a very short time of my arriving in France, I came to the conclusion that I was surrounded by absolute chaos—that there was no organization that was going to look after me or my interests. Gradually the conviction dawned on me that what happened to me from that point on would depend largely on what I did. In other words, I would have to take responsibility for myself and make the necessary decisions. I would have to decide what I wanted and work toward achieving it. I would have to use whatever opportunities presented themselves to fulfill those objectives, but it would be most important for me to have a clear idea about my goal, about my objectives and my destination. In short, I realized that my survival in the midst of chaos would depend primarily upon myself and that I would have to remain clear-headed, single-minded, and determined, perhaps even stubborn, in order to achieve my goals.

When we arrived at Blaringhem, we were told that it was too late to register and that we should come back the next day at eight o'clock. We began looking for somewhere to sleep. I met a man who was going to go to Le Havre, and in the course of our conversation he advised me to go to England! From that moment on the idea of reaching England never left me. This idea became more and more embedded in my mind as I surveyed the chaos surrounding me. I wrote in my diary "I want to go to Bloxham and I will do everything I have to do in order to get there." I realized, of course, that I was here in France because the Belgian government had ordered me to go, but I rationalized my plan to go to England by saying to myself, "I am sixteen years and nine days old and too young to be a soldier. I am a student and have no trade. There seems to be no organization that is in fact implementing the mobilization of young men. Therefore there is nothing for me to do in France." I am sure that this determination to go to England was a way of coping with my loneliness and the chaos surrounding me.

I had dinner in a military canteen with the two young men I had met earlier. After that we went to the town hall to find out where we might be able to spend the night and we were told to go to a barn. Before going to sleep that night, I asked a captain to whom we had talked earlier, whether he thought I might be able to reach England. He told me I could try, but the big question in my mind as I went to sleep was how to get there. Would I go to Le Havre or to Boulogne, to Calais or even to Dunkirk? I learned later that the Belgian government left Brussels today for Ostend, a city on the North Sea coast.

Friday, May 17. I slept in a barn, on straw, last night but I was very cold because, even though I was fully clothed, my blanket was not thick enough. I decided this morning I would go to Calais because Le Havre was too far away. However, in order to do so I learned that I would need a special pass, special identity papers, and traveling permits issued by the French authorities. After we had breakfast in the canteen, which consisted of a slice of bread and a cup of coffee, we went to the office to get our papers. We learned that no special passes would be issued in the morning except for pedestrians and that we would need to come back in the afternoon at two o'clock. I went to Hazebrouck to buy a map of northern France and to change a few Belgian francs into French money. After waiting in a long line for what seemed like an eternity, I then returned to Blaringhem. To my distress, I learned that my new friend, the man who had suggested I go to England, had left this morning by train for Le Havre. I felt very sad and lay in the grass by myself thinking about what I was going to do and writing in my diary.

MAIRIE DE BLARINGHEM (NORD)

No 1442

Nom : de Marneffe
Prénoms : Francis Laurent
Né le 7-5-1924 à Bruxelles
Nationalité : belge
Adresse à l'étranger : Bruxelles
Avenue Louise n° 497
se rend à en France Calais
Motif : Evacuation
Passeport No 923312
Mode de locomotion : bicyclette
Auto : No .... Marque ....
Signalement : ....
Observations : ....

Lieu, date et heure : du passage : Abeele
16-5-40 14h
de l'arrivée au centre : 16-5-40 17h
du départ : au plus tôt

BLARINGHEM, Nord

Figure 2. Pass issued in Blaringhem.

After lunch I went to the office at the town hall in order to get the required papers, for, more than ever, I was determined to do everything in my power to reach England. When the French captain responsible for giving out the papers arrived, the room was already completely full of people. He was very angry because under those circumstances he could not do his work. He ordered the room to be completely cleared. I managed to be one of the last ones to leave the room and I tried to look as distressed and helpless as I possibly could so he would take pity on me. I must have succeeded because he decided that I would be the first one to be served by the officials!

The pass which I was given *(Figure 2)* authorized me to go on bicycle toward Calais. I was surprised at this because I had heard that going into the Pas-de-Calais was forbidden as it was now considered a "military zone." But since I had an official pass, I left my two new friends, the young men I had met earlier, and went in the direction of Saint-Omer. A quarter of an hour later, a soldier who was guarding a crossroads stopped me and ordered me to take the road south going to Thérouanne. This was not the direction of Calais, and I did my best to convince him that I had permission to go to Calais, showing him my official papers. He told me that I would be stopped later anyway, but still I tried to convince him. I almost decided to ignore his orders, but he became rather threatening and I got somewhat scared because he had a rifle and appeared determined. I was afraid that he might shoot me. Therefore, I had no choice but to obey his orders and go through Thérouanne. At this moment I felt very discouraged and full of sadness and frustration at the obstacles I was finding in my way of reaching England.

I took National Road No. 28, which took me to Hesdin, but on the way down a hill I fell off my bicycle while I was holding onto the side of a car to help me to go faster and not have to work so hard. (I had had a lot of practice hanging onto the sides of cars or the backs of trucks because, since the age of six, my siblings and I had commuted every day to school on our bicycles along the Chaussée de Waterloo in Brussels—a trip of about five kilometers—and we often latched onto a truck. We had to be careful not to be caught by policemen since latching onto moving vehicles was illegal and the police manned some of the intersections on the Chaussée.) I took my bicycle with a bent pedal into a repair shop but was told that if it was straightened out it would break and they did not have a spare one. So I continued on with the damaged one until I reached the next town, where I would spend the night. When I reached Hesdin, I looked for a place to sleep but was told there was no more room. I took my bicycle to be repaired while I enjoyed some French-fried potatoes. After this, I left Hesdin to go to a farm on the outskirts of the town where I had been told I might find a place to sleep. It was now 7:00 P.M. I was very discouraged and trying to get used to the idea that it might not be possible to go to England and Bloxham, at least for the time being. A military sentry stopped me along the road and convinced me that the best thing would be for me to go to Abbeville, 18 kilometers further on, where there was a reception center for refugees such as myself. I took his advice and arrived at Abbeville at a quarter past nine. I found the refugee reception center and the living accommodations, as expected, very primitive. All of us were quartered in a barn, just simply lying in the hay. I fell asleep after an excellent meal with a quarter of a bottle of red wine.

Today the German Army occupied Brussels, thus preventing me from communicating with my family from now on. I had no idea whether my two postcards had reached my parents.[1]

Saturday, May 18. I woke up very early, at half past five, because I was cold. Since I intended to arrive in Rouen before the evening, I decided to get going right away. Since I hadn't washed or had a real bath or shower since I left Brussels, I was very happy to find the public baths. I left Abbeville at 6:45 A.M. without breakfast to save time. After an hour and a half of bicycling, I did stop for breakfast in a little café for very little money. During my journey to Rouen I grabbed repeatedly at various cars and trucks to pull me along. At half past twelve I decided to have lunch in a café and had a wonderful omelet and a bottle of beer.

Early in the afternoon I arrived in Rouen and went directly to the reception center, which turned out to be a French Army barracks, Caserne Talandier, that had been lent by the French Army to the Belgians. This was where all the young male refugees such as myself were being collected. I discovered after I entered this camp that you were not allowed to leave without a special pass. Upon my arrival, many men were just leaving the camp by train for Toulouse in the South of France. I was given the opportunity of leaving with them, but I decided to remain for a while in the hope of finding some friends from school. I also knew that 800 kilometers separated Rouen from Toulouse and that eventually I would have to choose between going on bicycle or going by train. I did not know what

[1] After the war, I learned that my mother had sporadically kept a diary of certain events. From her diary I learned that they had talked to one of their friends on June 10 who had seen me in Roulers on May 16. She also noted that this information was confirmed by my two postcards of May 15 and May 16, which they had received at the end of June (see Appendix A).

to do. On the one hand I hated the idea of abandoning my bicycle, which had served me so well and provided me with a great deal of independence, and yet the idea of bicycling another 800 kilometers alone to Toulouse did not appeal to me.

I left the room that I shared with ten other men, each of us lying on a mattress on the floor, and went to talk to the corporal in charge of the sentries at the gate. He was very kind, and I told him that I was due to leave by train for Toulouse and that I wanted to leave my bicycle with a "friend" in the neighborhood. He agreed to let me do so, and so I went to get my bicycle and gave the corporal my identity card as a guarantee of my return.

In the neighborhood of the barracks, I found a bicycle shop and tried to sell my bicycle. The man, however, did not wish to buy it, although he agreed to try and sell it for me. I was still very uncertain about my decision, so I gave him instructions to store it for me for the time being and not to sell it until I got in touch with him again in writing. He gave me a receipt for my bicycle. In the event I reached England, I gave the owner of the shop the address of Aunt Dorothy in Bloxham.

After having settled this matter of the bicycle, I returned to my room in the barracks and lay down on my mattress, feeling the weight of one of my concerns lifted off my shoulders. Spiritually, for a short time at least, I felt a lot better than I had earlier in the afternoon when I had first arrived in the camp. Suddenly, I began to feel that I had made a terrible mistake in giving up my bicycle. There was a lot of conversation in the room among the men about to leave by train for the South of France, mentioning some of the terrible things happening on the way to Toulouse. In particular, one man told me that I was an absolute fool to have given up my bicycle because the trains were being bombed and machine-gunned by enemy planes, and that it would be much safer for me to go on bicycle rather than by train. I did not know if these stories were true, but at this point, I felt quite confused about what to do. I was at a complete loss to figure out what would be in my best interest. An additional consideration of mine, was that by going to the South of France either by train or by bicycle, I would be getting further and further away from the ports of northern France from which I might embark for England.

Finally, in desperation, I decided to throw myself, so to speak, on the mercy of the commanding officer of the camp to help me decide, and I asked to speak to him. I was told that he was too busy to see me, but a lieutenant did agree to speak to me. He turned out to be Lieutenant Lambion, a man who was to play an important role in my life during the next several weeks and to whom I would owe a great deal for his help in enabling me to ultimately reach my destination. When I had first seen this lieutenant he was yelling at someone angrily, and that is why I wanted to talk to the commanding officer, a major, because I was too scared to approach the lieutenant. I made up a story which I told him and which fortunately he seemed to believe. I told him that I had left Belgium with my family, which was of course not true. I let him know who my father was and showed him one of his business cards, which he had given me for just such an occasion and which indicated that he was a general in the Belgian Army. I told him that my parents and I had become separated during our departure from Brussels and that here I was in France but that I had reason to believe that my father, mother, and sister were now in England. I asked him to help me rejoin them and told him, if he helped me, my father would be most appreciative and grateful. Lieutenant Lambion was very kind and reassuring, telling me that I shouldn't worry too much. He tried to comfort me, because I was obviously very distressed, and he said he was quite sure that I would be able to find my family again. He asked me whether I was a Boy Scout. This seemed at the time like a non sequitur, but I told him that I had never formally joined the Boy Scouts but that I had done many of the same activities and that I could be very helpful. Whereupon he said that there was a small group of Boy Scouts that the commanding officer and he, the second in command, were using as messengers to help in various ways. I accepted his offer to join this group with great relief and alacrity, went back to my room to pick up my luggage, and moved into the central building where the headquarters were located. As I went to sleep that night I felt a lot better because my hope of reaching England and going to Bloxham had been rekindled.

Sunday, May 19. Ten of us had slept in a very small room. We got up, had breakfast, and all started work. My assignment for the morning was to take messages from the headquarters building to various parts of the barracks and the camp. In addition, I left the camp a few times with the official motorcyclist of the headquarters and took messages to various parts of town. Another part of my job was to screen the people who wanted to see the commanding officer, Major Mercenier. I felt a lot better now being part of the staff, rather than being one of the hundreds of men who had little control over their fate, waiting to be told where to go. Then we had lunch together and in the afternoon I continued to do the same kind of work. As the day went by I was once again becoming discouraged and afraid that I would not be able to reach England, although Lieutenant Lambion continued to be very kind and encouraging. He did not seem to have lost the hope of helping me reach England. Part of my job that evening was to check the identity cards at the gate to make sure that the people coming into the camp were appropriate, that is, that they were between the ages of 16 and 35. From half past eleven to half past twelve, I was on duty in the command office, mostly answering the telephone, taking messages, and having them delivered to the major.

Monday, May 20. Last night I slept much better than before and throughout the day the work was essentially the same as the day before. I am beginning to enjoy myself. During the afternoon I was thinking about the future. As I looked at the map it occurred to me that, if I were to leave the barracks and go towards Le Havre, I might find a boat to take me to England.

Tuesday, May 21. This morning I was woken up at five o'clock by one of my colleagues and told that I was on duty from 5:00 to 6:00 A.M. There was already a great deal of activity in the courtyard of the barracks. Suddenly I noticed a lieutenant colonel walking in the courtyard and coming up the steps of the headquarters building. I recognized him by his bushy eyebrows! It was Lieutenant Colonel Tasnier, a great friend of my father! I introduced myself to him and he recognized me, because it was not very long ago that my parents, Pauline, and I were traveling in the Ardennes and we had stayed in the same hotel as Colonel Tasnier, who was the military correspondent of *Le Soir* and who was covering military maneuvers at the time. I told him I wished to get to England and he told me to get my luggage and follow him. I felt embarrassed about leaving the officers whom I had been serving these last few days and who had been so helpful to me, but Lieutenant Lambion understood this to be a wonderful opportunity for me. If Lieutenant Colonel Tasnier could help me reach England, he felt I should go with him without hesitation. I said goodbye to the Boy Scouts whose colleague and friend I had been these last few days.

As soon as we got out of the camp Colonel Tasnier gave me the address of his hotel where he was staying with his wife and I went to fetch my bicycle. Unfortunately, the bicycle shop was still closed at this hour. I rejoined the colonel and he decided to requisition a car. Both of us got on board and he asked the driver to take us to the hotel. At the hotel we met Madame Tasnier and the three of us had breakfast in a café. After breakfast, we went back to the hotel, where I had a bath in the bedroom of the colonel and his wife. He gave me a note which he tried to make official telling me to go to Le Havre and he also sewed on my jacket a tricolored piece of an armband that he himself had—black, yellow, and red, the colors of the Belgian flag—to make me look more official. His wife very kindly gave me 100 francs together with a letter for their daughters, of whom they were without news at the present time, in the event that I ran into them.

Just before I left the colonel he asked me my age, and he realized that I was indeed over 16. For a horrible moment, I was afraid he would say that I had to remain in France in response to the order initially given over the radio in Belgium. Fortunately, I was able to convince him that there was nothing for me to do in France since I didn't have a job in the midst of this chaos. Also, if a military front were to be established in France, even if I were in England I would be able to join the forces and do my duty. This seemed to convince him and we parted company. I was very grateful for the Tasniers' help, just as I had been for the help which the Belgian officers had given me. After the war, when I went back to Belgium, I learned that Colonel Tasnier had died shortly after on June 10, "extremely depressed at the military debacle which was unfolding."

After leaving the colonel and his wife, I picked up my bicycle at the bicycle shop and took the road to Le Havre. I was feeling on top of the

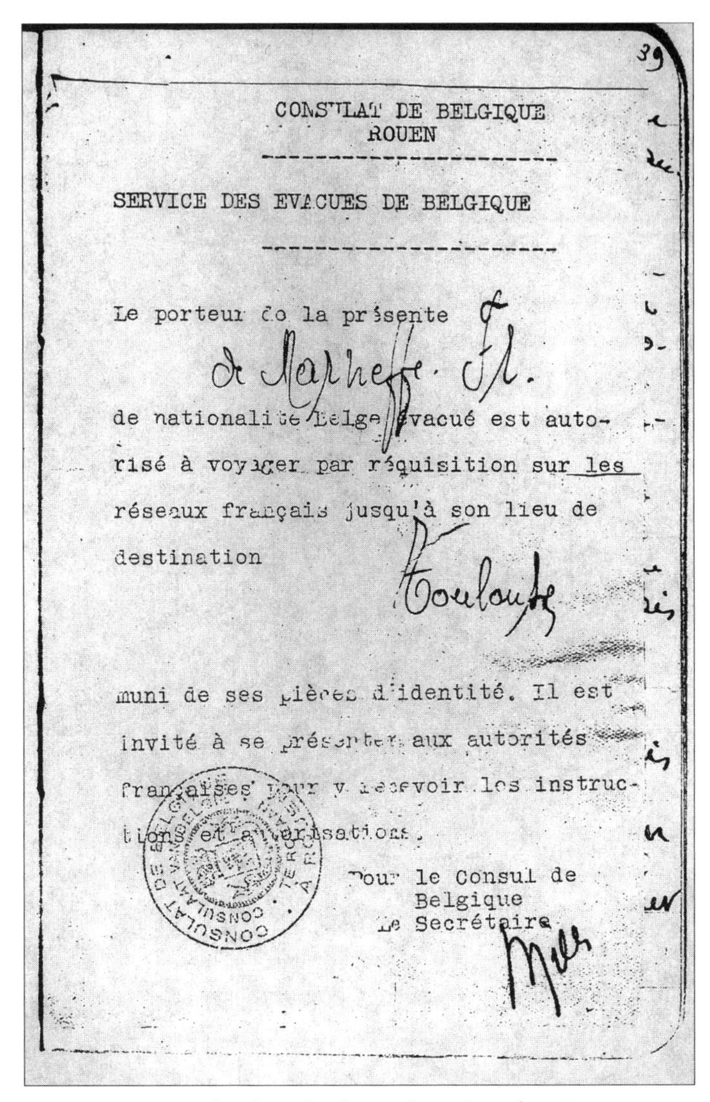

CONSULAT DE BELGIQUE
ROUEN

SERVICE DES EVACUES DE BELGIQUE

Le porteur de la présente

de nationalité Belge évacué est autorisé à voyager par réquisition sur les réseaux français jusqu'à son lieu de destination Toulouse

muni de ses pièces d'identité. Il est invité à se présenter aux autorités françaises pour y recevoir les instructions et autorisations.

Pour le Consul de Belgique
Le Secrétaire

Figure 3. Railroad voucher from Belgian Consulate, Rouen.

world, looking forward to arriving at Le Havre and finding a boat to take me to England. But it was not to be. Twenty kilometers from Le Havre I was stopped by French military personnel and told that I could not go to Le Havre. I produced the paper that the colonel had given me earlier that morning and I was taken to a French Army captain who was in charge. He informed me that Le Havre was now a restricted military area and out of bounds to all civilians. I indicated that going to Le Havre was not essential, and that all I was trying to do was to reach the coast. He informed me that I could not go south because all the bridges across the river Seine were closed and that the only place I could cross the river was back in Rouen. I tried desperately to convince him to let me go on. I produced the business card of my father showing him that he was a Belgian Army general, but I was afraid that, particularly at that stage of the war, a connection to the Belgian Army did not carry much weight with a French officer. I was terribly discouraged, as I would now have to return to Rouen. I cried with rage and frustration.

Fortunately, I found a couple of trucks that were willing to put my bicycle on top and carry me back with them to Rouen. When I arrived in Rouen, there seemed to be nothing left for me to do but to go to the Belgian consulate to get a railway pass to take me to Toulouse. A large part of my discouragement was because I knew that the barracks I had left just this morning were being evacuated by the Belgians. Therefore, I probably would not find my friends again, the Belgian officers and the Boy Scouts who had helped me so much in the last few days. I was afraid that I was once again one of the masses of Belgians in France, who would have to fend for himself without much help from anyone.

At the Belgian consulate, after queuing up for quite a long time, I was given a pass *(Figure 3)* permitting me to travel on the French railroad without payment from Rouen to Toulouse. Although I didn't know if I was going to use this ticket, I accepted it nonetheless. I tried to get the consulate staff to issue a pass and a ticket for me to go to the French coast. I had read in the morning paper that the Belgian government was at the present time at Saint-Adresse, on the coast near Le Havre, and I made up a story that Monsieur Gutt, the Belgian finance minister and the father of my good friend Etienne, was my uncle and was there waiting for me to join him. There was a moment of hesitation on the part of the staffperson. He made a couple of phone calls and then expressed his regret that he would not be able to give me a pass to go to the northern French coast because it was now a restricted military zone, as I already knew. His only choice was to give me an official ticket to go to Toulouse by train.

So, feeling very discouraged once again, I left the consulate, got on my bicycle, and went back to the Caserne Talandier, the one where I had spent the last several days. I confirmed with great regret and distress that, as I had feared, the lieutenant, the major, and the Boy Scouts had already moved out. I felt very low at this point, very discouraged and lonely. I had decided not to use the free railway pass given to me by the consulate. I still did not want to rule out the option of eventually getting to a port in northern France and finding a boat to take me to England. This ruled out getting on a train for Toulouse. But for now, with nothing else to do, I got on my bicycle and started the journey of 800 kilometers to Toulouse.

But luck was on my side. Half a mile outside of Rouen, along the road to Toulouse, I spotted Fernand, the motorcyclist who was the official messenger of the military headquarters and with whom I had ridden a few times. I caught his eye, and he stopped and asked me where I was going. I told him I had tried to go to Le Havre but had been stopped and was now on my way to Toulouse. He told me that he was waiting for Major Mercenier and Lieutenant Lambion. who were currently visiting General Vinçotte, the Belgian general in charge of army recruitment in Rouen. Fernand reassured me that I would be able to leave with them and not to worry. I felt that, once again, I had been saved from the terrible, lonely fate of bicycling to Toulouse alone. With this reassurance based on I don't know what, I took my bicycle once again to the shop where barely twelve hours earlier I had taken it out. After leaving my bicycle to be sold at that shop *(Figure 4)* I realized, to my horror, that I had left my luggage on the back of it, and I fetched it later.

I hoped that I could depend on the kindness of the officers and that they would continue to look after me. I noted in my diary that the military situation continued to get worse since the German Army had passed Amiens. Personally I felt that, provided I could stay with these Belgian officers, the chances of being caught by the Germans was very remote. since they would leave before the Germans arrived. When the officers came back later that evening I discovered that all the Boy Scouts except one, Marcel Peters, had been dismissed and were off on their own. There was some discussion among the two officers and Marcel as to what to do

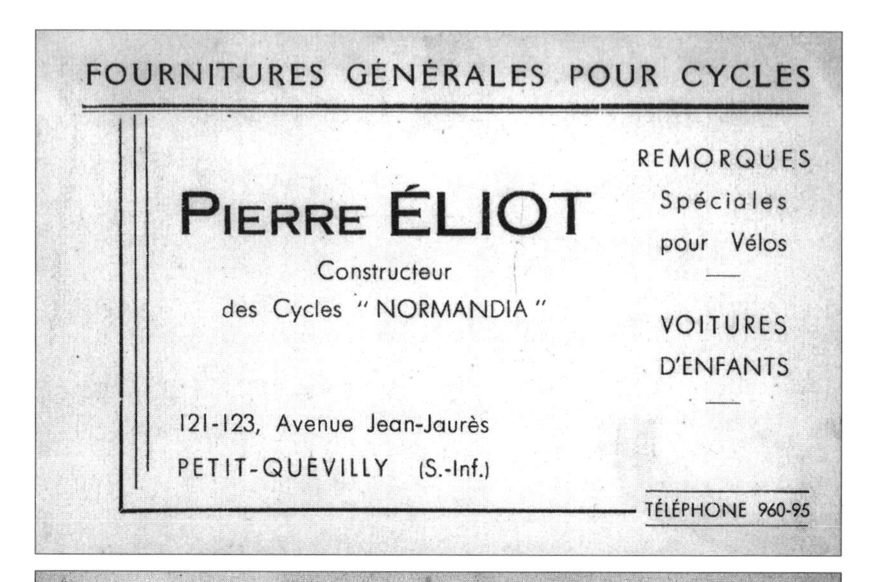

FOURNITURES GÉNÉRALES POUR CYCLES

PIERRE ÉLIOT

Constructeur
des Cycles " NORMANDIA "

121-123, Avenue Jean-Jaurès
PETIT-QUEVILLY (S.-Inf.)

REMORQUES
Spéciales
pour Vélos

VOITURES
D'ENFANTS

TÉLÉPHONE 960-95

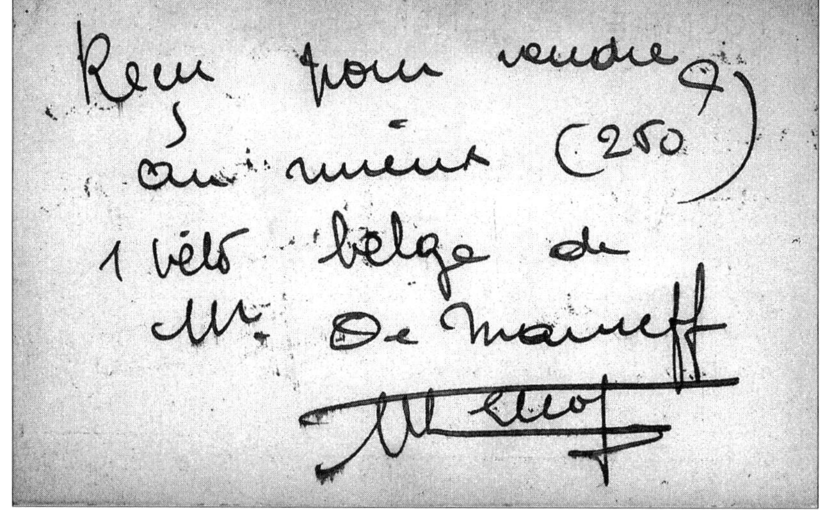

Reçu pour vendre
au mieux (250)
1 vélo belge de
Mr De Marneff

Figure 4. When I joined the staff of some Belgian officers in Rouen who had a car, I gave my bicycle to a bicycle shop to sell for me—here is the receipt. "Received for sale at best price (250 ff) one Belgian bicycle from M. de Marneffe." I never went back. Never saw that bicycle again. Never got the money!

with me. I was very relieved when Lieutenant Lambion decided there was room for me in his staff car. He would be the driver, and Major Mercenier, Marcel, and I would be the passengers. It was with great relief that I realized the four of us would still be together. That night I slept in the car with Marcel, and before we went to sleep we had supper with delicious croissants.

Wednesday, May 22. Last night I slept very well in the car, probably because I was not alone and could depend on my friends, the two officers and Marcel. We had breakfast with the remainder of the croissants of yesterday and made some coffee in the kitchen of the house where the officers had slept. After breakfast I was given the job of guarding the motorcycle and the staff car. I was glad to do this because it reassured me that I would leave with the car. The two officers, the major and the lieutenant, went to the headquarters of General Vinçotte and I stood guard over their car.

At twenty past noon, we left Rouen heading towards Poitiers, where, according to the newspapers, the Belgian government is staying. We took National Road No. 840 towards Elbeuf. The road was extremely crowded with refugees and traffic very slow. It was part of the job of the major and the lieutenant to police these roads, and at various times the major, Marcel, and I got out of the car and we directed traffic at crossroads. At one point while I was doing this, I saw the car disappear at a bend in the road behind a clump of trees. When I came around the bend, I was appalled to discover that the car was not there. My heart absolutely sank. I was terribly worried, because my worldly belongings were in the car, in the rucksack that I had been carrying since Brussels. I only had the clothes I stood in. To make things even worse, I did not know our exact destination. I was frantic and for quite a while I ran along the road, hoping against hope to find the car parked a little further behind one more bend, but to no avail. There was simply no car.

I wracked my brains to try and remember whether I had heard the name of the town where we were going. I had a vague feeling that the name ended with "-ches," something like it, or maybe "-onches." For the next several minutes, I jumped on the side of a moving car to ask for directions and look at the map that the driver had in his hand. Sometimes I was welcomed by the driver and was permitted to look at the map. Sometimes, however, there was a struggle between the driver and myself, the driver trying to push me off—even insulting me. Eventually I found somebody who was willing for me to have a good look at his map, and I found a town many miles further down along with a name ending in "-onches." It seemed to be the only town around with that ending, and I concluded hopefully that our destination was Conches. With a combination of walking, running, and jumping on cars, I arrived several hours later at Conches. Somewhere along the way, in my excitement and almost panic of running and crossing behind and in front of cars, I ripped my pants, badly enough to need new ones, which I bought later.

When I arrived in Conches, without much conviction that I would find the car, I went, for want of a better place, to the town hall. To my incredible joy I discovered the staff car there in the yard! My feelings were absolutely indescribable. I was relieved to retrieve my few belongings, but also to find the people who had befriended me. Quite frankly, I could not understand why they had left me behind. It reconfirmed for me the importance of looking after my own interests and underscored the fact that I could not trust or rely completely on someone else for my welfare. Although the officers were pleased to see me, they took my arrival rather matter-of-factly. They did not apologize for leaving me behind, but explained that they thought I knew our destination and perhaps they underestimated the distance. However, I have never understood why they acted in this way and was quite shocked and learned a very important lesson. After I met up on the second floor of the town hall with the lieutenant and the major, my duties were described to me. They were once again to be a messenger, to answer the phone, to give people directions to various parts of town, and, with Marcel, to make sure that the daily needs of the major and the lieutenant were satisfied. These two officers belonged to the Center for the Army Recruitment and their responsibilities included directing the thousands of Belgian refugees and military personnel trickling through the town to new destinations. Today we worked very late with the major and the lieutenant, and afterwards Marcel and I slept in the car once again.

Thursday, May 23. During the night I was called to take a wounded man to the doctor in town. All morning I crisscrossed Conches to make purchases for the various officers. Lieutenant Lambion was in a bad mood today because he didn't sleep at all last night. He asked us to get him some food, and whatever we got him he did not like. This afternoon my work was the same as this morning: more trips to various parts of town, answering the telephone, taking messages. This evening we had a good meal with macaroni, and later I was on duty for about four hours answering the phone and giving directions.

Friday, May 24. This morning the concierge kindly made hot coffee for us. While sitting in her kitchen I suddenly saw Roger Wattiez, a friend of my brother Robert in the courtyard! I ran out and asked him to tell Robert that I was in good health. I also asked where Robert was, and Roger told me that he had not seen Robert since they had lost each other in Abbeville several days earlier. They had been in a military train at Abbeville which was bombed and they had been ordered to scatter. It was every man for himself, they had gone in different directions, and he had not seen Robert since then. Throughout the day I looked for Robert in vain. Every time I saw a young soldier in the uniform of the Belgian Army Medical Corps I told him who I was and I asked him to tell my brother that I was well. Five years later, after I returned to Belgium, Robert told me that he had come within less than a mile of Conches, but had decided it looked too "military" for his liking and he decided to skirt around the town. Otherwise he and I would surely have met. He also told me that he did get my messages, via his friends. This was the first information he had of my whereabouts.[2]

Saturday, May 25. Last night I was on duty from 2:00 to 4:00 A.M., but unfortunately I went to sleep at midnight and I only woke up at 4:20 A.M.—two hours and twenty minutes later than I should have! From four o'clock on, another Boy Scout was supposed to be on duty but since we didn't know exactly where to find him I took over his duty and I slept as a matter of fact very well until half past six. Throughout the morning I rushed from shop to shop making purchases for the officers. At noon we had lunch as usual, with bread and butter and "monkey" [the slang term for the canned military food which in later years would be called Spam]. The afternoon was similar to the morning. One of the people we dealt with was a French

---

[2] See Appendix B for an account of Robert's 1940 journey.

captain who was very strange. When he explained his ideas he had an incredible stammer; he coughed, he sniffed, and he made many gestures with his hand. To complete the picture he had a monocle in his eye! We "requisitioned" abandoned bicycles today at the railroad station, and these should facilitate our work as we rush around this small town. I volunteered to be on night duty again because I have found that sleeping on the chairs in the office is just as comfortable as sleeping in the car.

Sunday, May 26. Today I did mostly the same work as I had done previously. Some of the time I rushed around the town buying food and preparing food for the officers. At other times I took various officers to different addresses and gave them directions. I am enjoying myself a great deal: I like the work and the people I am working with, and I feel useful. I feel that I am a participant in important events, and I like this military atmosphere.

This evening I took two sick military people and one wounded man to the infirmary. The only people staffing the infirmary at the moment are members of the Center of Instruction of the Army Medical Corps because all of the qualified physicians apparently have disappeared! In front of the building which served as the "hospital" I ran into some of Robert's friends and colleagues, who told me they had shared the same room with Robert. In the expectation that they would see him somewhere, again I gave them a letter for him telling him what had happened to me. Afterwards, I returned to the town hall, had supper, and slept in the car.

Monday, May 27. This morning I decided that it was time for me to bathe once again. However, the bath really wasn't very good because all I had available was to go to the fountain in the courtyard of the town hall, wash myself as best I could, and change my clothes. Basically today's work was the same as yesterday and nothing special occurred.

Tuesday, May 28. Last night I slept well. The news this morning was that the King of the Belgians had ordered the Belgian Army to surrender. It was a terrible shock. The whole of Belgium reduced to slavery for God knows how long! Paul Reynaud, the French prime minister spoke this morning on the radio, severely criticizing the Belgian King, but also from what I was told making many errors. As the morning wore on, many Belgian officers came to the town hall asking for information. Clearly the main issue was going to be the decision of the Belgian government. The situation seemed fairly clear in one way: the King could not capitulate, I am told, without abdicating, and the question is, has he abdicated? Clearly, this was not accurate, but we didn't have all the news and there was a dearth of information.

This evening Monsieur Pierlot, the Belgian prime minister, spoke on French radio and relieved all military personnel from their oath of allegiance to the Belgian King. Until half past eleven this evening I was rushing around the streets of Conches taking officers back to their houses. My duty ended at midnight.

Wednesday, May 29. The implication of the surrender of King Leopold is still unclear. I went to the cleaners to pick up clothes I had taken there two days before. We left Conches at eleven o'clock to return to Rouen. I was glad to be making by car the reverse journey that I had made on foot seven days previously! We arrived in Rouen at half past one in the afternoon and went to a restaurant for lunch. Of course we ordered a ham omelet and French-fried potatoes! What a treat! Afterwards, we went to the headquarters of General Vinçotte and stayed until eight o'clock. We learned that Rouen no longer tolerated Belgian refugees, and Lieutenant Lambion ordered us to remain in the army barracks where we are staying and not to come out until further notice.

We had some concern about returning to Rouen. Since we were last there the German Army had continued to advance. The city had become noticeably more deserted, and some of the bridges over the Seine had been blown up in an effort to delay the German advance.

Thursday, May 30. We slept very well last night on hay and straw! Since we had nothing else to do, we slumbered all day, and in the evening we went to the Café de Paris next door to the barracks.

Friday, May 31. Again we slumbered for most of the morning but, given the sad condition of my clothes, I decided to do some shopping. When I left Brussels I had taken my oldest clothes, expecting to be clothed by the army. Since this did not happen, my clothes had become rather tattered. With some trepidation at disobeying Lieutenant Lambion's orders, I left the barracks with one of our motorcycle drivers. We crossed a bridge and found the city rather deserted. We looked all over for an open shop and finally I found a pair of riding breeches for 135 French francs. At eleven o'clock we returned to the barracks for lunch. The food in this French barracks is absolutely excellent. After lunch we rested.

At four o'clock, Lieutenant Lambion appeared and told us to pack quickly, because in ten minutes we would have to leave the barracks. Unfortunately Billy, one of the Boy Scouts, had gone for a walk and we left without him. I felt very lucky that I had done my shopping in the morning. The lieutenant told us that we were going to Angers, where we should arrive at 8:00 P.M. The lieutenant, Marcel, and I were the only three people in the car. We drove through very beautiful countryside. We went through Bernay, Alençon, and Le Mans. The lieutenant drove very fast—mostly at 100 kilometers an hour, which on these roads was very fast indeed—and we finally arrived at Angers, stopping on the Boulevard Marechal Foch at the Credit Lyonnais. We were only a few doors from the seat of the Polish government-in-exile.

We were received at the Credit Lyonnais by the family of Lieutenant Lambion, and they were most gracious and welcoming. We had a most wonderful evening meal. It turned out that the lieutenant's father-in-law is the owner of the Hotel Osborn in Ostend, and that Madame Lambion, his wife, was treated a few years ago by my father! What a remarkable coincidence! Marcel and I spent the night sleeping on sofas in the living room.

Saturday, June 1. I slept very well last night. After breakfast, Marcel and I went to take a shower at the public baths. On our return—clean, fresh, well disposed, and with me wearing my new riding pants—we had a most wonderful meal. After lunch we loaded up the car and, after visiting friends of the lieutenant, we left Angers and headed towards Poitiers, 130 kilometers away. Once again we were racing through the French countryside, but at a slower pace than yesterday because Madame Lambion and her daughter were following us in a smaller car. Poitiers was at that time the seat of the Belgian government-in-exile, and I was hoping to find Monsieur Gutt, the Belgian finance minister, and my best friend's father.[3]

On arrival in Poitiers, we went looking for a place to stay. After a search of half an hour we found accommodations with a very kind and generous woman, at 5 Rue Jules Ferry. We parked the cars and had supper with the sandwiches which Madame Lambion had prepared in Angers. After dinner the Lieutenant went to find his instructions. I went to the Hotel de France, where I hoped to find Monsieur Gutt. It was difficult to get into the hotel, but I seized a moment when the policemen at the entrance were distracted to slip by them.

I went to the front desk in the lobby and asked for Monsieur Gutt. They told me that he was having dinner in the dining room. I peeked through the entrance of the dining room but I didn't see him. I went back to the desk and said I couldn't find him. They explained that he was at the far end of the dining room. I was dressed at the time with an open-necked shirt, a jacket that had seen better days, had holes at the elbows, my new riding britches, and hobnailed boots, which I had bought when my old shoes had worn out. I will never forget the embarrassed feeling of self-consciously walking through this long, crowded dining room, with its crystal chandeliers and well-dressed guests, almost slipping on the highly polished floor as I threaded my way between the tables towards the back of the room, where I saw Monsieur Gutt, his older son François, and another man having dinner.

When I arrived at their table, they, of course, immediately recognized

---

[3] In Appendix D, I will describe in greater detail the movements of the Belgian government and the decisions it took at various times during this period, but for now let me say that the government had left Brussels on May 16, the day before the Germans occupied the capital, and moved to Ostend while extensive discussions were going on between the government and the King prior to the King's capitulation on May 28. After it was no longer tenable for the government to remain on Belgian soil, it moved to France, first to St. Adresse near Le Havre (where, incidentally, it had been for many years during the First World War) and then on to Limoges, where many members of the Belgian parliament were staying at the time, and where a rump session of the parliament was held following the King's capitulation. Later, by arrangement with the French government, the government had established itself in the Hotel de France in Poitiers.

me. Monsieur Gutt was evidently in the middle of a very important conversation with the other man (whom I learned later was Monsieur Georges Janssen the president of the Belgian National Bank), and he suggested to François that he take me to the lobby. François and I went into the lobby, where I gave him a quick thumbnail sketch of what I had done since leaving Brussels. A short while later Monsieur Gutt joined us and asked me what I wanted to do, and gradually the conversation veered towards England. I will always be extremely grateful to Monsieur Gutt for his kindness and sensitivity to my situation. He immediately understood my wish to go to England. It was clear to him that I would need a passport and a British visa. He asked me whether I needed money and lent me 500 French francs and two English pounds. Before our conversation had ended it was clear that the Gutts would help me to get to England. I then returned to the house where I was staying and informed Lieutenant Lambion of my future plans.

Sunday, June 2. François Gutt and I had planned to meet at eight o'clock in the morning. When I arrived François had already spoken to Monsieur Van Langenhoven, the general secretary of the Ministry of Foreign Affairs, and asked him what would be needed for me to go to England. Monsieur Van Langenhoven had then given orders to Monsieur Costermans, the head of the Passport Department, to issue me a passport. François and I were told to go at ten o'clock to his office at No. 12 Rue St. Hilaire. In the meantime we went and had breakfast.

At ten o'clock we went to Mr. Costermans' office and he was there in person. While my passport was being prepared (I was very glad that I had taken with me some extra passport photographs from Belgium just in case!) M. Costermans told me that to obtain a British visa I would need a letter or telegram from my aunt certifying that she would look after me in England. I would also require a special permit to go as far as Bordeaux in southwest France and a special pass authorizing me to leave France.

The first priority, therefore, was to get a letter from Aunt Dorothy. So I went to the post office and sent her a telegram which stated, *To obtain visa need telegram confirming I am your nephew and allowed come live at your house. Stop.* I signed my name and wrote the address where I was staying:

No. 5 Rue Jules Ferry, Poitiers. The post office informed me that the telegram would need a special stamp from the chief of police. We ran to the police station, and finally the telegram was sent to England. I was shocked at the telegram costing me 86 French francs, but reassured that my contact with the Gutt family might provide the money I needed. While François went to buy some food to eat, I went back to the house to again thank the Lambion family and Marcel Peters, who had been so kind to me, so welcoming, and so helpful since we had met. Unfortunately, Major Mercenier and the motorcyclist Fernand were not there, and I was not able to say goodbye to them at that time.

After François returned with the food, we went to the river, approximately twenty minutes away from the hotel, where we ran into the Van Langenhoven family and we all picnicked together. This marked the beginning of an incredible two weeks during which, even though we had daily reminders of the deteriorating military situation, we were leading a life in some ways completely removed from these world-shaking events. We usually went to the river to swim in the beautiful weather and brilliant sunshine. There was a very unreal quality about the whole experience. On this particular day we ate French bread and cheese on the banks of this lovely river Léthée and after lunch went swimming in the river. We eventually returned to the Hotel de France, and while I wrote in my diary François mended his clothes. At seven o'clock we went in search of a little restaurant and finally found a very enchanting one where we had dinner. We then returned to the hotel and, because there was hot water, I was able to take a bath. After that I returned to my temporary abode at 5 Rue Jules Ferry.

Monday, June 3. I slept very well last night but this morning Madame Sicard, the owner of the house, suggested I obtain a residence permit to stay in Poitiers because, according to her, Belgians were no longer allowed to remain in town. François and I had breakfast in a little café. My only task today was to wait for the telegram from Aunt Dorothy and to obtain a residence permit. We went in search of the Belgian chief of police, who was very helpful and pleasant. He confided in us that he himself did not have a permit to be in Poitiers, and that it was only through a governmental department that one could obtain such a permit.

After this we went food shopping and then on to the river. We again had a swim in brilliant sunshine followed by lunch. At two o'clock, François left to find Monsieur Lebon, Chief Secretary of the Ministry of Finance. An hour later he returned to say that we could not get a residence permit, but that Monsieur Lebon had told him that if we ran into trouble we should contact him to straighten out our problems. François and I also talked about his work. This morning he had gone to a factory called Forces Motrices de la Vienne and had applied for employment as an engineer.

At six o'clock we returned to the hotel very sunburned, and, in order to reassure myself, I borrowed François' bicycle to go and see whether Madame Sicard had received a telegram addressed to me and to brief her about the residence permit. Unbelievably, a telegram had arrived! What incredible luck and what speed! It was hard to believe that in the midst of the chaos of war my telegram had reached Aunt Dorothy so quickly, and even more surprising that her reply had reached me so quickly. With almost unbearable pleasure and tension I opened the telegram , which was written in French and which said, *I confirm that Francis de Marneffe is my nephew. I wish to have him come and live with me. Stop. Dorothy Loveday. Bloxham, Banbury.*

I returned to the hotel and shared my good news with François. It was too late by then to pursue the matter of the visa and so we left the hotel and had supper in the same café as yesterday. On our return to the hotel I ran into Monsieur Costermans and showed him the telegram. He told me that he had seen Mr. Lambert, who was the secretary of the British embassy and the person currently in charge because Sir Lancelot Oliphant, the British ambassador to the Belgian government, had disappeared, apparently taken prisoner by the Germans. Mr. Lambert told Monsieur Costermans that he did not know where one should apply for a British visa at the present time. This was extremely disappointing, and on that worrisome news I went back to the house to sleep.

In 1984 as a result of certain unexpected events, which I will describe later, the letters which François wrote almost daily to Janine, the person who later became his fiancée, came into my possession. There are many references to me in them. François was at the time 23 years of age, a graduate in engineering of the University of Brussels, and in love with Janine, a 19-year-old medical student also at the University of Brussels. She was, at the time he wrote to her, in Bordeaux in southwest France. François' perception of me and his comments, not always flattering, about our days together at the time are an unexpected enrichment of my story. The first letter, dated June 3, reads:

> My very dear Janine,
>
> Saturday evening while I was dining with Papa we saw a person whom we did not expect, i.e., Francis de Marneffe. When I received, on Tuesday May 14th, the order to leave Brussels, I almost telephoned him to ask him to join me on my journey. Unfortunately for him, I did not do it because Etienne thought Francis was not yet 16. The poor boy left alone with 400 francs, believing as I did that we would be mobilized at Ypres. When he discovered that that was not the case, he tried to get to England but 15 km from Le Havre he was turned back, military zone. Crying like a new-born lamb, he covered once again the 70 kms to Rouen when he had the good fortune to meet a lieutenant with a heart of gold who adopted him and employed him as an orderly together with another boy. Passing through Poitiers he came to see Papa in the hope of obtaining some dough. Gutt [that's what François called his father] has given me the mission, in addition, of getting him the necessary papers to join his aunt in England. We already have the passport, all we need now is a visa, a special pass, an exit permit and a boat!"

Tuesday, June 4. Last night, again, I slept well and had arranged to meet François. François and I had breakfast at half past eight, then I bought a map of England and we went to the post office to telephone the British embassy as recommended by Monsieur Costermans. Unfortunately, the number that he had given us was inaccurate, but we finally tracked down the right number and were advised that my application for a visa would have to be made in Paris. We discussed how to get me to Paris but decided to wait for Monsieur Gutt's return from Paris in a few days' time, when he was scheduled to attend the meeting of the Council of Ministers next Saturday in Poitiers. While François shopped for food I had a snooze in his bedroom at the Hotel de France. We then went to the river for lunch and a swim. I learned that Etienne, my friend and François' brother was now at Rugby School in England and only 40 kilometers from Bloxham where I was hoping to go.

Today we learned that the whole of Belgium was now in the hands of the Germans with the exception of La Panne. When we returned to the hotel, we ran into Monsieur Costermans, who told me that he should take my passport back since he feels that he was not, based on new regulations, authorized to issue it. However, he did not do so. As time went on, I began to feel that he was playing a mean game with me, counteracting my hopes of getting to England and predicting that I would never make it.

François wrote to Janine today:

> Dear Janine,
>
> Throughout yesterday, Francis de M reminded me of Leon [an adopted brother] who asked Mummy every day, "When will I be promoted to 2nd Lieutenant?" Similarly, Francis asked me at least 15 times, "Do you think I will get to England?" Fortunately in the evening, the famous telegram from his aunt arrived certifying that he could join her in England. During the evening he took the telegram out of his wallet at least 10 times and savored reading it.

And further on in the letter:

> Personally and selfishly I don't regret at all Francis' arrival in Poitiers with his strong Belgian accent and his obsession about going to England. His company is more pleasant and lively than [that of others around here].

Wednesday, June 5. Madame Sicard, the kind owner of the house where I have been sleeping since arriving in Poitiers without paying anything, informed me that she would be welcoming refugees from the north of

France and that she would no longer be able to put me up. She recommended that I go to her aunt a short distance away, but it was clear to me that if I went it would be very inconvenient for her. I asked her for some other suggestions. She suggested another address, and when I went there I found an elderly lady who suggested that I go to No. 5 Rue St. Nicholas. I explained my situation to the lady who owned the house at No. 5 and eventually she gave me permission to sleep there. The accommodation was a straw mattress on a camp bed, which was very adequate for my purposes. Satisfied with the new arrangement, I returned to the Hotel de France to find François. We once again followed our daily routine: after buying French bread, salad, cheese, and fruit we went to the river, where we met Monsieur Nicaise. He is Janine's father, whom I had met once or twice before the war. Monsieur Nicaise was a physics professor and the author of the standard textbook we used at school. Janine, I discovered later, is François' fiancée. That evening François received a letter from his father informing him that he would be returning to Poitiers from Paris in two days. We went out for dinner and on our return we did some laundry.

Thursday, June 6. I had a very strange experience last night. I was asleep in bed when I suddenly woke up and I was convinced that somebody had entered the room. I thought it might be a thief who had entered through the window. I was convinced I had seen him, and for a period of time I was very frightened, but eventually I went back to sleep. I met François for breakfast and some shopping. As we returned to the hotel I ran into Major Mercenier and Lieutenant Lambion and brought them up to date with my plans to go to England. François and I did some writing and then went to the river for lunch and swimming.

François wrote to Janine as follows today:

> Dear Janine,
>
> Francis is not yet used to simple fare and he has regrettably expensive tastes. I must tighten the purse strings permanently to stay in the realm of the possible.

Friday, June 7. I slept well last night without experiencing any new strange presence in the room. François received a letter from his father informing him that he was returning to Poitiers this afternoon. Today we followed the same schedule as on other days with lunch, the river, and a return to the hotel. Unfortunately Monsieur Gutt has not yet returned. His return was particularly important to me because we had sent him my passport in the hopes that he would be able to obtain my British visa while in Paris.

François wrote to Janine:

> Yesterday Francis and I found the ideal spot along the river to eat, to swim, to sleep. Within two hours the news had spread so that we were soon joined by a judge advocate from the military, a young diplomat, [and] the whole of the Van Langenhoven family, who are as short of cash as Francis and me. Francis finds all these people unbearable and declares they are the worst snobs. One can see that he has not met the ones who are really snobs, like the nobility and the nouveau riche. It is evident that all those people from the Ministry of Foreign Affairs have to behave, because of their jobs, in ways that remind one only distantly of the banks of the Canal de Willebroeck. [This was a reference to the canal where the Gutts and my family did their rowing.] The literary culture of Francis encompasses only spy stories and mysteries. Since he had nothing to read, I bought him *Servitude et Grandeur Militaire* (by Alfred de Vigny[4]), which is sufficiently dramatic to sustain his interest and which will be a more important acquisition than *The Drama of the Stolen Key* and other masterpieces. Yesterday I was close to being depressed and wanted to be alone so I ordered Francis not to join me. Perhaps he imagined I was going to spend a most immoral evening! Until Francis arrived in Poitiers, I had lunch and dinner at the Lyceum. As Francis is not a University student we cannot eat there and since I don't want him to have to wander by himself in Poitiers I accompany him and we eat as best we can here and there. Yesterday, Madame Van Langenhoven's nephew

[4] François wrote on the front page, "In order to perfect the literary education of Francis, and to encourage him to be patient, with all my heart, François Gutt."

was not going to have dinner so Francis took his place and Marie Rose gave me hers. It is frightening to see how many potatoes Francis can put away and also chocolate cake (it has been more than a week since we had any potato). At certain times Francis is very rough. He has already damaged my bicycle pump and my gears, which I was able to repair.

Saturday, June 8. We went to the river as usual and ran into Madame Van Langenhoven, who told me that she had found somebody to accompany me to England! It was Baron Boel, the Belgian military attaché at the embassy in London. He was going to London the following day, and his wife and family would follow in two weeks. I very much appreciated this information, and my hopes rose that perhaps my plans would work out after all. Monsieur Gutt has returned; there was a meeting of the Belgian cabinet in the afternoon in the Hotel de France. Monsieur Gutt told me that he had my passport but that in order to obtain the visa I would have to personally appear at the British embassy in Paris. Since he was returning to Paris within a day or two it was decided that I would accompany him. From Paris I would go to Bordeaux, where hopefully I would find a boat. I told him of my conversation with Madame Van Langenhoven: that the Baronne Boel would be leaving for England in a few days to rejoin her husband and that it had been suggested that I might accompany her. Monsieur Gutt told me he would speak to her husband.

Sunday, June 9. I received a letter from Robert through the intermediary of Monsieur Gutt! This was the first news I had received from my brother since I had last seen him in Ghent many weeks ago. He informed us that he had been caught in the bombardments of Calais, Boulogne, and Abbeville, where he and his companions had almost been taken prisoner by the Germans.

Monsieur Gutt informed me that he was going to Paris the following day and that I could accompany him. We went to the river and François convinced his father to come too. The war news was very bad. The Germans have reached Compiègne, about 75 kilometers north of Paris, and General Weygand, the new Commander-in-Chief of the Allied armies, issued an order of the day stating that the fate of France and its allies would be decided in the next quarter of an hour and ordering the armies to resist at all costs. The Germans are approaching. Later I wrote a letter to Robert who was near Nantes at La Chesnaie pres d'Olonne. Then I had dinner in the Lycée [a school] with Madame Van Langenhoven and after that went to bed.

Monday, June 10. The military situation is extremely serious and the Germans are encircling Paris. Monsieur Gutt decided not to go to Paris since it had been announced that the embassies were being evacuated. Therefore there was no point in our going. So, goodbye to my visa!—at least for the moment. We shall have to wait until the situation settles down and the location of the Diplomatic Corps is clarified before trying again to get a visa.

François has gotten a job as a workman in a factory building military equipment. He has a very busy schedule, working twelve hours a day including Sundays. In order to save time, I bought the food, met him at the river, and had lunch during his free half hour. Since in coming days François is going to be busy all day at work, he had the wonderful idea of renting a canoe to celebrate his new job.

Monsieur Gutt, to my distress, informed me that there was nothing else that could be done at the present time to obtain a visa. We will have to see where the British embassy relocates itself. In great discouragement, I wrote a letter to Aunt Dorothy and to Etienne Gutt at Rugby.

Monsieur Gutt informed me that he was going to give me a letter of recommendation for the British military attaché, who is now located at Nantes or perhaps Bordeaux. I decided that if I go through Nantes I will try to see Robert, who is nearby. Since François was busy I went and had supper by myself with some croissant and hot chocolate at our usual little café. I returned to the hotel and stayed in François' room until his return at ten past nine, at which time he informed me that, beginning at midnight Italy is declaring war on Britain and France.

Earlier in the day François wrote a long letter to Janine while sitting on the riverbank describing the previous evening, which he had spent with his father, and also various events of today.

As the latest developments prevent a return to Paris, Francis stays here until further notice. He has finished Vigny and now I will give him Balzac to read. Today I bought for Francis, *Les Contes de Voltaire* and the *Lettres Persannes* [by Montesquieu]. A while ago, after returning the canoe to its owner, we swam against the current to rejoin our clothes on the banks of the river. At the place where the current was strongest, Francis and I swam absolutely flat out and stayed in exactly the same place! We decided in order to preserve ourselves as future soldiers, to cover the rest of the distance on foot along the riverbank.

Tuesday, June 11. Since François needed his bicycle to go to work I did all the shopping on foot today. After breakfast, I took a letter at Monsieur Gutt's request to Monsieur Lebon, his chief of staff. I then went to the Ministry of Education in order to register Robert for university exams, in case he can take them. After shopping, I met François at the river. He has been promoted to draftsman, which means that he will not have to work such long hours. I ran into Jean-Michel Romain, a high-school classmate of mine in Brussels. He is the first person from school I have run into since I left Brussels. We described to each other our adventures since we left home. We arranged to meet again tomorrow. He told me he did not know where his father was, his father being a senior Belgian Army officer. On returning to the hotel, I wrote in my diary waiting for François and then I went back to my abode and was criticized understandably by Madame Proidal for returning very late.

Wednesday, June 12. I got up very rested and went to the Café Bar Calmont where I met François and the whole family Van Langenhoven, who also have breakfast there every day. Marie-Rose Van Langenhoven and I went to the reception center for refugees, which is located close to the railroad station. On the way I ran into Jacqueline Berger, the sister of Simone, whom I knew from gymnastics classes in Brussels. Marie-Rose and I went to the canteen of the reception center and served food to the refugees for several hours. Then we went shopping for food and ate in

François' hotel room. I went to my meeting with Jean-Michel Romain, but he did not show up. I got a haircut, bought a cheap shirt at Prixunix [the French equivalent of Woolworth's], had a bath at the hotel, changed my clothes, and did my laundry. François was still working, so I walked around the town and ate at an inexpensive restaurant. I am increasingly worried about money at this point because I can see all the money that I have, including the sum I borrowed from Monsieur Gutt, disappearing very quickly. I went back to François' room at the hotel, and wrote in my war diary while waiting for François. The news tonight was that the Italians had bombed Malta, and it was expected that Egypt would in all probability enter the war on the side of the Allies. It was also announced that the Belgian merchant marine had been mentioned with honor by the French Navy for its part in the evacuation of the Allied troops from Dunkirk.

Thursday, June 13. I decided to visit Lieutenant Lambion and his family and all my friends at the Bolin Farm in Jardres, which was serving as General Vinçotte's headquarters. It took me an hour and a half to cover the 20 kilometers. Upon my arrival in these bucolic surroundings, I was pressed with questions about what was happening in Poitiers and what the Belgian government was going to do. We had a magnificent meal and afterwards I read in the sunshine. Marcel, the chief scout, is now earning some money, 15 francs per day to work on the farm. Janine, the daughter of Lieutenant Lambion, informed me that she had seen in a newspaper that they had news from an A. de Marneffe. This was my father's first initial, and I was very puzzled because my family had made it very clear that they were intending to stay in Brussels. After lunch we picked cherries, which were delicious. At six o'clock I left to go back to Poitiers. I had borrowed François' bicycle to come to this village and on the way back I was lucky enough to hang onto a whole series of trucks, which helped me to cover the distance much faster than in the morning.

The military situation is extremely serious. The Germans are at the gates of Paris. This evening François invited me to have dinner with him in an excellent restaurant. For the fun of it François wore his white coveralls, which were already quite dirty with grease, but it amused him to show the other guests in the restaurant that he was "a working man."

Friday, June 14. After breakfast in our little café, I tried to look up some of Marcel's companions whom we had known in Rouen. I wrote two airmail letters, which I sent certified mail to Robert and Aunt Dorothy, hoping they would receive them.

Paul Reynaud, the French prime minister spoke on the radio last night. He described the desperate plight of France and the need of more support from the Allies. He appealed to the United States and President Roosevelt to support France. He claimed that this present struggle was nothing short of a the battle for Western civilization.

Later on, I saw Monsieur Gutt, who told me that after listening to the speech by Paul Reynaud, he expected France to surrender to the Germans! This was shattering news! If France surrenders, the Belgians in France will in all probability have to return to Belgium, but I was absolutely determined not to return to Belgium to live under German occupation. It was, however, likely that the Belgian government would not remain in France but rather would go to England, and I hoped to go with it. I was very frightened and I begged François not to abandon me in such a situation. If ever he were to abandon me I would have only two options left: either for a third time ask for the help of Lieutenant Lambion and his friends; or, my last option, to fend for myself and try and get to England on my own. We had dinner in Room 109 at the Hotel de France, but as François was going to start work the next day at 4:00 A.M., we decided to go to bed early. I went back to my own abode.

It was announced late tonight that Paris has now been occupied by the German Army. The Queen of England spoke this evening, appealing to the women of France in French. The Italians haven't budged and were bombarded by the British in Abyssinia and in Libya.

Saturday, June 15. This morning I went directly to François' factory to meet him. When I arrived, to my horror, I discovered that he was not there! I was terrified that he had left Poitiers without letting me know!

And yet, as I thought of it, I could not believe that he would do such a thing. My next thought was that his alarm clock hadn't worked, and I rushed back to the hotel and went to his room. I found him in bed, ill, and not going to work today and perhaps not even tomorrow. His father went to a cabinet meeting at noon.

The big issue for the Belgian government now is to decide, in the expectation that France will surrender to the Germans, whether to continue in the war and go to England or to follow the example of France and lay down its arms. Monsieur Gutt told us at the end of the cabinet meeting that he had managed to convince the rest of the Belgian government to continue the war and go to England. François and I are thus preparing ourselves to leave Poitiers with Monsieur Gutt. Apparently the British government has offered twenty-four places on board a seaplane to take the Belgian government to England. Some ministers were in favor of accepting this offer, but others were not because they did not wish to leave their families behind. Some of the Belgian ministers have many children, including the prime minister, Monsieur Pierlot, who has six children.

Since we are expecting to leave tomorrow, I decided to visit once again the Lambion family and the major and Marcel to say goodbye and thank them for all the help they have given me in this great adventure. François had asked me not to divulge what I had heard in Poitiers about the plans of the government, but once I was with my friends I felt a certain obligation to share some of the information for their own safety. The best guess was that the French Army would capitulate, and I suggested that they should begin to plan for their own future.

At the end of the day, I returned to Poitiers and to the Hotel de France. I reflected on the day's events and reassessed my own situation. With the approach of the German Army, it was clear that the Belgian government might suddenly decide to leave Poitiers on very short notice, and with the fear I had experienced this morning when I found that François was not at his factory still fresh in my mind, I realized that circumstances might develop that would require François and Monsieur Gutt to leave Poitiers, and that they might not have the time to look for me, since obviously the affairs of state which Monsieur Gutt was responsible for would take precedence. Much as I treasured their friendship and knew of their affection for me, I was realistic enough to realize that it might not be possible for them to track me down before leaving Poitiers. I therefore decided that from now on I would sleep in Monsieur Gutt's car. I went to get my things at the house where I had been living and brought them to the hotel. Tonight I slept on the back seat of the Lincoln with the official government number plate A8, which was a ministerial car and the one which Monsieur Gutt would certainly use to leave Poitiers when the time came.

[Although I continued to write in my diary in subsequent days, at the suggestion of François I removed all the pages that I wrote at the time in order to avoid their being read in the event we were taken prisoner by the Germans or even if we fell into the hands of soldiers or officials of a supposedly "neutral" country, such as Spain or Portugal. Once I reached England and it was safe, I reconstructed the few pages of my diary with my vivid recollection of these incredible events.]

Sunday, June 16. I didn't sleep well in the car, and because of the smell of gasoline I woke up with a terrible headache. The smell of gasoline was due to the fact that Monsieur Gutt's chauffeur, Omer, had made sure to have always enough gasoline, and the space between the front and back seats was filled with cans of gasoline. I went up to the hotel room and ran into Monsieur Gutt in the corridor. He told me that François had a document for me and some more specific instructions. I found François in Room 109, which Monsieur Gutt had just left, and he gave me a piece of paper *(Figure 5)*, which read, in French:

> PASS
>
> Mr. de Marneffe, nephew of Monsieur Gutt, Minister of Finance of Belgium, is accompanying the latter to England via La Rochelle or Bordeaux.
>
> Please let him pass.
>
> Signed the Minister of Finance
>
> Gutt
>
> June 15, 1940.

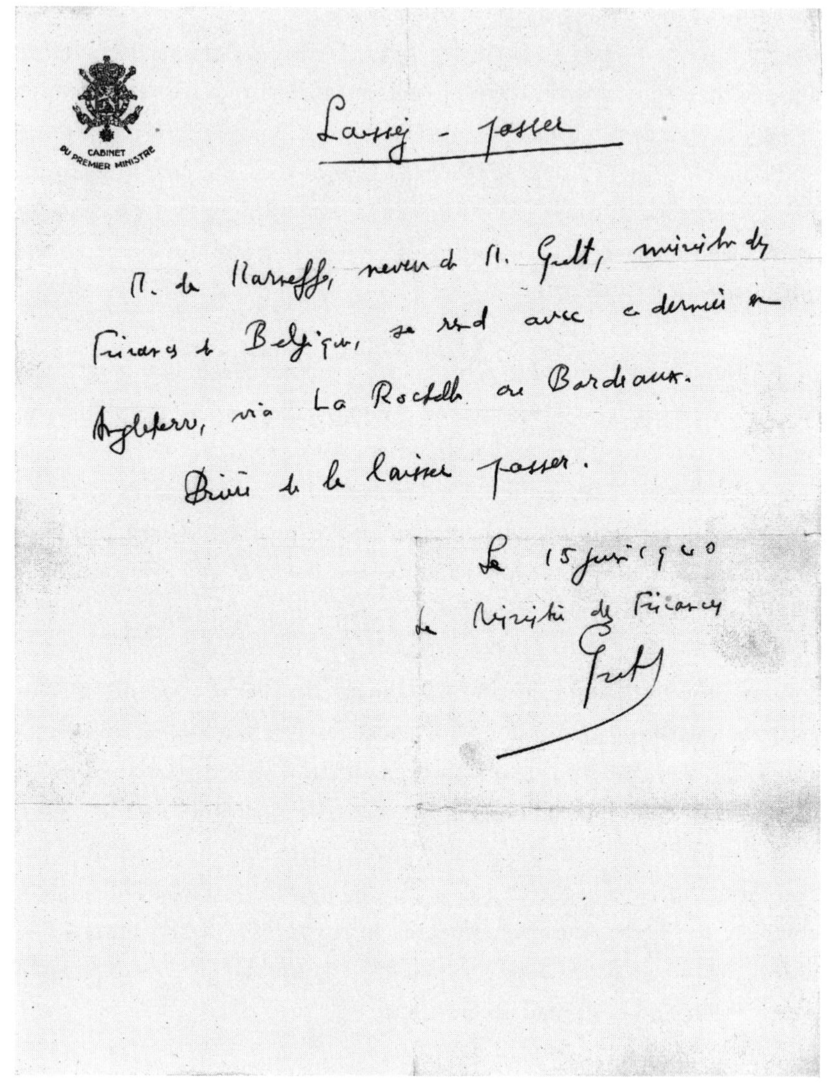

CABINET DU PREMIER MINISTRE

Laissez-passer

M. de Marneffe, neveu de M. Gutt, ministre des Finances de Belgique, se rend avec ce dernier en Angleterre, via La Rochelle ou Bordeaux.

Prière de le laisser passer.

Le 15 juin 1940

Le Ministre des Finances

Gutt

Figure 5. The pass from Monsieur Gutt.

François told me that we were probably going to leave for Bordeaux, but that he was waiting for a reply to the telegram he had sent to Janine in Toulouse asking her to come to Poitiers. The telegram arrived shortly afterwards telling him that she was taking the train from Bordeaux with her parents at three o'clock in the afternoon. François went to the railroad station to get further information but he found no train. Later on, we learned that a British destroyer had been offered to the Belgian government with nine places on board. But again, because there were thirteen ministers the government refused the offer. Monsieur Gutt told us that he had decided to leave the following day for Bordeaux.

At eight o'clock I went to the railroad station at François' request to wait for Janine. But the train for Bordeaux still had not arrived at half past eleven, so I gave up and went back to the hotel and reported to François. I learned that Messieurs Gutt and Janssen, the president of the Belgian National Bank would leave tomorrow at half past four for Bordeaux. In the meantime we were waiting for Janine. Tonight, I slept once again in the car.

Monday, June 17. Messieurs Gutt and Janssen left this morning at half past five. After I left the car, I slept on a camp bed above the garage of the hotel. Subsequently, I ended the night in Mr. Gutt's bedroom with François. The train from Bordeaux still hadn't arrived, and at ten o'clock François received a telegram addressed to his father. With some misgivings, he opened it, and it was in fact meant for him and had been sent by Janine. She informed him that she would be waiting in Bordeaux at No. 1 Rue Blanc Dutrouilh. We prepared to leave in a few minutes and François went to Lebon, the secretary of the Ministry of Finance to get an official stamp put on our pass. He told François that a car from the Ministry of Finance would be leaving for Bordeaux in five minutes. We quickly returned to the hotel to pick up Monsieur Gutt's other car (the 572) and to join the car from the Ministry of Finance. As we passed the Hotel de France I saw my classmate Jean-Michel Romain again and had time to yell goodbye at him through the window.

We drove at high speed toward Bordeaux. The driver, Omer, was Monsieur Gutt's chauffeur, who was available to us since Monsieur Gutt was driving his own car. An hour and a half after leaving Poitiers, we stopped in a small café for lunch. We had a delicious omelet and French-fried potatoes, and then we heard on the radio that the French government had proposed an armistice to the Germans. It was announced that General Huntziger was on his way to German headquarters to discuss the conditions of an armistice. François and I had discussed a number of times what we would do in different circumstances. We thought that time had so far been on our side, but that from the moment the French asked for an armistice, this would no longer be the case. We decided to cut short our meal and leave, though François encountered some objections from Omer, who, as a true Belgian, wanted to finish his meal without hurrying. Finally, François had to be blunt with him and imply that we were prepared to leave without him. Omer was determined to return to Belgium and be with his family. He could not have cared less about the war and he had no intention of going to England. In fact he had made sure that for every gallon of gas he bought to go south away from Brussels, he bought another gallon at the same time in order to drive north after an armistice and return home. This was the reason why there were many gasoline cans in the A8, which had caused my headaches at night as I slept. Finally, Omer elected to come with us, and we continued our journey towards Bordeaux.

As we drew near to Bordeaux the traffic was bumper to bumper for miles. There were long delays at the bridge which spans the Garonne River and François and I decided to leave Omer with the car and cover the last few miles on foot. Monsieur Gutt had arranged for us to meet him at the Hotel de France in Bordeaux, but there was no such place. After further inquiries about where the Belgian ministries might be, we learned from a policeman that they were at 1 Rue Blanc Dutrouilh, the same address that Janine had mentioned in her telegram. When we reached that address we found Monsieur Gutt, who told us that he had received Janine's address, but he couldn't find it and had lost it!

Monsieur Gutt, although extremely tired, invited us to dinner. We went to a very elegant restaurant, the Pavilion Bleu, for a most remarkable meal attended by a substantial number of the Belgian ministers. At the table was Paul-Emile Janson, a leading minister of many Belgian governments, and currently a minister of state [who was to die in a German extermination camp]; Monsieur Gutt; Ganshof Van der Meersch, the Belgian Judge Advocate General; and many other ministers. Altogether there were ten or twelve of us. After dinner the Belgian government met in executive session with all the ministers to continue their discussions and to decide whether to go on with the war and go to England or not. During this meeting François and I waited in the car until after midnight.

Eventually Monsieur Gutt came out with Ganshof Van der Meersch and drove us all to the *Baudouinville*, the largest ship in the Belgian merchant marine, to spend the night. This ship, the pride of the Belgian fleet, is anchored in Bordeaux harbor. This ship could take the whole of the Belgian government to England, but the shipping company is scared after the loss of three of its ships: the *Leopoldville* was sunk outside of Le Havre, and the *Periapolis* and *Elizabethville* at Antwerp. What a change from my living conditions in recent days! When we arrived on board, we were each given a beautiful cabin with real bunks and real sheets—what luxury! During the night Bordeaux harbor was bombed and I got very scared.

Tuesday, June 18. I slept well later in the night but earlier, around one o'clock, there was an air raid, and I was so scared I went to François' cabin next to mine. François was extremely worried about Janine, whom he had not seen as a result of Monsieur Gutt losing her address. In some ways his mind was not on our planning. I felt that it was up to me to get him to concentrate on the steps we would need to take to get to England. I thought we had a number of choices, which we discussed during the night. The ideal would be to find a boat in Bordeaux to take us directly to England. The next best would be for Monsieur Gutt to give us one of his cars, preferably the one with the special ministerial number plate, and all the necessary passes, and we would take it to the Atlantic coast on the Bay of Biscay. There we would either buy a boat—a sailing boat or a motor boat or even exchange the car for a boat—and sail along the French and Spanish coasts until we reached Portugal, and from there get a boat to take us to England. The third and least desirable plan was to drive M. Gutt's car into Spain as rapidly as possible, hoping not to be arrested by the Spaniards—who officially were neutral but as fascists were leaning towards the Germans—and to get into Portugal by land, and from there to England.

At breakfast we sat at a table with Monsieur Gutt and Marcel-Henri Jaspar, the Belgian minister of health. The captain of the ship came over and talked to Monsieur Gutt. Monsieur Gutt tried to convince him to take his ship to England, but the captain claimed he didn't have enough diesel fuel to do that. So Monsieur Gutt assured him that he could get all the fuel he needed. The captain clearly did not want to risk taking the ship out of the harbor. There was a rumor that there were two Italian submarines in the estuary just outside Bordeaux, and the captain was scared that his ship might be sunk. [We learned later that the Germans had seized the *Baudouinville* and converted it into an armed merchant cruiser, and that it was sunk by the Allies.]

Monsieur Gutt went to a cabinet meeting this morning, and François and I waited for Janine to join us. She arrived at 9:30 A.M. to François' great relief, and it became clear to me at that point that Janine and François were very much in love and that she was in fact his fiancée.

Yesterday we had filled out a questionnaire to permit us to leave France and go to England via Spain and Portugal, and today we went to get this permit, but it had not yet arrived. Monsieur Gutt asked me to go next door to the British consulate and let him know when the British ambassador to the French government arrived. I went to the consulate, and when a distinguished-looking gentlemen whom I thought might be the ambassador arrived, I inquired and learned it was indeed the ambassador. I left the British consulate and went a block away back to the house on Rue Blanc Dutrouilh, where the Belgian cabinet was meeting in executive session. I walked up to the second floor without being stopped by a policeman. It was a very simple, medium-sized room with a long table in the middle, a few chairs on the side, and packing cases, on which some of the ministers were sitting. It was very poorly furnished and had no decoration on the walls.

To my amazement the Belgian cabinet with thirteen ministers was meeting in executive session, still trying to decide whether to go on with the war! I went over to Monsieur Gutt and informed him that the British ambassador had arrived. He got up, offered his apologies to the prime minister, and left the room with me. We went together next door to the British consulate, where François and Janine were waiting for us. Monsieur Gutt asked us for our passports and Janine's identity card. For the next hour or so Gutt was in a private meeting with the ambassador. When he returned with the ambassador, the latter said, "Monsieur Gutt, I cannot tell you how grateful we are for what you have done, and is there anything I can do for you?" Gutt said there was, and pointing to François he said François was his son, Janine François' fiancée, and pointing to me said I was his "nephew," and that we all three wanted to go to England and that if he could provide us with British visas we would be very grateful. The ambassador called an assistant to issue the visas and we left the building.

We learned that Gutt had been engaged in a very crucial transaction with the ambassador, hence the latter's gratitude. Monsieur Gutt had lent the whole of the Belgian gold reserve to the British government for the duration of the war! Ninety percent of the gold we were told had been traveling in fourteen trucks from Belgium to Bordeaux,[5] and ten percent was in Paris. [During the war the Belgian government sued the Vichy government of France in federal court in New York for the gold, which they had refused to return to the Belgians. The court ruled in favor of Belgium. That use of the Belgian gold by the British was crucial to the conduct of the war, because these were the days of "Cash and Carry"—in other words, only for cash would the Americans supply arms to the British. This "Cash and Carry" policy officially continued until March 11, 1941, when President Roosevelt signed the Lend-Lease Act.] Three visas for the Belgian gold! These must have indeed been the most expensive visas in history![6]

Now that we had our visas the next hurdle was to find a boat to get to England. François was very engrossed in his relationship with Janine, and

---

[5] The trucks did not identify their contents. But whenever they stopped, Belgian police would prevent passersby from getting too close by telling them, "Stay away, stay away, that is the Belgian Gold . . . !"

[6] In his memoirs, which he wrote after the war, Monsieur Gutt gives a rather different story than what I understood at the time. Apparently much of the Belgian gold had already been transferred to England and also to the United States, and it was the portion of the gold which had been left in Paris which the French government had promised to hand over to the Belgian government that was the subject of the discussion with the British ambassador on June 18. A British destroyer with a Captain Onslow was standing by to carry the Belgian gold to England, and Monsieur Gutt describes in his memoirs how the French government betrayed the Belgians by not handing over the gold that was in Paris at the time and that was only subsequently obtained as a result of the lawsuit in New York.

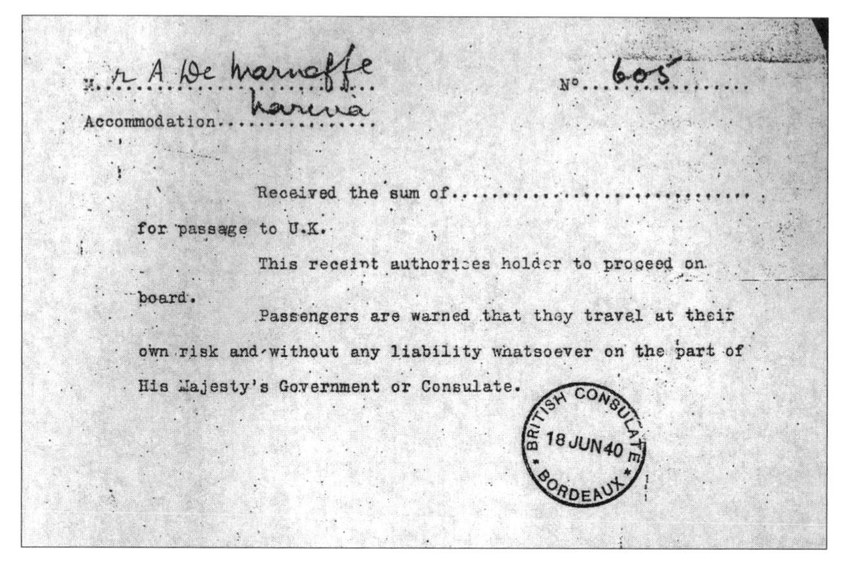

Mr A De Marneffe No. 605

Accommodation Mariva

Received the sum of ....

for passage to U.K.

This receipt authorizes holder to proceed on board.

Passengers are warned that they travel at their own risk and without any liability whatsoever on the part of His Majesty's Government or Consulate.

BRITISH CONSULATE 18 JUN 40 BORDEAUX

Figure 6. Boarding pass for the SS Mariva.

was so delighted to have found her again that he was not paying much attention to the next steps. I felt that I was the one who must keep his eyes open to the opportunities to leave France. While I was standing outside the British consulate I noticed a blackboard with an announcement that the SS *Mariva* was available to British subjects wishing to return to England at Le Verdon, in the estuary of the Gironde on the Atlantic Coast. We obtained a pass *(Figure 6)* giving each of us permission to board the SS *Mariva*. We did not have much time to get to the ship and we were very grateful that Monsieur Gutt drove us to the railroad station to take a train for Le Verdon. On the way to the Gare Saint Louis, he seemed to be very despondent and told us that the Belgian government had decided to return to Brussels, probably in the next two weeks. I was very sorry to hear of this decision. Nevertheless, I took advantage of it and quickly wrote a letter, part of which I had already prepared ahead of time, addressed to my parents to let them know what had happened to me. Until this moment there had been no communication from me to my parents except my two postcards early on, which might not have reached them. I knew they must be very worried about me and I wanted them to know that I was on my way to England.

It took us two and a half hours to reach Le Verdon. We boarded a ferry boat to take us to the SS *Mariva*. We spent an hour and a half looking all over the harbor for the *Mariva*. When we finally found it, we were denied permission to come on board! Eventually, we arrived at another ship, the SS *Madura*, which was already full of refugees. These two ships which belonged to the P & O (Pacific & Orient Line) were in the Mediterranean, on their way back from India, when Italy declared war on June 10. They were ordered to stop in Bordeaux to pick up as many last-minute refugees as possible and bring them to England.

I will remember all my life the tremendous relief I felt as I arrived on board this ship. We were immediately handed a small mimeographed piece of paper that informed us of the two times of the day when we would be fed. After a long month in the chaos of France, boarding this British ship was an incredible relief. Somebody was in charge who knew what to do, and I felt I was in good hands. Nevertheless, we were by no means out of danger. Shortly after boarding a German plane flew over us, which we were told was shot down by three French fighter planes.

The *Madura* had been built to accommodate 300 passengers in cabins who were traveling from England to India; now it had 1,600 people on board and most people had to stay on the deck. The crew had suspended large tarpaulins from the ship's cranes, thus covering the decks in case of rain. François, Janine, and I found a place on the rear deck; this was to be our home and sleeping quarters for our journey to England. François, with great wisdom, pointed out that with all the people on board there were clearly not enough lifeboats for everyone, and that if the ship were sunk we would be in trouble. We went in search of a wooden table and found one near where we had spread our blankets to sleep. Our plan was that, in the event of the ship being torpedoed or hitting a mine, one of us would immediately retrieve this table; if we had to abandon ship we would throw the table into the sea and hang onto it until we were rescued.

Later that evening we went to eat our meal. Although it was reassuring to get two meals a day they were certainly very Spartan ones consisting of one slice of canned Spam, one boiled potato, and some bread. After supper we went to our "sleeping quarters" on deck under the tarpaulin and spread out. While I read Voltaire before going to sleep, François and Janine, the lovers, went to sleep right away in each others' arms.

Wednesday, June 19. When we woke up this morning we were on the high seas and at first we seemed very much alone and were worried about German submarines and mines. Coming back from breakfast, however, we were very happy to see that we now had a British destroyer escort, which stayed with us for the rest of the journey. As we were walking on deck, we ran into Marcel-Henri Jaspar, the Belgian minister of health with whom we had eaten breakfast yesterday morning. We were very surprised to see him because Monsieur Gutt had told us that the Belgian government had decided to return to Belgium. We were shocked to see that he had abandoned the government. There was some conversation between François and Monsieur Jaspar, and the latter expressed surprise that François' father was not going to England. François explained that his father had a great sense of solidarity with and loyalty towards the Prime Minister. Jaspar implied that there was a time when it was too late for loyalty. François was very tempted to tell him that that moment had not yet arrived.[7]

Today I spent some time sleeping, lying in the sun, and writing in my diary. Around two o'clock a young man with whom I had been talking offered me a sandwich, which was very nice since I was hungry. At half

[7] When Jaspar arrived in England he did not apparently know that his portfolio as a minister had been withdrawn by the government in Bordeaux when they discovered that he had abandoned his post without notice. It was Gutt who informed him a few months later upon his arrival in London. He tried to be a Belgian de Gaulle. He made speeches trying to raise the standard of Free Belgium in England. Jaspar wrote of this time in his autobiography titled *Souvenirs sans Retouches,* which I will refer to again later. It is clear that he had despaired, based on what he had heard at the cabinet meeting on June 17, about the Belgian government's intentions about the war. The latest he had heard was that the prime minister and the rest of the government had decided to stay in France for now and eventually return to Brussels if allowed to do so by the Germans and by the King. Therefore, in his despair and total disagreement with that decision, and because of his belief that the war should be continued, he elected to, unilaterally, depart for England. He was criticized by his colleagues for not telling them of his decision. In fairness to him, given that his wife was Jewish, it was important for them to avoid being caught by the Germans. During the war, although stripped of his portfolio as a minister, Jaspar served Belgium well and honorably as ambassador to exiled Allied governments located in London.

past four, we went to the dining room below deck for dinner and had baked potatoes, rice, and some meat. We heard that we were going towards Falmouth in Cornwall and wondered whether we would arrive tomorrow or the next day. We eventually went to sleep.

Thursday, June 20. I did not sleep very well last night. We were struck by the fact that seagulls were flying over the ship, suggesting that we were approaching land. At 8:35 A.M. we saw the English coast! What an incredible relief it was to arrive in England at long last after so many weeks of planning and worry—England was in view! We washed and got ready to land. Arriving at Falmouth in Cornwall was no easy matter for the captain because he had to avoid mines, and we picked up a pilot. Eventually, we dropped anchor in the bay at ten o'clock. By half past one we still had not disembarked and, being hungry, we went to the Indian crew and bought some of their own Indian food. It was a very expensive meal because they did not have any change and we gave them our cash. It was a typical Indian meal with rice and curry. We spent the rest of the day walking around the deck and observing the various activities performed by the crew in preparation for landing. At half past seven, we went to the dining room for a meal, still wondering when we were going to get off the ship.

At twenty past eight several tugboats came alongside the ship. The first people off the boat were the newspaper reporters, war correspondents, and various VIPs. We had heard during our trip that the Polish government-in-exile was on board and also Eve Curie, a war correspondent and the daughter of the Nobel Prize winners. Marcel-Henri Jaspar was also taken off on the first boat. We were fortunate to get on the second boat, and when we landed we were taken by bus to a reception center where our passports were inspected. The inspector commented that the photograph on my passport was rather old and he wanted to know where I had learned English. They examined our luggage very briefly, simply saying, "Any cigarettes, any revolvers, any cameras? All right." We were told that a train would be leaving tomorrow at ten o'clock for London. At the reception center we were very well taken care of. We were lent blankets on which to lie on the lawn; it was fortunately a beautiful night and the weather, which had been so dry and sunny for the past month was continuing. Friendly English ladies provided us with food and tea and couldn't have been kinder. Their attitude was that we had gone through hell on the Continent but now they were telling us that we could relax and rest all we wanted. That is not what we wanted to hear since we were very eager to get to London and get on with our lives. I was impressed by the remarkable organization and efficiency and the calm with which the British were behaving. What a difference from the chaos in France! I wondered out loud to an English lady, "What is England going to do now that the great, supposedly invincible French Army has been defeated and France is out of the war?" I will never forget her reply, which was, "Well yes, dear, isn't it nice there is no one left to let us down?" What a spirit!

Friday, June 21. We all slept very well on the lawn. While we were still lying "in bed" we were brought a cup of soup which was nice and warm. When we got up, we washed under a tap and packed our bags. François, Janine, and I went to the railroad station to find out when the train for London would be leaving. We learned that there would be one leaving at 9:55 A.M. which would arrive in London at 5:30 P.M. I thought that if I took that train I could catch a train later that evening to Banbury. When we went back to the reception center, to our surprise we had to talk our way back in because they wondered how we had gotten out. That is the point at which we began to realize that, without being very obvious about it, the English were keeping close tabs on us refugees: we were told that we were really not supposed to leave the center without permission. On our return, still marveling at the excellent organization of this center for the reception of refugees, we learned that an official train would leave later in the day and would not cost us anything. We decided to wait and leave with the rest of the refugees.

I went to Lloyd's Bank to change the rest of my French money, at least up to the amount authorized. I was allowed to change 2,600 French francs at the rate of 178 francs to the pound. François and I discussed our finances and he lent me two pounds. We discovered that Janine had not received a very important document, so we inquired about it and looked for a particular employee. After dinner, François and Janine went to the bank to change their money, but the bank was closed. We were still concerned about Janine's important document, which had not arrived, when the officer in question arrived and told us that after all it really wasn't that important. We learned that the six o'clock train to London would accept foreigners like us, at which point we jumped in the bus to go to the station. We found some very good seats near the corridor. I marveled again at the remarkable organization which the British had established. There was a YMCA at the entrance to the station, which distributed free food on the platform and in the train.

At twenty minutes past six the train left the station and we were on our way. We went through Devonport, where we saw naval ships anchored in the bay and balloon barrages over the town to prevent dive-bombing. After that we went through Plymouth, but as the evening wore on and it got dark, I found a more comfortable area in which to sleep in the carriage that housed the post office. I spread the blanket and was able to sleep lying on the floor. Finally we went to sleep and at dawn we arrived in London.

Saturday, June 22. On arrival in London, we were given sandwiches and a cup of tea on the train. When I had finished eating, I wanted to stretch my legs and left my carriage to deposit the cup on a bench on the platform. After I had taken a few steps, a tall English policeman touched my elbow and very politely said that he would take care of the cup and that I should return to my carriage. This again reinforced our impression that we were under very close supervision. Clearly the English were determined to protect themselves effectively from any Fifth Column activity, and were not going to let refugees such as ourselves scatter around the English countryside without some very careful screening. Later that morning we were, railroad car by railroad car, put on double-decker buses, each with a policeman guarding the exit, and driven across London to North London near Crystal Palace.

When we arrived at the reception center, we were given some food and a bed. This is where we were going to be registered and questioned, and we began to feel once again very impatient. What François, Janine, and I wanted to do was to leave and get on with our lives, but things were not going to be that simple. We spent the rest of the morning walking around, and after lunch we went to the offices where we had to show our passports, were interviewed by doctors, and the police examined our luggage. We were then interviewed by the Belgian consul, who informed François that he was not allowed to leave because he is of military age and will have to serve in the Belgian forces. The consul went to telephone the embassy to find out whether something special could be done for the son of a Belgian minister, but it being Saturday the embassy was closed.

Apparently, when I had filled out the questionnaire form on arrival at this reception center, I had written my birth date as 1924, but the 4 had appeared to the reader as a 7. When I was interviewed, he said, "Well, you were born in 1927 and you are only 13, and therefore you are free to leave." I had a very difficult debate within myself at that moment. Was I going to try and get away with this, or was I going to clarify that I was in fact born in 1924? I decided, partly out of honesty and partly in order to stay with François to level with them and clarify that I was 16. They said, "Ah, well, you too are not allowed to leave since you are between the ages of 16 and 35!" So once again having reached England essentially under our own steam we were confronted by the "16 to 35" issue which had begun in Belgium and which had led to my leaving home in the first place. My arrival in Bloxham would be delayed. [In retrospect, it is strange that I did not telephone my aunts the moment I arrived in England. I believe that I was so eager to surprise them personally that I did not think sufficiently of the worry that they must have been feeling at not having heard from me since they had received my telegram many weeks before.]

We asked for permission for Janine, who was allowed to leave, to stay one more night in the reception center. Although the consul had contacted the ambassador we decided that tomorrow Janine would go to the embassy to explain our situation. It seemed to us that we had two ways of getting out of this camp. The Belgian ambassador in London at that time, the Baron de Cartier de Marchienne, the dean of the diplomatic corps, was a great friend of Monsieur Gutt, and we believed that if he knew that François was here he would help us. Another option was for me to renounce my Belgian nationality and to become a British subject, something I was already beginning to think about even if I got out of the camp.

I also realized that if François and Janine were to get married they would be free to leave, and on that note we all went to sleep on our camp beds.

Sunday, June 23. After breakfast I gave Janine a letter for her to mail to Aunt Dorothy. Janine left for the embassy and François and I lay down on our beds. I wrote in my diary, read *The Hounds of the Baskervilles*, and around ten o'clock that morning I went to sleep and woke up at one o'clock, just in time for lunch. During dessert, Janine entered the dining room and informed us that she had come back from the embassy, with an embassy counselor, Jean Nieuwenhuis, who would do everything possible to get us out of the reception center. He told us that he was going to speak to "the head of the prison." After this conversation, though, he apologized for having given us false hopes, and he admitted having difficulty in finding out where the order to hold us had come from. After lunch he was going to speak to the British Home Office and Scotland Yard. He admitted that it would be difficult since this was a Sunday, but he thought he would have some news for us by tomorrow afternoon. Janine left the camp with Monsieur Nieuwenhuis and François and I sat down in the sun in front of the building and read our books.

At around half past five an officer informed us that we could leave and that a car was on its way to fetch us! We packed our luggage very quickly and gave the address where we three were going to be staying. The driver of the car was Monsieur Nieuwenhuis himself, and he drove us to the Belgian embassy in Eaton Square. François went to see his father's friend, the ambassador, and the military attaché, who informed him that he would not be called into the army until some time in the future, and that I would have to present myself to the embassy when I reached the age of 17. Jean Nieuwenhuis then drove us to the Regent Palace Hotel near Picadilly Circus, where François and Janine were going to stay. After this he drove me to Paddington Station. I bought some chocolate, sandwiches, and lemonade, and at half past seven I boarded the train for Banbury. I met an English soldier with whom I spoke throughout the journey. We gave each other some souvenirs and he promised to send me some English emblems. We passed through familiar places, Reading and

Oxford, where the English soldier got off. He told me that he was on his way to Bampton where my Aunt Lilias [the mother of John Loveday, who had died aboard the HMS *Exmouth*] lived, and I gave him a little note to give to Aunt Lilias. I arrived in Banbury having been given an RA (Royal Artillery) button by a soldier.

Upon arriving at Banbury Station I took a taxi in the middle of the night and arrived at Bloxham at the front door of Nut Tree Cottage shortly after midnight. I rang the bell, and at first there was no answer, so I rang the bell again and finally Aunt Dorothy opened the upstairs window. I told her who I was and she couldn't quite grasp it, so I repeated it and eventually she said, "Francis—what? What? Well, I never!" She came downstairs with Aunt Katherine, opened the door, and I quickly gave them a thumbnail sketch of my trip and my adventure. Aunt Dorothy gave me some lemonade and congratulated me on arriving safely. They told me that they had given up hope of seeing me when it was announced over the radio that the last boat from Bordeaux had arrived and they hadn't heard from me. We went upstairs to the attic and we made up my bed in the bedroom where Jacques Piraux and I had slept the previous summer.

Aunt Dorothy told me that she had sent me and Robert some money. I hadn't received any, and I had very much hoped that Robert had because I was sure that he needed it.[8] It turned out that today, the 24th of June, was Aunt Dorothy's birthday, and she always told me in later years that she could not have had a nicer birthday present. This phase of my adventure was over. It had begun one month and ten days ago in Brussels.

[8] After the war, I saw a letter Robert had written to M. Gutt at Poitiers, asking to borrow some money, but I don't believe he received any. He did however receive the two pounds from Aunt Dorothy.

CHAPTER V

THE ENGLISH SCHOOLBOY

June 1940 – January 1943

MY ARRIVAL AT Bloxham on the 24th of June 1940 opened a new, exciting chapter in my life. It was a momentous time, not only because of my personal experiences, but because 1940 and 1941 were incredible and dramatic years for Britain. With the whole of Western Europe occupied by Germany, England stood alone. We all felt that, upon the forthcoming Battle of Britain—and battle *for* Britain—the future of our world, as we knew it, would be decided. The British people showed an unconquerable spirit articulated magnificently by Winston Churchill, the prime minister, who

> I would say to the House [of Commons], as I said to those who have joined this government: "I have nothing to offer but blood, toil, tears and sweat.
>
> We have before us an ordeal of the most grievous kind. We have before us many, many long months of struggle and suffering. You ask, what is our policy? I will say: it is to wage war by sea, land, and air, with all our might and with all the strength that God can give us: to wage war against a monstrous tyranny, never surpassed in the dark, lamentable catalogue of human crime. That is our policy. You ask, what is our aim? I can answer in one word: Victory—victory at all costs, victory in spite of all terror, victory, however long and hard the road may be; for without victory, there is no survival.
>
> PRIME MINISTER WINSTON CHURCHILL,
> *speaking in the British House of Commons, May 13, 1940*

Nut Tree Cottage, Bloxham, near Banbury in Oxfordshire. The thatched roof cottage where I lived with my aunts Dorothy and Katherine during World War II.

used his oratory to inspire the British people to great efforts and great courage. Even today, his speeches are deeply moving and still strike a most responsive chord in all who heard them during World War II. I for one used to be able to quote verbatim from his major speeches, and still get goose bumps when I read or hear them now. We expected the Germans to try and invade Britain. We knew that the British Army had lost most of its equipment during the evacuation from Dunkirk. The way ahead was very uncertain and, although we didn't think about it most of the time, we knew that on the result of the invasion of Britain would depend our whole future.

Churchill did not disguise the seriousness of the situation, but by his own courage and determination he inspired us all to believe that, if there were an invasion, we would fight to the bitter end and perhaps survive as a nation. We believed that if we could hang on and avoid defeat, something, somehow, would happen that would bring other nations into the war on our side, especially the United States. Over the years, whenever people hear that I lived in England between 1940 and 1950, they often comment that 1940 and 1941 must have been terrible years. My response is always, "Not at all." For in spite of the bombing, the thousands of deaths and destruction, and the dangers we encountered, 1940 and '41 were glorious years in England, ones in which there was a unity of purpose and determination on the part of the people in all walks of life. It was for me a most wonderful experience to have lived in England during that time. I would not have missed it for anything in the world. It was a time, in some ways, of contradiction because our lives went on, on a day-to-day basis, as if we were confident that there would be a tomorrow, and yet we were daily preoccupied with the course of the war. We listened to the BBC news, usually four times a day, and every day the 6:00 P.M. and 9:00 P.M. news during the Battle of Britain gave the number of German aircraft shot down and the number of our planes lost and British pilots saved.

This is how I looked upon arriving in England from France, June 1940.

I could not have been more fortunate in arriving in Bloxham to be looked after by my aunts Dorothy and Katherine. They were two of my mother's younger sisters, both unmarried and in their late fifties. They had led very different lives and were very different people, but both of them were warm, caring and loving, and they looked after me in a most generous and thoughtful way. I had met both of them many times over the years in London, Brussels, and at Bloxham. (On our family's visits to England in earlier years our first stop was usually at 22 Cheniston Gardens in the Kensington section of London, where Dorothy and her mother, Grandy, lived. My grandmother died in 1936, and after that Dorothy and Katherine moved to Bloxham.)

Dorothy, a year younger than my mother at 57, was a remarkable woman. As my cousin Norah Nicholls wrote so accurately in 1980:

"She could turn her hand to anything and make something beautiful of it, including gardens, but there was never time or money for her to develop her full potential in any single field of work.

"She was first educated for architecture, but finding no prospects likely in that line, she did hand bookbinding in a workshop with a friend for several years with considerable success and had some pupils.

"During the First World War, at first she did munitions factory work, then spent most of the time in the W.A.A.C. [Woman's Auxiliary Army Corps] and became an excellent motor mechanic under very severe conditions with ambulances in the front line.

"Later on, after the war [WWI], she studied sculpture at the Polytechnic on Regent Street, in London, and this was where her talent came to fruition. Wood was her favourite medium; she exhibited at the Royal Academy and sold some of her work. She also taught handicrafts at a boarding school in Ascot. She counts, therefore, as a professional artist, though the family claims always prevented her from having the full career she deserved."[1]

Katherine, then 56, had been a teacher and had served for a number of years as a governess for children of prominent families in India and the Middle East. She had traveled extensively as governess to the children of General Clayton (the brother of Jack Clayton, who was married to Florence, a cousin of mine—about whom more later) and she had also been in the Middle East during the First World War, meeting T. E. Lawrence (Lawrence of Arabia) and General Allenby, the Commander-in-Chief of the British forces in the Middle East. She had attended the wedding in the early twenties of Lord Louis Mountbatten, later Earl Mountbatten of Burma. She had had a most interesting life, and there is even a reference to her in one of the books written by Lawrence of Arabia.

Nut Tree Cottage had a thatched roof and a lovely garden, lovingly tended by my aunts, and there was separate from it a garage and studio in which Dorothy did her work. Dorothy was the head of the Women's Voluntary Service in Bloxham. The WVS was a volunteer organization with a

[1] In 1940 she began an altar piece (in which Clement and I were models!) which she gave to Coventry Cathedral after it was destroyed and rebuilt. When my family and I visited Coventry Cathedral in 1994 we saw the altar piece in one of the chapels.

We shall go on to the end, we shall fight in France, we shall fight on the seas and oceans, we shall fight with growing confidence and growing strength in the air, we shall defend our island, whatever the cost may be, we shall fight on the beaches, we shall fight on the landing grounds, we shall fight in the fields and in the streets, we shall fight in the hills; we shall never surrender, and even if, which I do not for a moment believe, this island or a large part of it were subjugated and starving, then our Empire beyond the seas, armed and guarded by the British Fleet, would carry on the struggle, until, in God's good time, the New World, with all its power and might, steps forth to the rescue and liberation of the old.

PRIME MINISTER WINSTON CHURCHILL,
speaking in the British House of Commons, June 4, 1940

very large membership nationally which, in each village and town, organized the important civilian services for the war. For instance, Dorothy was responsible for the billeting of the children and teachers evacuated from London to avoid the bombing. Thus it was that in Nut Tree Cottage itself, in addition to Dorothy, Katherine, and my great-aunt Laura, there was a Miss Walton ("Meduck" by nickname), who was a teacher who had been evacuated from London. As part of the war effort, paper, aluminum, and other metals were saved and recycled, and it was up to Aunt Dorothy to organize this effort. The woodshed at the end of the garden was where the people of the village dropped off their paper, cardboard, and aluminum, etc. Each week members of the WVS came to do the sorting, for instance, separating one kind of paper from another, and periodically these materials would be collected by the authorities.[2]

---

[2] One day when I returned from school, I was told the following story by my aunts. One of the WVS volunteers, a Mrs. Jackson, who lived in a nearby village, had come to our house with her sister, Unity Mitford, to sort through some of the waste paper for recycling. Unity Mitford was quite notorious because she had been a close friend of Adolf Hitler and had at the beginning of the war in September 1939 made a suicide attempt in Germany because of her distress at the war between Britain and Germany. Hitler had put his private train at her disposal to pass through Holland on her way to England. Another Mitford sister, formerly married to Lord Moyne, was now married to Sir Oswald Moseley, the founder of

The day following my arrival at Bloxham was a very busy one, Several important tasks had to be accomplished as rapidly as possible. Given the very dilapidated state of my clothes, one of the first tasks was to get some decent clothes to begin school. Aunt Dorothy was very enterprising and collected some clothing from relatives and neighbors, but some still had to be bought. Another task was to register with the police in Banbury and get my Alien Registration Certificate. The British had learned a lesson from the debacle in France and were very careful about registering foreigners and limiting their activities. In addition to the Alien Registration Certificate I had to get a special permit to bicycle and only within a radius of five miles. Whenever I had to go beyond the five-mile limit, I had to get an additional special permit from the police in Banbury and the police at my destination.

Another important task was to arrange my entrance to Bloxham School. Some preliminary planning had been done in earlier years. After my parents had decided in 1938 that, in the event of war, my sister and I would go to England, my aunts had spoken to Mr. Armitage, the then headmaster about my admission as a day boy. The school had been very helpful and willing to make an exception to some of its rules. The school was part of the Woodard Group founded in the past century and very High Anglican Church. Mr. Armitage was made aware of my own lack of religious affiliation, but in spite of that he was willing to admit me provided I would attend daily chapel as every other boy. Mr. Armitage was now in the armed forces and his successor was Mr. K. T. Dewey, who enrolled me after he and I met. I was impressed by the friendly reception I received at the school. There were three houses at Bloxham: Wilberforce (mine), named after a religious man, Wilson, and Crake. On my first day of school, the housemaster accompanied me and introduced me to the

---

the British Union of Fascists, and they were both interned as potential security risks by the British authorities in May of 1940. Unity Mitford, who was considered mentally ill, was put in the custody of various members of her family, including her sister, Mrs. Jackson. My aunts reported rather strange behavior on Unity's part. They had all tried to avoid any discussion of the war, but suddenly, out of the blue, Unity exclaimed, "Ah, Hitler, how I love that man!" to the embarrassment of all concerned. I was sorry to have missed this event by having to attend school.

master and the students in my class, explaining that I was Belgian and had just come over from the Continent because of the war. Since I still expected to go to the University of Brussels and probably study medicine, I believed that I should take Latin, Greek, physics, and chemistry in order to qualify for that program, as I had been doing in Belgium. Other school activities involved swimming, and early on I was asked to join the school swimming team. We often visited other schools for swimming competitions.

The English Schoolboy wearing his Bloxham School blazer, Summer 1941.

Soon after I arrived at Bloxham, I wrote to Etienne Gutt, who was at Rugby School, about 30 miles away. Thus began a most remarkable correspondence, a quite unique experience in my life. Over the next two years, Etienne and I wrote to each other practically every week, and I still have all his letters. Much of our news related to our respective school experiences, how we were doing in the classroom, in our various exams, in our sporting activities, (swimming, cricket, rugger)—but also sharing our views about the war. In the first letter I received from him, three days after my arrival, he asked me if I knew where his father was. All I could tell him was that I had last seen him in Bordeaux on June 18, and that at that time he had thought he might be going back to Belgium. This correspondence solidified our friendship started before the war, sculling on the canal. Both of us were far from our families, his mother in Belgium and planning to remain there doing her Red Cross work and his father with an uncertain future as far as we knew at that time. The only member of his family in England was François, whom he hadn't seen yet. Three days after my arrival, François and Janine left London and, on their way to Rugby to see Etienne, they came and spent the night with us at Bloxham.

I expect that the Battle of Britain is about to begin. Upon this battle depends the survival of Christian civilisation. Upon it depends our own British life, and the long continuity of our institutions and our Empire. The whole fury and might of the enemy must very soon be turned on us. Hitler knows that he will have to break us in this island or lose the war. If we can stand up to him all Europe may be free and the life of the world may move forward into broad, sunlit uplands. But if we fail, then the whole world, including the United States, including all that we have known and care for, will sink into the abyss of a new Dark Age made more sinister, and perhaps more protracted, by the lights of perverted science. Let us therefore brace ourselves to our duties, and so bear ourselves that, if the British Empire and its Commonwealth last for a thousand years, men will still say, "This was their finest hour."

PRIME MINISTER WINSTON CHURCHILL,
broadcasting on June 18, 1940

Another very important activity was going to the Gibbs farm at Milcombe, a nearby village, where in previous visits to Bloxham I had ridden ponies and befriended the four Gibbs brothers—Harold, William, Joe, and one other—who had all served in the British Army in the First World War and knew France and Belgium. Over the next year and a half, I was to spend a lot of my free time at the farm: riding ponies, helping with farm work during the haymaking season and the harvest, milking cows, and mending fences.

Shortly after the 10th of May, when it appeared that France was in trouble and that Britain might be the next target of Hitler, the Local Defense Volunteers (LDV) was created by the British government as a militia, a citizen army. The plan was that, in the event of an invasion, every town, village, and hamlet would be defended by the LDV. Eventually this group was renamed the Home Guard and had millions of people in it. I wanted to volunteer but being only 16 and an alien, I was not allowed to join officially. Initially the LDVs had no arms or uniforms.

They wore an LDV armband and trained with brooms. I was, however, unofficially enrolled as a messenger, and on many occasions I carried messages from one section of the LDV to another. Captain Fox lived in a big house in Bloxham and was in charge of the local LDV. He had been a captain in World War I and was an important individual in the community. I visited him and his wife many times and I used to go horseback riding on his property, sometimes with his attractive 11-year-old niece, Daphne, whose father had been killed in the RAF during the Battle of Britain.[3]

As the summer wore on, we anticipated an invasion. Many barges had been spotted on the northern coasts of France and Belgium, presumably in preparation for an invasion of England. There was a high degree of LDV alert, and on several nights I accompanied the Gibbs brothers on all-night patrols. There was a small hut on a hill in South Newington, a village about five miles from Bloxham in which we spent the night, alert to the possibility of German paratroopers landing. Periodically we left the hut and patrolled the roads, sometimes stopping and investigating cars, motorcycles, and bicycles.

Other security measures were also in force at this time. There was a complete blackout, and the church bells were silent—only to be rung in the event of an invasion.[4] As the summer wore on the Royal Air Force inflicted very heavy casualties on the German Luftwaffe. Every day more German planes were shot down than were lost by the British. In addition, if a British fighter plane was shot down over Britain there was a fairly good chance that the pilot would bail out and survive to fight again, often

---

[3] Daphne was a very attractive and precocious 11-year-old girl with whom I went riding. On one occasion we had a picnic in a field under brilliant sunshine. Our ponies were next to us and she and I became rather amorous and kissing in a very innocent way. One of the horses came over and started nudging us and Daphne said, "He is jealous that you are making love to me!" I believe she was the first girl I ever kissed. Returning home, I felt very guilty about having been attracted to her and worst of all kissing her. I did not know what to do. Finally I decided to talk to Dorothy, my spinster aunt. But, what to say? Nothing had really happened, we were fully clothed and only kissed, probably only on the cheek! Yet I was so inept and embarrassed at describing what I had done that Dorothy was really worried. I finally had to reassure her that we had not had sexual intercourse! Dorothy was very reassured and reassuring.

[4] Rattles were only to be used to signal a poison gas attack, and people kept weapons such as kitchen knives available to kill Germans and pepper to throw in their eyes.

on the same day. The Battle of Britain was won by a very, very narrow margin. When Churchill went to the headquarters of the 11th Fighter Group, which bore the brunt of the German attack, and he was following the progress of the aerial battle he asked, "Where are the reserves?" and was told there were none. Every available British fighter plane was in the air. That, fortunately, was the turning point of the Battle of Britain.

Our debt to the fighter pilots was well expressed by Winston Churchill on August 20 when he said in the House of Commons, "Never in the field of human conflict was so much owed by so many to so few."

As a result of the destruction of so many German planes, Air Marshal Hermann Goering decided to change his strategy and switched from daylight attacks to bombing British cities indiscriminately at night. Although over the months thousands of civilians were killed and wounded and much destruction occurred, this change in tactics probably saved England. It was basically impossible to completely destroy a city such as London. The success of any German invasion depended upon two factors: the control of the sea around Britain and the control of the air. The Germans achieved neither. Although there were some military targets in London and other cities, the indiscriminate bombing of cities was an attempt to destroy the morale of the British people. However, the net effect of the bombing was to arouse the anger of the British people in a way that had not been the case before, and it did not break their morale.

My uncle Clement Loveday, the youngest of my mother's siblings, also came occasionally to stay in Bloxham. He was the third owner of Nut Tree Cottage, and in 1940 was living in Newcastle in the north of England working for an insurance company and serving as an auxiliary fireman. Auxiliary firemen were volunteers recruited to assist in putting out fires from the bombing. I also had other relatives in the neighborhood. My Aunt Mamie and Uncle Arthur, who was an older brother of my mother's, lived at Aynho, a village about 10 miles from Bloxham, and at Deddington, a few miles from Bloxham, there were some second cousins. From time to time I visited them and they too were very generous towards me. My Uncle Arthur lent me many books to read. I went to tea a number of times to visit my cousins at Deddington—Mary, Nell, Jack, and Bill—all of whom were unmarried.

One of the school-related challenges I faced early on was the fact that, in the summer of 1941, I should be taking the School Certificate Examination, which permitted a student, if he did well, to enter a university. The class I was in, the fifth form, took school certificate on a trial run shortly after I arrived. I soon discovered how difficult it was going to be for me. My whole education had until then been in French. Although I could speak some English, I did not know how to read or write much English. My vocabulary was very limited and my grammar very poor. Later that summer, my determination to learn English was reinforced by a comment of Uncle Clement. He pointed out that in the future I would be serving, in all probability, in the Belgian forces and would be speaking mostly French. "Therefore," he said, "why don't you really make the effort to learn English?" By that time I was rather proud of my English and was hurt by his remarks. I took it to heart, however, and acted accordingly, working very hard at learning English and especially the right pronunciation. The challenge was how to learn English not only from a conversational point of view but also how to do arithmetic, physics, chemistry, Greek and Latin, and other subjects in English. In the trial examination I did very, very poorly in everything except French.[5]

Another concern of mine was whether my family had learned that I was in England.[6] On July 22 a letter from Etienne informed me that his mother had been told through the Papal Nuncio that we were all well, and it was presumed that they knew by then that I had arrived in England.

On July 30 I bicycled to Rugby to fetch Etienne and bring him to Bloxham, where we spent a week together. We went to the farm, rode ponies,

---

[5] This is the point at which my attitude toward studying changed drastically. As a child growing up in Belgium I was a poor student, usually ranking twenty-ninth or thirtieth in a class of thirty-five, and doing just enough studying to avoid having to repeat a grade or to repeat an exam. My family did not encourage school studying. My image of myself was that I was not very intelligent and not a good student. Now, alone in England, with a very uncertain future and in the aftermath of my adventure in Belgium and France, it became very clear to me that my future would depend on my own effort and that my education was of paramount importance. I was galvanized into radically changing my attitude towards education, and I began to apply myself vigorously and became in fact a very good student, which served me well in the months and years ahead.

[6] I describe in Appendix A the various pieces of information my parents received which gave them some idea of what had happened to me.

milked cows, and rode to Broughton Castle.[7] Shortly after his visit, he informed me that on August 9 his father had arrived in London and with Monsieur De Vleeschauwer, the minister for the colonies, had established the Belgian government-in-exile. They were also hoping that Prime Minister Pierlot and Foreign Minister Spaak would soon join them in England.

Later that summer the eldest sister of my mother, Aunt Cary (who was my mother's half sister) invited me to Bulwell, her house near Maidenhead in Berkshire for the two weeks of her gardener's vacation. I enjoyed my stay, and she was very kind to me. There were also two young German girls, Jewish refugees living there, as well as the man we called "Egypt," who was my aunt's friend and lover, and who had been private secretary in earlier years to her husband, Arthur Schuster. Eric Whitehead, my cousin and grandson of the noted mathematician and philosopher Alfred North Whitehead, was also a guest, and we played tennis together.[8]

---

[7] At this time, I did not know the owners of Broughton Castle, so that when I rode my pony on their land, as I occasionally did, I was in fact trespassing and hoped I would not be found out.

In 1982 we met Susannah Fiennes in Dublin, NH and were helpful to her. Her parents, Lord and Lady Saye and Sele, the owners of Broughton, were most appreciative and invited us to stay with them. Nat and Mariette have been warm, wonderful friends ever since and we have stayed with them several times and they have joined us for dinner many times in Broadway and Woodstock.

This has renewed a family contact going back more than a century. My mother and her sisters, as they were growing up at Wardington in the 1890s, used to go to Broughton in their pony trap to play and have tea with the children living there.

[8] Aunt Cary was the widow of Sir Arthur Schuster, a distinguished scientist, Fellow of the Royal Society, and professor at the University of Manchester. He had found a job in Manchester for Chaim Weitzmann, the Zionist leader when he first arrived in England. Weitzmann was the first president of Israel. Uncle Arthur had died in 1936.

Cary Schuster was a remarkable woman: authoritarian, powerful, very intelligent, determined and very confident. She was very fond of my mother, had been very generous to Robert in inviting him to Yeldall and Bulwell every summer for ten years running before the war. Now I was the beneficiary of her generosity. Throughout the war, we wrote to each other a great deal. Her handwriting was almost illegible!

She had discovered—thanks to her half brother, Arthur—that she was sixth cousin twice removed of George Washington and she made much of this connection, sometimes in an exaggerated way.

When I came to America she told me that my Washington connection should facilitate establishing myself as a professional! Also, she told her granddaughter, Sheila Gilmore,

During the two weeks of my stay at Bulwell I had a job, replacing the gardener. This meant polishing the shoes of the people in the house, watering the garden in the morning, picking vegetables for the meals, etc. For this I was paid 15 shillings a week. In the afternoon I enjoyed the social life of the house, and I was very grateful for this opportunity. To reach Bulwell, I went on my bicycle from Bloxham to Maidenhead via Oxford, passing by Benson Aerodrome and going through Henley. On August 20 I received from Etienne a short letter from my mother, signed also by my father and Pauline and written on the 19th of July, telling me that they were well and knew where I was.

I attended Uncle Arthur's daughter Patsy's wedding, in Aynho on September 1 with Aunt Cary. From time to time during those months at Bloxham there was bombing nearby. Banbury was bombed on September 7; bombs also fell on a village near Bloxham. We heard periodically the air

---

that this connection should let her become a member of the Daughters of the American Revolution (DAR)—not exactly one of Sheila's ambitions!

Aunt Cary showed her unconquerable determination and self-confidence in connection with the dedication of the Washington ancestral home at Old Hall, Washington, County Durham, on September 28, 1955 by Winthrop Aldrich, the American ambassador to the Court of St. James. The headline in the *Manchester Guardian* on September 29 read "US Ambassador Reopens Past President's First Home." "Member of the Washington family at ceremony."

Aunt Cary was amused by the whole episode and wrote me a letter.

"My dear Francis:

I think the enclosed will amuse you. They are full of little inaccuracies. The one that annoyed me was saying that I had not had an invitation as nothing could be further from the truth. It sounds most discourteous on my part to say. I hope none of the Committee who organized the show saw it but they probably did as all the papers had it except the *Daily Telegraph*. Sheila sent me an amusing cutting from *Time* in which I am described as prim and grey haired, neither of which are true. I had a wonderful time and never had such a fuss made of me in my life before. Luckily the weather was fine and warm as the whole ceremony was out of doors in front of the Hall and we had no seats. I got there early and was standing for two and a half hours and was *not tired* which also pleased me as I feel it proves how fit I am."

When I read the People Section in *Time* magazine of October 10, 1955, that she had been a gate crasher at the party, I wrote *Time* a letter pointing out the discrepancy between their story and my information. I received a call from the *Time* office in Boston asking me what my connection and interest were in the matter. I told them that Lady Schuster was my aunt and they said they would get back to me after investigating, which they did. We were both right. She had not received the original gold-engraved invitation, but when she identified herself she was invited to attend.

My Aunt Cary, my mother's oldest sibling (half sister) who generously invited me to stay with her many times in the summer during World War II. Here she is at age 90, five years before she died. At the home of her sisters, Dorothy and Katherine, Nut Tree Cottage, Bloxham, 1957.

raid warning, but only occasionally was the neighborhood itself bombed. On September 8 the blitz on London began in earnest. This signified a turning point in the war between Germany and Britain. On September 15 there was a very big raid on London and 185 German planes were destroyed.

My school life got into a certain routine in the new term: I went to school every day except Sunday, but we had a half holiday on Wednesdays and Saturdays. We played sports every afternoon. I learned to play rugby football, but was not allowed to play in rugger matches because I was bigger and older than my skills justified in being in a particular division, and I was considered to be too rough.

It was announced on October 23 that ministers Spaak and Pierlot had arrived in London, thus completing the Belgian government-in-exile. On November 15 Coventry was severely bombed. I stood in our garden and heard the bombs and explosions, and saw the sky lit up by the fires of Coventry. Coventry Cathedral was totally destroyed. On November 30 I attended the wedding of Penelope, my first cousin, in Oxford. She was my Uncle Francis' and Aunt Lilias' daughter and married a surgeon, Randle Lunt, who was in the army.

On December 2, 1940 I received a message from home through the Red Cross which had taken months to reach me. Another message came in a letter received on December 11 from Zurich from a woman called Lilly Österberg, a Swedish friend of my mother's. They had known each other as students in Stockholm in their youth at the Royal Institute of Massage and Gymnastics. As a result of this letter, we created a channel of communication between England and Belgium which lasted through the next three years of the war. Initially, Lilly in Zurich, upon receiving a letter from my family, transcribed it onto a postcard or a letter and forwarded it to me. Letters which I wrote to her were transcribed also and then sent on to my family in Belgium. As time went on, we became bolder and the actual letters we wrote were forwarded directly in a new envelope. We had to be very careful about what we wrote because the letters were subject to both British and German censorship. It was crucial that the Germans not realize that my parents were communicating with somebody in an enemy country, i.e., England. On one occasion my parents were fined, but could have been imprisoned or worse. We had to use very subtle language, very general language which would avoid identifying the country of origin of the letters.[9] The British censors also took a dim view of my communicating with enemy-occupied territory, and usually in the letters from Belgium there was a statement to that effect from the British censors.

At the end of 1940, my Great-Aunt Laura died peacefully in her sleep, at 86, and Aunt Dorothy, Aunt Katherine, Uncle Clement, and I, plus the maid, walked from the house to the churchyard behind the simple horse-drawn carriage bearing the coffin. Around this time I had invited Etienne to visit me at Bloxham. Instead I was invited to spend a week with him at his father's house. This proved to be a most interesting experience. The house where they lived in Surrey, which M. Gutt had rented with Janine his daughter-in-law running it as the lady of the house, was also occupied by M. Pierlot and M. Paul-Henri Spaak—in other words, three-fourths of the Belgian government-in-exile. I spent a wonderful and interesting week there. Pierlot, Spaak, Etienne, and I played cards in the evening. We played Cheatums, which required lying! M. Pierlot and I discovered that we had a common de Marneffe cousin, the Burgomaster of Chimay.[10] Another per-

[9] I learned after the war that I had made a very serious mistake in one of my letters when I wrote that I had seen the latest Chaplin film. In January of 1941 I went with Etienne to see *The Great Dictator* in London, which was a film about Hitler. My family feared that they would be punished by the Germans, since it was such a giveaway that London was the only place in Europe where the movie was being shown. Luckily the German censors missed it.

[10] In 1998, thanks to a mutual friend in Belgium, Marie Anne Beauduin, I learned that Pierlot's daughter, Cecile Strugnell, was living in Winchester, a suburb of Boston. I invited her to lunch to meet her and later she came to dinner at our house while Etienne and Catherine Gutt were staying with us in October of 1998.

son who was there initially was M. Niewenhuis, the first secretary at the Belgian embassy in London and the man who had "rescued" us from the reception center when François, Janine, and I first arrived in London.

Etienne and I had not seen each other for some time, and we had the giggles when we first met. M. Gutt got annoyed with us because we couldn't stop laughing through dinner the first night I arrived. This led M. Spaak to say at one point, "Don't worry Gutt, they are laughing at my mug." In the midst of my laughter I agreed with him! For many months afterwards, I was quite embarrassed about my behavior and my seeming lack of respect towards this distinguished man. Etienne tried to reassure me that my behavior had not been so bad and that it was all forgotten and forgiven. I also met the children of M. Pierlot, who had just arrived with their mother from Portugal. Unfortunately a few months later two of them were killed in a tragic accident. There was a fire on the train in which they were traveling to return to their public school in Yorkshire and they were killed. It was, of course, a terrible blow to M. Pierlot.[11]

During this week, Etienne and I frequently went to London, often driven by Spaak in the Jaguar previously owned by M. Camus, the president of the Union Boat Club in Brussels (our club), and a senior official in the Belgian colonial office, whom I knew and who had been killed by a bomb in the Carlton Hotel a few weeks earlier. I was impressed by Spaak's oratory and his ability to declaim poetry by the page. On one occasion, I mentioned that I had heard that the French had criticized the Belgians for opposing their continuing the Maginot Line along the Belgian border, thereby facilitating the German breakthrough into France during the battle in May. Spaak was angry at that suggestion and remembered clearly, when he was foreign minister in the late thirties, urging the French to continue the Maginot Line to the sea, since there would have been less reason for the Germans to invade Belgium.

When we went to London, we walked around and met one another for lunch. I also met Etienne's oldest brother, Jean Max Gutt, who had arrived from the Belgian Congo and was trying to join the RAF. Sadly, he

[11] I wrote to Monsieur Pierlot expressing my sympathy and received from him a very nice letter of thanks.

was killed in a training accident in the RAF a few months later. On January 7 Etienne and I went to London in Gutt's car. Gutt was having lunch with General de Gaulle and Etienne asked him to try and get his autograph for the album Etienne had given me for Christmas. I had already collected autographs from Pierlot, Spaak, and Gutt. Unfortunately he did not get one.

On January 11, 1941 I returned to Bloxham. I also paid back M. Gutt the two pounds which he had lent me in Poitiers. When I had parted company with François in London in June, he had lent me a 50-pound note, which I had previously returned. I was told that M. Gutt said to his family that this was the first time anybody had borrowed money from him and paid him back! On February 21, 1941, I received another letter from Lilly Österberg, who told me that she had received my letter in twenty days. So our new communications system was working well.

As 1940 came to an end, we began to feel more secure. Germany had perhaps missed its opportunity of invading England. Every month that went by England grew stronger and was in a better position to repeal any invasion. We did not then know that the Germans had given up the idea of invading Britain and had turned their attention towards the east and an invasion of the Soviet Union.

Life in 1941 continued much as it had been in the latter part of 1940. I continued to go to school. I planned to take the School Certificate Exam in the summer of 1941, but discovered that I was not taking all the required subjects and had to add geography. I went to school every day, studied very hard at night, and often got up early in the morning and studied before school. I had by then moved into Aunt Laura's room, a more comfortable room and more suitable for studying. I often went to the farm and worked, and I participated in Home Guard activities. In the summer of 1941, I again went to Bulwell for three weeks to stay with Aunt Cary. Another cousin, Anthony Schuster, who was the grandson of Aunt Cary, was also in the house during my visit: he was to die in the Italian campaign while a captain in the Welsh Guards. Aunt Cary after the war gave a Della Robbia terracotta relief as a memorial to him, which stands at the entrance to the chapel in Eton College. We continued communicating with Belgium through Lilly Österberg in Zurich. That channel of communication was opened up to Etienne: I sent him the letters for him I received from Belgium and he sent me letters to be forwarded to his mother. We tried to avoid overloading the system and arousing the suspicion of the German or British censors.

My big achievement was passing the school certificate exam in the summer of 1941 in such a way that I could be admitted to university. To accomplish this I needed a "credit" as opposed to a mere "pass" in at least five subjects. I achieved this in English, Mathematics, Geography, Chemistry, and an even higher mark—very good—in French (surprise, surprise!).

I decided to stay at Bloxham School another term to convert my pass in Latin to a credit and pass in Physics and Greek, which I did in December, thus improving my chances of admission to university.

During 1940 and 1941, with the help of M. Gutt, we tried to get the money that my mother had inherited from her mother, which was in Lloyd's Bank in London, released to alleviate the financial burden on my aunts of looking after and educating me. This had proved so far to be impossible because the bank had not received a letter my mother had sent them authorizing the release of the funds to her sisters. I was very much aware of the financial burden my stay had placed on my aunts. It was only in 1942 that the Belgian government made funds available to Belgian students for their education. Eventually, though, Lloyd's did release the funds to my aunts.

Having passed my school certificate exam, the next question was where and when to go to university. Hovering over me was the issue of when I was going to be called into the Belgian armed forces. In my communications with Etienne, and through him with his father (now, in addition, the minister of national defense), it seemed that Belgians were not to be called up earlier than British students, that is, before the age of 19. There was some advantage to volunteering before being called up, primarily the ability to choose the branch of service in which one wished to serve.

My first choice of university was either Oxford or Cambridge, but the financial burden for my aunts was too great and we ruled them out.

King's College of the University of London had been evacuated to Birmingham, and I had a cousin, Elizabeth Loveday, who lived there with her husband, William Kenrick, and her son Martin. William Kenrick belonged to a distinguished Birmingham family, his father having been Lord Mayor of Birmingham, the second city in England. He was the head of the family company, which in peacetime had produced casters for furniture but now had been converted into a war factory. This was Elizabeth's second marriage. She had in the early thirties married a free spirit, somewhat of a Bohemian, and they had traveled for a few months on the rivers of the Continent, but then the marriage had been annulled and eventually she married William in Bloxham Church in the late thirties. The Kenricks were related to the Chamberlains, also a Birmingham family, and at the time of her wedding Neville Chamberlain was the prime minister of England. When the forthcoming marriage was announced there was a lot of excitement in Bloxham because it was hoped by the villagers that the prime minister might attend the wedding, but he did not. Elizabeth was my first cousin, the daughter of my Uncle Francis—mentioned before, and after whom I was named—and of Aunt Lilias, and she was the sister of John, who had been lost early in 1940 when the destroyer on which he served as navigating officer was sunk in the North Sea. She was also the sister of Penelope, whose wedding I had attended in Oxford in late 1940. At any rate, Aunt Dorothy asked Elizabeth if I could live with them while attending university and she agreed.

Etienne Gutt with me at Bloxham, 1942.

Although I was accepted at King's College in Birmingham, my actual work in order to take my first MB—the first examination for medical degrees—was to be done at the Edgbaston School of Science, which would provide me with education in biology, physics, and chemistry.

I went to Birmingham in January of 1942, lived in the Edgbaston section of Birmingham, and I was very well taken care of by Elizabeth and William. They were most kind and generous. Occasionally I saw Penelope, who by then had a son. Birmingham was bombed occasionally but not often. It was a very happy time during which I studied very hard and prepared my examination. I took the examination, the first MB, in the summer of 1942, passed in physics and chemistry and got what was called a "deferment" in biology. This meant that I would have to take the biology exam again. It was announced in the late spring of 1942 that King's College would return to London in the fall. During the summer I went to camp for two weeks with the Officer Training Corps (OTC) of Birmingham University and took Certificate B, which meant that if I joined the British Army, I would automatically go to officers' school rather than serve in the ranks. I did not, at the time, know what my military future would be.

After the OTC camp I left Birmingham and returned to Bloxham, my "home base," where I spent the rest of the summer doing my usual activities of going to the farm, working, haymaking, harvesting, riding ponies, and seeing my friends the Gibbs. I again saw something of Etienne that summer. We went into Oxford and did some sculling. I also once again went to Bulwell to help out while the gardener was on vacation. I still communicated with my family in Belgium through Lilly in Zurich and kept them informed of my doings.

In September 1942, I moved to London, first to a room near Victoria Station, off Vauxhall Bridge Road, and then to South Kensington at 54 Cranley Gardens. It was very cold and I had to put pennies and sixpences in the gas meter in order to heat the room. I met some very nice people, other medical students, one of whom was John Ogilvie Macglagen Wedderburn, a Scotsman who kindly invited me to spend a week at his parents' house in Edinburgh between Christmas and New Year's. I was officially a student of King's College, but since King's was not offering the course, I went to the Chelsea Polytechnic to brush up on biology and prepare for the exam in December. I passed the examination and had completed my first MB. By December of 1942, I was 18 years and six months old and I had made some decisions about my immediate future.[12]

Some Belgian medical students whom I met had decided to ignore any calling up by the Belgian government to serve in the armed forces. The Belgian government had in reality no "police power" (no power of coercion on British soil), and since British medical students could defer their military service until after they had completed their medical training, they thought they should also be able to do that. This behavior did not appeal to me at all. I felt that I was one of the lucky few people, who had been able to get out of Belgium and reach England. It seemed to me inappropriate for a Belgian, one of the few Belgians in Britain, to avoid military service in the middle of a war on the grounds that he was a medical student. Therefore, I decided to interrupt my medical training in order to serve in the armed forces. That was my primary motivation, but in addition I thought that a moratorium on my medical studies would allow me to explore other career possibilities and give me more time to think about my future. Basically, however, I knew I would feel embarrassed and ashamed to spend the war as a medical student.

The question then became, which armed forces? I did not particularly want to serve in the Belgian forces for various reasons. I was very much of an Anglophile, and I had thought many times that I would eventually become a naturalized British subject. I thought it doubtful that I would go back to Belgium permanently. Therefore, I preferred to serve in the British forces, and I explored various possibilities. I found that I could not join the Royal Navy and, since there was a Belgian Army in England, the British Army would not take me. Therefore, I decided to join the Royal Air Force, in which many Belgians already served. However, the way in which I achieved it was rather complicated.

---

[12] One lunch hour in the fall I joined a sizeable crowd on the sidewalk of the Strand, a short distance from King's College. We were there to cheer VIPs on their way to a luncheon at the Mansion House. One of them was Winston Churchill, in an open car on this sunny day waving to the crowd. I was struck by how very blue his eyes were.

I was reminded of the evanescence of fame when another man, with a beautiful head of white hair, went by and someone said, "Who's he?" Very few recognized him. It was Lloyd George, the great British prime minister during the First World War.

I went to a recruiting station and signed up for the RAF. I passed my first physical examination, but when I was due for my second physical examination, I was told that I needed a release from the Belgian authorities to join the RAF. I was almost sure that I could not to get such a release, but nevertheless tried to get one. I went to Belgian headquarters in Eaton Square in London and spoke to Commandant de Ryckman de Betz and asked him for one. He was outraged at my request and tried to shame me when he heard my name and knew that my father was a retired general in the Belgian Army. He said, "What would your father think if he knew that you were trying to avoid service in the Belgian forces and preferred to serve in the British forces?" I told him that my father was in Belgium and wouldn't know about any of this for quite a while! But as expected, permission was denied. I was informed that I could volunteer for the Belgian Army and then request transfer to the Belgian Air Force and thence to the RAF. I indicated I would think about it.

To help me decide what to do I wrote to M. Gutt, and he very kindly responded to my inquiries. One of my concerns was the belief that if I served in the Belgian forces I would be demobilized at the end of the war, later than if I served in the British forces. M. Gutt reassured me on that point in a very nice letter dated January 18 *(Figure 7)*. He wrote that he wished he could help me to join the British forces but that he could not, and that if I wanted to serve, I had no choice but to serve in the Belgian forces. He also indicated that the Belgian Air Force was an integral part of the RAF.

My family already knew that I was pursuing my medical studies, but I felt that I should let them know that I was going to join the air force. The problem was how to phrase the information so that they would understand but the German censors would not. The German censors would not have been pleased, and there would have been serious retaliation against my parents if the authorities realized that their son was joining the Royal Air Force, i.e., their enemy. I communicated my plans by writing that I was going to do the kind of work my cousin Roger had performed in the early thirties. Roger Teale, one of my first cousins, had been an officer in the Royal Air Force and had unfortunately been killed while preparing to compete in the Schneider Trophy in the early 1930s.

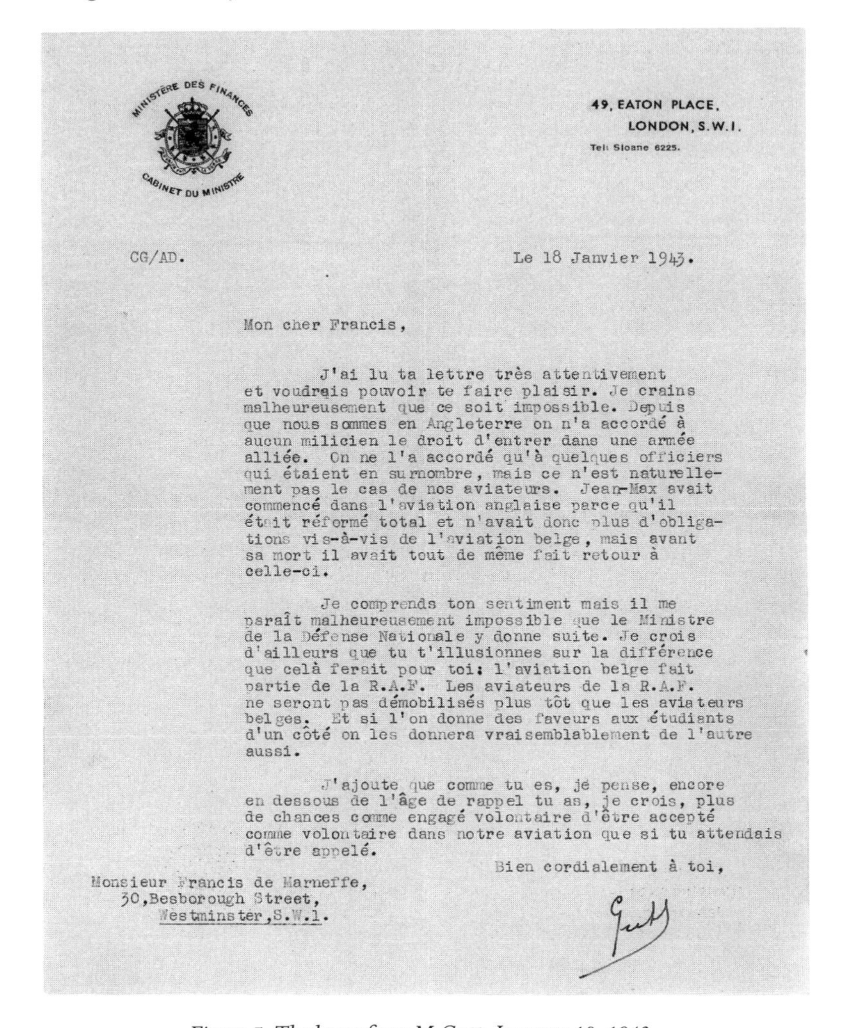

MINISTÈRE DES FINANCES
CABINET DU MINISTRE

49, EATON PLACE,
LONDON, S.W.1.
Tel: Sloane 6225.

CG/AD. Le 18 Janvier 1943.

Mon cher Francis,

J'ai lu ta lettre très attentivement et voudrais pouvoir te faire plaisir. Je crains malheureusement que ce soit impossible. Depuis que nous sommes en Angleterre on n'a accordé à aucun milicien le droit d'entrer dans une armée alliée. On ne l'a accordé qu'à quelques officiers qui étaient en surnombre, mais ce n'est naturellement pas le cas de nos aviateurs. Jean-Max avait commencé dans l'aviation anglaise parce qu'il était réformé total et n'avait donc plus d'obligations vis-à-vis de l'aviation belge, mais avant sa mort il avait tout de même fait retour à celle-ci.

Je comprends ton sentiment mais il me paraît malheureusement impossible que le Ministre de la Défense Nationale y donne suite. Je crois d'ailleurs que tu t'illusionnes sur la différence que celà ferait pour toi; l'aviation belge fait partie de la R.A.F. Les aviateurs de la R.A.F. ne seront pas démobilisés plus tôt que les aviateurs belges. Et si l'on donne des faveurs aux étudiants d'un côté on les donnera vraisemblablement de l'autre aussi.

J'ajoute que comme tu es, je pense, encore en dessous de l'âge de rappel tu as, je crois, plus de chances comme engagé volontaire d'être accepté comme volontaire dans notre aviation que si tu attendais d'être appelé.

Bien cordialement à toi,

Gutt

Monsieur Francis de Marneffe,
30, Besborough Street,
Westminster, S.W.1.

Figure 7. The letter from M.Gutt, January 18, 1943.

Kingdom of Belgium, Ministry of Finance, Office of the Minister

49 Eaton Place, London SW1

January 18, 1943

My dear Francis,

I have read your letter with great care and would like to be able to please you. Unfortunately, I am afraid it is impossible. Since we arrived in England we have given permission to no one to join an allied army. We have given permission only to a few officers who were supernumeraries, but it is of course not the case with the Air Force Personnel. Jean-Max [Gutt's eldest son] had started in the British Air Force but he had no further military obligations to Belgium, but before his death he had nevertheless rejoined the Belgian Air Force.

I understand your feelings but it seems to me unfortunately impossible for me as the Minister of National Defense to satisfy them. In addition I believe you are mistaken in

My parents understood my message and were very unhappy about it. They tried very hard to dissuade me. I received many letters from them urging me to continue my medical training and not to pursue a career in the air force. I understood their motivation. I think they were afraid I would be killed and thought that it would be better for my long-term future to continue my medical studies. I understood that it was out of love for me that my parents wanted to spare me the dangers and possible death of being a pilot in the Royal Air Force. But I also felt that, as a result of the occupation in Belgium, they were out of touch with what was going on in England and the way in which the whole country was mobilized, not only to survive, but also to eventually achieve victory. My English family had already suffered a number of losses. My first cousin John had been lost at sea early in 1940; my first cousin Hilgrove, Roger and Meg's brother, had also been lost in the fall of 1942 over the Mediterranean during the invasion of North Africa. He had served as an observer in the Royal Air Force also. Therefore the war was touching us very closely, and it was unthinkable for me not to participate in the war in an active way. In any event, their views notwithstanding, I proceeded with my plans.

Eventually I received letters from my mother and father withdrawing or at least muting their criticism of me for interrupting my studies and joining the RAF. They said they understood and wanted to reassure me that I should not be concerned about their earlier comments. This was an example of my mother's very generous nature, as she explained that she did not want me to worry but wanted me to enjoy to the fullest extent my new adventure. I think my mother imagined my being up in the air and worrying about their opinion, and hence increasing my danger. However, in the last few months before the liberation of Brussels, because letters from me did not reach them, they were very concerned that I had been killed without their knowing it.

I informed King's College that I would be leaving in order to join the

---

thinking it will make a difference for you. The Belgian Air Force is part of the Royal Air Force. The RAF Airmen will not be demobilized earlier than the Belgian airmen. And if advantages are given to students in one air force they would also be given in the other.

I would add that since you are, I believe, below calling up age, you would have a better chance of being accepted in our air force as a volunteer than if you waited to be drafted.

Very cordially, Gutt

Belgian Army and hopefully the Royal Air Force. Professor Stibbe, the Acting Dean, who had accepted me originally and had been very kind, assured me that there would always be a place for me after the war. He put a statement to that effect in my file and gave me a letter to confirm it.

The entry in my diary on January 19, 1943, (the day after M. Gutt's first letter was written) says: *After being rejected by the RAF, I joined the Belgian forces. Saw Stibbe, who promised me a place at King's after the war.*

The following day I went to King's and attended some lectures. It was hard to concentrate because I loved being at King's and I hated to leave, but I told myself I would be coming back. The following day, January 21, I went to the Belgian Armed Forces Depot at Goring-on-Thames, which was located in a hotel requisitioned by the government. I was excited to be there, met some nice chaps, passed my physical, and returned to London. On January 22, I got my army kit and uniform and went to King's. Many people seemed to envy me, and I was looking forward to a grand time. On Saturday, January 23 I went rowing at Thames Rowing Club in the afternoon and then went to Mitchum for a college dance. The following day, Sunday the 24th, I packed my things, went to Milton Court in South Kensington, and had dinner with Florence Clayton, my cousin.[13] Monday, January 25, was my last day at King's. I rang up Jacqueline Payne, a fellow

---

[13] Florence Clayton was a daughter of Aunt Cary and was married to Jack Clayton, a rear admiral who was stationed at Naval Headquarters in London.

Jack Clayton had a distinguished career in the Royal Navy during and after WWI. On the 11th of December 1936 he was senior officer on duty at Portsmouth Naval Base and was ordered to prepare a destroyer to take a VIP to France. The VIP turned out to be the Duke of Windsor, who had that afternoon abdicated as King Edward VIII. Jack saw him off on his exile. It was very cold that night and Jack had the good judgment to stay indoors and be notified by telephone as the ex-king's railway car passed each of the stations on its way from Windsor to Portsmouth. And he didn't step out until the train was near Portsmouth. On the other hand, the poor admiral in command at Portsmouth paced up and down the platform in the freezing cold waiting for the arrival of his former sovereign. Unfortunately he caught a cold and died of pneumonia shortly thereafter.

Jack and Florence had a flat in South Kensington, and many times during the war they very generously invited me to stay with them when I had a weekend leave. They had two children: one son, Richard, was attending at that time Dartmouth Naval College, and after the war had a brilliant career in the Royal Navy. He ended up as Second Sea Lord after being Fourth Sea Lord, Comptroller of the Navy, was knighted, and then retired from the navy. Sadly, he was killed in a motorcycle accident in the 1980s. He never married. One daughter, Jocelyn, married John King, had three children, and was a nurse by training.

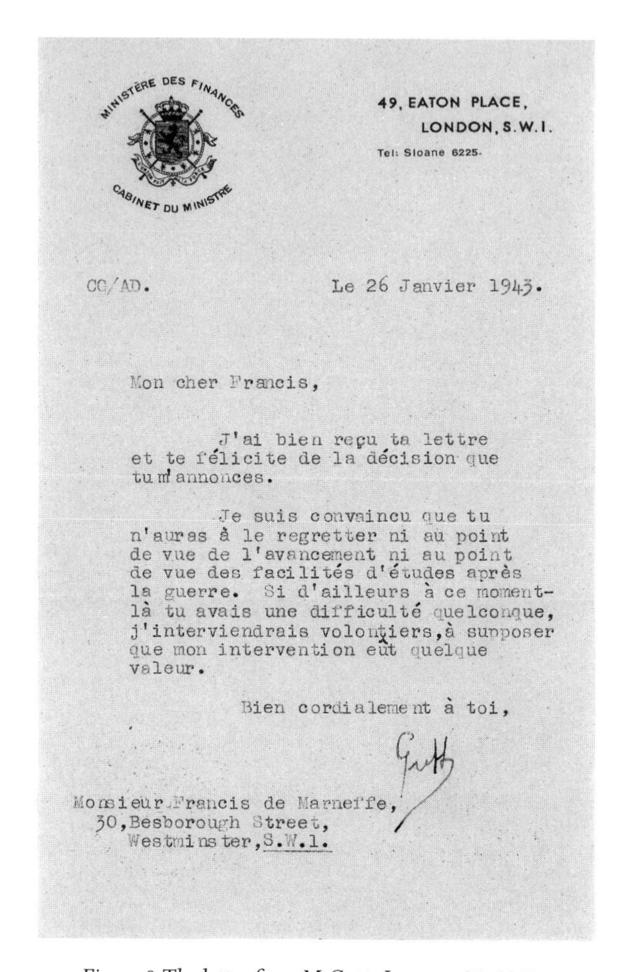

MINISTÈRE DES FINANCES
CABINET DU MINISTRE

49, EATON PLACE,
LONDON, S.W.I.
Tel: Sloane 6225.

CG/AD. Le 26 Janvier 1943.

Mon cher Francis,

J'ai bien reçu ta lettre et te félicite de la décision que tu m'annonces.

Je suis convaincu que tu n'auras à le regretter ni au point de vue de l'avancement ni au point de vue des facilités d'études après la guerre. Si d'ailleurs à ce moment-là tu avais une difficulté quelconque, j'interviendrais volontiers, à supposer que mon intervention eût quelque valeur.

Bien cordialement à toi,

Gutt

Monsieur Francis de Marneffe,
30, Besborough Street,
Westminster, S.W.1.

Figure 8.The letter from M.Gutt, January 26, 1943.

Kingdom of Belgium, Ministry of Finance, Office of the Minister

49 Eaton Place, London SW1

January 26, 1943

My dear Francis,

Thank you for your letter and I congratulate you on your decision.

I am convinced that you won't regret it. Neither in terms of promotions nor from the point of view of being a student after the war. In any event if at that time you had any kind of problem I would gladly intervene, assuming that my intervention would have any value.

Very cordially, Gutt

student whom I was very fond of, though she was never my girlfriend, *sadly*! I felt sorry that I was leaving, but I also felt quite proud of myself. On Tuesday, January 26 I went to Goring-on-Thames and began my military career. On January 26 I also received a very nice letter from M. Gutt in answer to mine informing him of my decision to join the Belgian forces as a step towards joining the Royal Air Force *(Figure 8)*.

CHAPTER VI

MY SERVICE IN THE ROYAL AIR FORCE

January 19, 1943 – October 1, 1945

NOW A VOLUNTEER in the Belgian Army, I was sent to Goring-on-Thames, the gathering place for Belgians who were joining the air force. We were billeted in a hotel on the banks of the Thames, in a charming village which, before the war, must have been a most enjoyable place to spend weekends. It was now very Spartan; all the carpets and hotel furniture had been removed, and it was furnished with army furniture. Nevertheless, the month I spent there was pleasant and I met some nice Belgians.

Of particular note were Pierre-Jean Goemaere and Ghislain de Mevius. Pierre-Jean had just arrived from Portugal, where he had been living with his family since 1940. His father was a well-known Belgian writer, and Pierre-Jean did not know any English, so Ghislain and I helped him along with his English exam.[1] While at Goring, I usually spent my weekends in London with my cousin Florence Clayton in South Kensington, and I sometimes attended dances at King's College. On occasion I also posed for a sculptor, Count Guy van der Steen, whom somebody had put me in touch with, and this was a source of additional income. Some Belgians living in England were ashamed of their nationality for a variety of reasons—some probably because the King had surrendered after only eighteen days of fighting, others because, compared to England, Belgium was considered a minor country in the war effort. Some also criticized the Belgian government, and on a number of occasions I found myself

[1] Pierre-Jean was to remain my friend on and off throughout my life. After losing contact for many years, he and his charming wife Yolande and we were frequently together beginning in the 1980s at their Chateau de Betz, in Brussels, England, Cambridge, Massachusetts, or Dublin, New Hampshire.

defending Gutt for his position on the war. I had many sore throats during this time, so many in fact that I began to be concerned about it, because to be found fit for flying one had to be healthy. Fortunately, on the 15th of February, I had my physical examination and was found fit for all flying duties.

One of the highlights of my stay at Goring-on-Thames was the lecture at the end of February given by Squadron Leader de Sellis Longchamps, who described his exploits over Brussels on January 20, 1943. About one block from my house on the Avenue Louise the tall building of the Gestapo headquarters for Belgium was located. Opposite, a wide avenue met Avenue Louise at an angle. De Sellis Longchamps swooped down at treetop level in his fighter plane and opened fire with his guns and hit the building, creating havoc and killing many Germans. This attack lifted the spirits of the Belgians, as it was the first Belgian attack against the Germans since the defeat of 1940. After the war, I learned additional facts.[2] Immediately after the attack, panic seized the Germans, who rushed out and scattered in all directions, but shortly thereafter somebody took command of the situation and they became extremely vicious. A very old, retired Belgian general, known to my father, who was accustomed to walking along the avenue every afternoon happened, unfortunately, to be passing the Gestapo building at this time. He was one of many Belgians who were rounded up, taken into the building, and severely beaten. He eventually died as a result of his injuries. My father was on his way home on bicycle when he encountered a Belgian policeman who knew him and warned him to make a detour to avoid the chaos at the Gestapo headquarters and the German retaliation. Sadly, de Sellis Longchamps was killed in action later in the war.[3]

[2] Another tragic consequence of this brave attack was the death of Martial Van Schelle. He was a well-known man in Brussels, owner of a swimming pool and skating rink. He was shunned by Belgians during the German occupation because he was frequently seen in the company of senior German officers and beautiful women. One German who was killed in the Gestapo headquarters had in his pocket a piece of paper incriminating Van Schelle. In spite of appearances, Van Schelle was in fact an Allied secret agent, and he was executed by the Germans. A very brave man.

[3] On January 20, 1993, fifty years after this action, a monument was unveiled on the square in honor of de Sellis and a plaque commemorating the attack placed on the building wall.

In early March our group went to Euston House in London to be formally inducted into the Royal Air Force and to swear allegiance to King George VI, his heirs and successors. While in London I took Pierre-Jean around, showed him the sights, and we participated in a Wings for Victory parade in Trafalgar Square where Anthony Eden (the British foreign secretary) took the salute.

On March 15 we left Goring for the Air Crew Receiving Center (ACRC) in Regent's Park, London. We spent three weeks in a large apartment building, where we attended some elementary lectures in navigation, Morse code, etc. I saw a lot of my uncles Clement and Arthur, and we often went to the movies and frequented Rose Restaurant, a Belgian restaurant in Soho, which served excellent horse-meat steaks and French-fried potatoes.

In early April, our serious training began when we went to the Initial Training Wing (ITW) in Scarborough, Yorkshire. We were located in a requisitioned hotel on the sea front. The doors of our room, which accommodated four, were nailed open, and we underwent a lot of physical training, exercises, and drills. We daily took lectures in armory, navigation, Morse code, aircraft recognition, etc., and the discipline was strict. The days were long, but we still could go out in the evening and meet people. I was quite disciplined throughout my air force service. Part of my motivation was the hope that, when I graduated as a pilot, I would receive a commission as an officer. Unlike the United States Air Force, in the RAF only one-tenth of the pilots were commissioned as officers at graduation. The others were sergeants. My performance was noted, because I received the white lanyard which identified me as a leader. This might have lead to my becoming the leader of the whole flight, but on one occasion I failed to make my bed the right way and I did not become flight leader. During my stay in Scarborough I had one short leave, and Pierre-Jean and I went to Bloxham. After he left Bloxham, I went to Bulwell to see Aunt Cary.

The three months in Scarborough were followed by a posting to Grading School at Sywell near Northampton. The purpose of Grading School was to weed out the people who were not suitable to become pilots but who might then become observers, navigators, or machine gunners. This was my first flying experience. We flew the Tiger Moth, the De-

Haviland 82A, a biplane with an open cockpit and wings and fuselage covered with cloth and not metal. On my first flight with my instructor I was fascinated by being up in the air and seeing the earth from a totally different perspective. I wondered not only how one could fly this plane, but how one could fight in it. The big concern at Grading School was whether one would go solo in an acceptable number of hours. This was the test of whether one could become a pilot. I successfully mastered most of the procedures and exercises but had trouble at first in judging some distances and making good landings. After I was tested to go solo, my instructor required me to make three successful takeoffs and landings in order to fly solo. The great day came on August 3 when I went up by myself. I soloed after eleven hours and twenty minutes of dual instruction, and so passed the grading test to train as a fighter pilot.

We left Sywell in early August and went to Heaton Park in Manchester in the north of England. Here air crews were gathered before going to either South Africa, Rhodesia, or Canada for the next phase of pilot training. Manchester was drenched in rain, day after day, but we were given leave and I went to London, Bloxham, Bulwell, and also saw Etienne and his father at Oxford. I also visited Jacqueline Payne in Devon for three days. Jackie was a student at King's College. I was very fond of her, but she was in love with another student; however, she always was very nice to me and we had a good time together.

On the 4th of September we arrived at Gourock in Scotland and boarded the *Queen Mary*, the beautiful Cunard Line ship which had been converted into a troop ship. It was capable of transporting over 20,000 troops. We slept in narrow metal bunks in three or four tiers. Strict blackout was enforced, and no cigarette smoking was allowed on deck at night. The regular Cunard staff was manning the ship, except that naval crews manned guns in various parts of the deck, ready to fire at any German plane or submarine which showed up. We had no naval escort; the ship relied on its high speed and a constantly changing zigzag course to avoid submarines. We felt fairly safe since we understood that only by pure chance could a submarine happen to be on the course of the ship. And no other ship could catch up with the *Queen Mary*, since at the time it was probably the fastest ship afloat.

We learned that, on the ship's previous trip across the Atlantic, Winston Churchill and his whole staff had been on board, on his way to the Quebec Conference. We often watched movies and also had duties assigned to us. My duties were to be part of a small group of twelve airmen who every midnight had to clean some stairways. It was a disgusting activity because many passengers were sick on the stairways after eating their meals. Another problem was that although we had to report there every midnight, the time changed and, because it was only 11:00 P.M., we had to wait to begin and kill time for an hour! We had daily lifeboat drills in case the ship was hit and we had to take to the lifeboats. During our trip, we learned that Mussolini had been overthrown and that Italy was now out of the war.

Our journey ended successfully, and on the 10th of September we arrived in New York harbor. I wrote in my diary that day:

> At five o'clock this morning, I was already on deck watching the lightships sending their signals across the night and showing us the way into New York harbor. As dawn broke and the sun rose the ship continued slowly on its course and the skyscrapers of New York became visible in the distance. As it became lighter there developed one of the most beautiful sights I have ever witnessed. On my left two small islands covered with trees and a few large spacious houses, and on my right parts of Long Island and Coney Island could be distinguished, but the most thrilling sight of all was seeing springing from a small island the famous and so much heard of monument, the Statue of Liberty. The ship went on slowly up the Hudson River and very tall skyscrapers could be seen. This indeed was New York! With its Empire State Building, the tallest building in the world.
>
> We then passed many docks, and after passing the new *Mauritania, Aquitania,* and saddest sight of all the *Normandie,* lying half sunk at an angle of 30 degrees and with powerful pumps emptying it of water as much as possible. There was no longer those marvelous structures on deck which once

were the pride of France. Now no funnel, just the bare sight of rusty steel, the remnant of an all-consuming fire. After a rapid maneuver we docked at 8:10 A.M. and thus ended our Atlantic crossing. An American Army band was on the quay to welcome us, and there was indeed more enthusiasm than I had seen for a long time. American military policemen came on board and took over. I strolled on deck watching the disembarkation operation. I feel that I am going to like the Americans. I am terribly excited. Who would have thought that I would have come to New York on the *Queen Mary*!

We landed on American soil at 1:45 P.M. and a ferry took us to the station to board the Canadian Pacific Railway train where we received magazines and oranges. There then developed before my eyes the most beautiful scenery I have ever seen. We ran parallel to the Hudson River, bordered by thickly wooded hills, among which could be seen picturesquely painted houses. The sight of those small villages and towns just by the Hudson River with fast-moving, silent modern cars—the contrast was simply staggering. As night approached we made a halt at Kingston, and at Albany, where we saw the Hudson River for the last time. By the time we raced through Saratoga it was completely dark, and after three and a half years in blacked-out Britain, to see rows of well-lit bright streets with colored advertisements was indeed cheering. This was the last sight of this most eventful day, one of the best in my life. I will be back here one day!

On September 11, I wrote:

During the night we crossed into Canada and after a very good night and breakfast we made a halt at Lac-Megantic in Quebec. Here we had our first contact with French Canadians; we spoke French and bought oranges, ice cream, and magazines. All day we went on, surrounded by marvelous scenery, and eventually we arrived in Moncton, New Brunswick, the camp where we will be staying for a short while. With my arrival in Moncton ended a ten-day voyage which will live forever as one of my greatest adventures.

Moncton was our gathering place before our departure for western Canada. We went on parade, we went into town, to the movies—we did not do much work. On September 28, we boarded a Canadian Pacific Railroad train for western Canada. This too was a remarkable experience, much more comfortable and luxurious than we had anticipated. The food was excellent; we had a sleeper car, which attendants prepared for us every evening, and we slept very well. In the morning the attendants reconverted the compartments from sleepers into club cars. The scenery was magnificent as we rode west by Montreal; along the banks of Lake Superior through Port Arthur and Port William, into Winnipeg in Manitoba, where there was a glorious welcome for us. Then Moose Jaw, Saskatchewan, and, on the 2nd of October, we arrived in Calgary, Alberta, and were taken by bus to De Winton. On our journey, from time to time, we disembarked from our train and marched through towns, partly to get some exercise but partly to "show the flag." There were often bands, parades, welcoming flags, and cheering by the population of the small towns we were in.

De Winton was a civilian air field which had been taken over by the Air Force as the 31st Elementary Flying Training School (EFTS), and it was located 20 miles from Calgary in the foothills of the Rocky Mountains. From the camp we could see the beautiful Rockies. The plane we trained on was a Cornell and my instructor was Caird Wilson, a very intelligent, well-educated, attractive man who had been student at Cambridge. At first I found it difficult to land the Cornell, but I eventually did well and also became very good at aerobatics. I soloed after seven hours fifty minutes, which was considered very good, and I was successful in passing my final exam. For some breach of discipline which I have forgotten I was confined to camp for fourteen days as a punishment, which interfered with my leave. I had been having many colds throughout the year, and I was told that I should have my tonsils out, so I decided to take advantage of being confined to camp to be sent by the medical officer to a hospital in Calgary for a tonsillectomy. Subsequently, in early December, I got some leave and I went to Vancouver, British Columbia, for six days, and again was impressed by the beautiful scenery as the train passed through the Rocky Mountains over the Continental Divide. In Vancouver, I went to the United Services Club, got the address of somewhere I could stay, and met some wonderful people—Mr. and Mrs. Jukes and Mrs. Rochfort, who entertained me beautifully. I was impressed by the setting of the University of British Columbia overlooking the Pacific. I was taken to the Capilano Golf Club by the Jukeses. I returned to Calgary again through the Rockies and through Lake Louise and Banff. A few days later we moved to Medicine Hat, Alberta, for our very long course at the 34th Service Flying Training School (SFTS). Medicine Hat, which lies east of Calgary, was a small town in the middle of the prairie, which at first seemed very bare and uninteresting, but which, as time went on, I came to love. To our dismay, we were told on arrival that we would not start flying for another six weeks. This was due to the fact that the course was being extended because many pilots were accumulating in England, which caused a backup.[4] Although we were very disappointed, we made the best of it and obtained two weeks leave. Pierre-Jean Goemaere, Ghislain de Mevius, Jan, a Dutchman, and I rented a cottage in Banff and spent our time skiing. We took turns preparing meals. We skied every day at Norquay Ski Lodge and sometimes we skated. We discovered the Jukeses, from Vancouver, were staying at the Royal Mount Hotel in Banff with a daughter and a niece, Rachel and Rosemary, and we spent some time with them. The Jukeses were most hospitable and invited us to their hotel for the Christmas festivities. On the 1st of January we swam in the sulfur springs at Banff Springs Hotel, surrounded by snow.

As 1943 ended, I wrote in my diary:

> This has been a year full of changes for me. I have spent most of it in the Air Force and often during that year I have wondered what the post-war years will hold in store for me. Since I left Belgium, nearly four years ago, I have been through interesting experiences which have opened my eyes

[4] RAF fighter pilots had not been lost in recent months at the rate which had been anticipated, and therefore there was an oversupply in England.

to new opportunities. My hopes, as they are now, are quite simple: to graduate as a pilot and then get on operations as soon as possible, and as long as possible. When the war is finished in Europe, indeed I might miss the European theater altogether, then go to the Far East and finish the job over there. Then I wonder what? Shall I be able to get accustomed to Belgium again? Whether I shall study medicine or not; whether it will be in Belgium, England, or anywhere else; whether I shall settle down in Belgium, England, Canada or another part of the Globe, is for the time being an entire mystery.

If I can become a doctor, as indeed I hope to one day, and then decide to go to England and make my home there, there will, I fear, be difficult times explaining my point of view at home. But, no doubt, Mummy will understand that, after leading an entirely different life since the age of 16 from that I had been accustomed to, it is hard to return to my former life! Brussels has for me some of the sweetest memory, that old red brick house which was my home for 16 years! I would like to do medicine, for it seems to me to be the only profession that would satisfy me. To dedicate one's life to medicine, what an ideal! But will it be possible for me to do so, can I start before 1946? And will I be young enough? I think that if I want it enough when the time comes I will get it. Last night I lay in bed thinking of the next five years, and I was thrilled to think that within those years I would get the answer to at least some of my questions. Indeed, this is going to be a very interesting life.

I also sometimes wonder when I am going to get married. I am nearly 20 and not yet have I had a real love affair. There are girls I have liked, and even thought I was in love with, but never yet have I had time to give the question much thought. The trouble is that in the Air Force you can only meet nice girls through introduction, and then it is only to know them for a few days before moving on. Very abnormal life.

> Vancouver has for me great charm and I shouldn't wonder if I went back there one day. But England is the country I love. However, "time will show." All these questions are secondary for the time being. Most important of all the war must be won and the European countries liberated. Once again must the people in Europe walk freely—free from want, from fear. I think Germany will be beaten this year, then after that we shall see. I have a whole lifetime before me and I know that it is going to be interesting and full of adventure. That is what I want it to be.

We returned to Medicine Hat from Banff to start our course in early January 1944, only to learn that there was a further delay in starting our course, No. 89. I received a letter from Etienne Gutt informing me that he had joined the Royal Air Force, but would be trained in England. He had been admitted into the RAF under a special dispensation because he had bad eyes and they wanted to experiment with new kinds of goggles. A Belgian, Louis Van Arenbergh, was assigned to me as my instructor, but after a few days, since I knew English, I was switched to an English instructor, Flying Officer Sykes, because Louis was needed to instruct a Frenchman who hardly knew any English. We flew AT6's as they are called in the US Air Force, but the British called them Harvards. It was a very heavy single-engine plane, but turned out to be easier to fly than expected. At first, I couldn't stand Flying Officer Sykes because he was a nitpicker. When he told me to climb at 65 mph and I was flying at 67 mph, he would criticize me, or if I was flying at 63 mph he would criticize me constantly. Whenever I went up with him, I complained to Louis Van Arenbergh that I couldn't stand the man and wanted to change instructors. However, after a while I realized that if anyone could teach me how to fly well Sykes would do it, because he was so exacting. I soloed after seven hours and ten minutes, which was considered very good.

During my eight months in Medicine Hat, winter changed to spring and spring into summer. Winter was extremely cold, but it was very dry and we were issued very warm clothing, and there was something very bracing and healthy about the atmosphere. I pursued many extracurricu-

The author flying in formation in Harvard No 65. Canada, Spring 1944.

lar activities. I was on the basketball team of the base and acted in some plays. I met some very nice people. I was introduced by the Jukeses in Vancouver to Mr. and Mrs. Cory, who had a nice house in town which I visited many times, sometimes staying for the night, and also went to their country house in Elk Water.

On one occasion I was reprimanded for having landed my plane in spite of the fact that several red flares had been fired into the air telling me not to land because I was landing across wind. I managed to cover up my mistake by saying that I was running low on fuel. New Belgians joined us in Medicine Hat: Antoine de Ligne and Gaston de Gerlache. Antoine was the heir to the number one princely family of Belgium (non-royal); and Gaston was a baron. I became friendly with both of them, and our friendship continued after the war. In April I received a sad letter from Aunt Cary informing me that my cousin Anthony Schuster was missing in Italy, presumed killed. Subsequently, I learned the circumstances under which he was killed in the Italian campaign. In his capacity as captain in the Welsh Guards, after many soldiers in his company had been killed, he decided to charge, almost single-handed, a German machine gun nest and was killed in the action.

I continued to work very hard at my flying and my ground lectures, and I was also involved in extracurricular activities, partly to increase my chances of being commissioned as an officer on completion of the course. According to my instructor, I was very good at most things in flying, including aerobatics. The only thing I had some trouble with was forced landings. In the event that your engine suddenly failed one had to identify a field, quickly, that was appropriate for making an emergency landing. In my final test I got 78 percent and in my ground exams I got 78½ percent. The one thing in my final test I had trouble with was again forced landings, but I still ended second out of eighty-five students in my course. In early June we were informed that our course was to be further extended by eight weeks, which was a tremendous disappointment to us all. On June 6, we were thrilled to hear that the Allies had invaded Normandy. "D-Day" had arrived at last.

In June I continued to see the Corys, and then I met their next-door neighbors—Mr. and Mrs. Taylor and their two daughters, Margaret and Adele. Adele was a good friend of Toby Overton, an instructor with whom I had flown a few times. On the 10th of June, Ross Van Rillaer, a Belgian in our course, and Toby Overton were killed. They had gone on a cross-country flight, the kind I had taken with Toby a few days earlier, and Toby unwisely had decided to fly very low over the river and had hit one of the cables that spanned the river. Their bodies were found a week later, and their military funerals followed. I and the other Belgians in our class carried Ross' coffin.

In early July, our group went to the Calgary Stampede. I had grown very fond of, if not in love with, Margaret Taylor, and I spent as much time as possible with her. We listened to music and we talked a lot and, although for months I had been looking forward to leaving Medicine Hat and returning to England, at this time I began to dread the separation.

As early August approached it was a confusing time. On August 11 I received my wings and a commission, which was the culmination of more than eighteen months of hard work, yet at the same time I had to tear myself away from someone I had grown very fond of. Also, in early August I received a letter from Etienne, written from Heaton Park near Manchester and dated July 24, informing me that François, his brother,

Barbara de Marneffe

Visiting the British Military Cemetery of St. Manvieux at Cheux (Calvados) near Caen in Normandy, where François Gutt is buried, in 1984, the fortieth anniversary of the Normandy invasion.

had been killed in Normandy.[5] François was in a Royal Artillery regiment and had participated in the Normandy invasion, which had started on June 6. I learned later that he had been killed on June 26 in the ferocious battles around Caen.

At the end of that momentous day, when I received my wings and my commission, I said goodbye to Margaret and boarded the train to go east. Pierre-Jean Goemaere and I commiserated with each other on our departure from Medicine Hat, since he had become very fond of Dell Taylor,

---

[5] In 1984 I visited the beaches of the Normandy invasion and contacted Etienne Gutt to find out where François was buried. I visited the British Military Cemetery at St. Manvieu at Cheux (Calvados), near Caen. I also received a letter from Tom Gutt, François' son, born in England during the war, telling me that he knew of my existence from the letters his father had written to his mother (Janine) in early June 1940. He very kindly and generously sent me copies of these letters, which contained the many comments about me which I included in the memoirs covering my stay in Poitiers. I met Tom and his wife when we visited Etienne in Belgium in the summer of 1984.

Prior to 1984, I had not seen Etienne since 1950 and it is really quite incredible that, given how close we had been before and during the war, we had lost touch with each other for 34 years. But, after 1984, we did see each other whenever I went to Belgium and, fortunately, in 1998 he visited us in Cambridge, Massachusetts, and Dublin, New Hampshire.

Barbara de Marneffe

The grave of François Gutt in the British Military Cemetery of St. Manvieux at Cheux (Calvados), near Caen in Normandy. "How do you recognize that the fruit is ripe? The way it leaves the branch."

and so we shared our misery at the separation. While my friends continued east, I stopped off in Toronto to visit Patsy Dunlop, who was attending Toronto Medical School, and with whom I had stayed ten years earlier in Sussex (England) on a vacation with my sister. I spent two days in Toronto and visited Niagara Falls. After that I visited Portland, Maine, and stayed for a couple of days in the summer house on Little Sebago Lake with my cousin Margaret Whitehead, her daughter, Sheila Gilmore, and Sheila's two young children. Then I went to Boston for a few hours to see Margaret's husband, North Whitehead, and visited his father and mother, Alfred North Whitehead and Evelyn. Alfred North Whitehead was, of course, a very famous philosopher and professor of philosophy at Harvard, who had come to America in the late 1920s after he anticipated having to retire from his position at the University of London. I spent the evening with them, and I was struck by Whitehead's effort to put himself at my level, by asking me a question such as, "I've always wondered how a plane can stay up in the air." He was a most distinguished man who subsequently received the Order of Merit from the King of England. In the early part of the century, he had written *Principia Mathematica* with Bertrand Russell. North and Margaret Whitehead had earlier in the war been living in London, and I used to visit them and have meals with them occasionally in the fall of 1942. I had been reading books on philosophy by C.E.M. Joad, a Professor of Philosophy at Birbeck College in the University of London, and I had an amusing interchange with Margaret which revealed my ignorance. Over dinner one day she told me, "You know, Francis, if you're really interested in philosophy, you should read some of North's father's books." Since I had never heard of Alfred North Whitehead I nodded and said that I would, but inwardly I thought to myself, "Isn't it wonderful this family loyalty, where she's urging me to read the books written by her father-in-law!"[6]

After leaving Boston, I joined Pierre-Jean and Ghislain in New York City for thirty-six hours. During this time, I visited Fifth Avenue, Park Avenue, the Empire State Building, and Radio City, and we went for a meal at the Brussels Restaurant, which was managed by Mr. Pagani, the former manager of the Carlton Restaurant in Brussels. He gave us an excellent meal at very, very reduced prices because we were Belgian soldiers. We visited the Copacabana and El Morocco, but then, exhausted, we returned north to Moncton, New Brunswick, waiting to depart for England. I was missing Margaret tremendously.

On the 29th of August we boarded the *Aquitania* in Halifax, Nova Sco-

---

[6] When I lived in Cambridge in the 1950s and 1960s, and Evelyn Whitehead, now a widow, lived with North and his second wife, Harriet, on Linnean Street, I used to go over and read to her because she had become blind. I used to ask her what she wanted me to read and she invariably said, "Read me a chapter from Alfred's books," which I did. She would listen to me with her eyes closed and, when the chapter ended, she usually said with a smile, "You know, Alfred was a rather intelligent man." (After ten years of blindness, Mrs. Whitehead, one afternoon ordered a taxi, went to an oculist in Harvard Square, and got a pair of glasses with which she was again able to see! Miraculous.)

The family was very glad Whitehead was awarded the Order of Merit (the year before Winston Churchill), shortly before he died. They had thought that, since he had emigrated to the USA in the late 1920s, he might have been forgotten by the Crown.

Another story Mrs. Whitehead told me was how Bertrand Russell had to be constantly reminded by Alfred to work on *Principia* instead of getting involved on tangential issues.

How North Whitehead (A.N. Whitehead's son) happened to be in England during the war is interesting.

He, too, was living in Cambridge, Massachusetts, throughout the 1930s—married to my cousin, Margaret, Aunt Cary's daughter. He had been teaching at Harvard for many years but was still an officer in the British Territorial Army, and when war was declared in September 1939, he assumed he had to return to England to go on active duty. During the Atlantic crossing, he wrote a very long letter to a friend in the Foreign Office in London analyzing the political situation in the US and the chances of it entering the war on the Allied side. This friend thought it was a great letter and showed it to his boss, who showed it to his boss, and eventually Lord Halifax, the Foreign Secretary, read it. He said, "We must have this man in the Foreign Office." On his arrival in England, North was told that he was not wanted in the armed forces and could have stayed in America! Therefore, he joined the Foreign Office and his job was to do everything possible to insure that the US would enter the war sooner or later.

tia and headed for England. Since I was now an officer, I was in the officers' quarters, and I shared a cabin with Australian and Canadian officers, but I spent as much time as I could below deck with my friends. On the 4th of September, while we were in the middle of the Atlantic, we learned that Brussels had been liberated. We all cheered and wondered what kinds of experiences our families were having in Brussels, and wondered how soon we would see them again. The next day, we arrived at Gourock and were impressed by the beautiful green countryside as we approached. After landing at Gourock, we went to Harrogate in Yorkshire, where we had to wait for our next posting. I sent a letter for my family to Monsieur Gutt, who was still in England, anticipating that he would shortly be returning to Brussels with the government.

As a pilot officer in the Royal Air Force, September 1944, age 20.

When we arrived in Harrogate, we were horrified to learn that the trainees that we had followed in Medicine Hat eight months earlier were still waiting for their next assignment, namely to the Advanced Flying Unit (AFU). That meant that we would have to wait a long time for further operational training. I was particularly disappointed since I had voluntarily interrupted my medical studies, which I could have elected to continue as other Belgians had done. Now it looked as if this was all going to be a waste of time, and that I was never going to be able to see action in the air force during this war.

During my leave in London, I went to Belgian Headquarters and, having previously learned from my instructor, Flying Officer Sykes, that because of my good flying performance he had recommended me to become an instructor, I asked them whether there was an opening. They were delighted because they were about to recreate, in England, an integrated Belgian Air Force and open a training station where young Belgians, coming out of liberated Belgium, would be trained. I also went to King's College and saw my old friend Phyllis McBain, the secretary to the dean, and reminded her that they had promised me a place after the war. I also learned at this time that M. Gutt had taken my letter to my family.

During this leave I met Betty and Frank, the sister and brother-in-law of Margaret Taylor, and I spent some time with Etienne. I also spent a lot of time with Jackie Payne, whom I hadn't seen since the year before in Devon. One evening while at the movies in Harrogate, I learned that Pierre-Jean and Ghislain had in fact been posted to their next station, and I felt terrible that I had prematurely chosen to become an instructor. I abandoned my date in the movies, took the midnight train to London, went to Belgian Headquarters, and asked them to undo my posting to instructor school. I got a dressing-down from the Commander-in-Chief of the Belgian Air Force, who rather sternly told me, "Once you're in the service you do what you're told and not always what you want." Therefore, my fate was sealed: I was going to become an instructor while my friends were going to go on with their training, move on to Hurricanes and Spitfires, and I was going to be left behind. I was very disappointed and thought I had made a terrible mistake. While in Harrogate, I began receiving letters from the family describing the liberation of Brussels, what their life under the occupation had been like, and their relief that I had survived the war (see Appendix C).

I was posted to Theale in Berkshire, where I flew Tiger Moths. I spent a month in Theale and often went to London on weekends, visited Bulwell and Bloxham. I also began receiving letters directly from home. I went to Belgian HQ at 107 Eaton Square in London attempting to arrange a visit to Brussels. There was no regular transportation to Brussels yet, and what I had to do was to try and be given a military mission or be a diplomatic courier with governmental documents to Brussels. Towards the end of November, I was posted to Flying Instructor School (FIS) at Woodley, also in Berkshire. I also finally got together with Aline Monnom, a graduate of my parents' massage and gymnastics school, who was working near Woodley, and I spent many evenings with her having wonderful discussions, listening to music, visiting some of her friends, and making new friends.[7]

One other Belgian flying officer was also training at Woodley to be a flying instructor. Jacques Pastur was a tall, handsome man about ten years older than I who had before the war been in the regular Belgian Army, serving in one of the elite cavalry regiments. He had escaped from Belgium during the war and had come to England and joined the RAF. He was currently married to a young South African woman, whom he had met in England—a woman from a very good family who now lived south of London and whom he visited from time to time on weekends. When we first met and he heard my name, he told me that my name was familiar to him, but that he couldn't quite remember in what connection. After a few days he told me, "I remembered where I heard your name. Your father is a Freemason." Since I knew of course that Freemasonry was a secret society and that my parents had always been very careful about maintaining the secrecy of their membership in that organization, I denied it, but he kept after me, kept saying that "Yes, that's where I remember your name," in spite of the fact that I continued to deny it.

As 1944 came to an end, I wrote in my diary:

> A great year. The long-awaited invasion of Western Europe and the liberation of Belgium and France. Once again those people are free and the reception of the British troops in Brussels comes to my mind. Once again we can write freely and say what we think to the people in Belgium; they have had an awful time. Starvation and mental anguish and torture from the Gestapo. As victory is in sight, the problems of making a lasting peace become more real and imperative, and yet there seems to be misunderstanding and mistrust between Britain, the USA and USSR, and yet it is upon those that will depend the future peace of the world. We

---

[7] Angela Blight was a charming young girl who worked with Aline Monnom at the Miles Aeronautical Technical School nearby. Together we enjoyed many dinners at the "Green Monkey," dances, plays, and movies. In the year 2000 she wrote to us and I had lunch with her in London in February 2001.

must build a society in which men may live freely and happily. What a cause and what an opportunity.

This year has been a wonderful one for me. I met Margaret in Canada and I have had feelings which must have been love. She understood me and taught me what life could be like with love and beauty; she showed me that beauty was expressed in the countryside, music and poetry. I shall never forget the Warsaw Concerto, Tchaikovsky, Beethoven, Mozart, Rupert Brook, etc. I shall never forget the evenings in which she and I lay under the clear Canadian sky watching the moon and stars and talking in soft whispers. Memories like these remain forever in our thoughts.

As to the future, there is no telling. When I have finished my job as instructor, I don't know what I shall turn my energies to. I don't think I will stay in the Air Force. I want a free life and more interesting; I want to do medicine and practice somewhere in the world. It may well be in Belgium, in spite of all that I have said, and yet it may be in England or Canada. I am interested in many things—poetry, music and politics, especially international affairs—and I really wonder what the situation is, and is there a place for me in the field of politics where I can help and do something towards the world order which must come after this terrible war. Time will show.

I want very much to see all my family in Brussels and understand them. We must make up almost five years of separation. How much longer will it be? For there is no doubt that there is scope in the world for work and goodwill, and every ounce of energy of everyone will be necessary to bring about a "new order" in the world. In years from now, we shall look back upon 1944 and think of the great deeds. But let us be true to the legacy of those who have died and endured hardship and have left us, and let us make sure that never again must men face such tyranny—this will only be achieved by understanding each other among nations. Let us

> think less as nationals and more as Europeans and world citizens; otherwise we won't have peace in the world. The success or failure of this mission of world peace depends on our generation.

As 1945 began, I received more letters from home, including one from my sister Pauline, who described what the occupation had been like. Eventually, in March, I graduated as a flying instructor. Throughout these months, my family and I had become increasingly frustrated and disappointed that I was not able to visit them in Brussels. Finally, on the 22nd of March, I flew into Brussels. I was, as a government courier, carrying bags of documents which I delivered to the ministries in Brussels, and that is how it was possible for me to fly to Brussels on a "diplomatic mission." It was very strange to be finally arriving in Brussels after almost five years. I landed at the military airport in Brussels and telephoned my family to let them know I had arrived. My father answered the phone, and when I told him who I was, he couldn't quite take it in and said "Who?" I said, "Francis." He said, "Who?" I said, "Francis!" Once again, he said, "Who?" Finally I yelled into the phone, "Francis, your son!" Whereupon, he said, "Ah, Francis, oh, okay, where are you?" I said, "I'm at Brussels Airport," at which point he passed me on to my mother!

A staff car which had picked me up at the airport first took me to the ministries, where I dropped off the bags of documents, and then the driver kindly took me to my house on the Avenue Louise. It was understandably a very emotional reunion, and yet one in which I felt quite inadequate. I rang the doorbell and my father, my mother, and my sister came downstairs to open the door and we hugged each other. They were all crying, but I felt very badly that I wasn't. I felt rather embarrassed by all this emotion. The front door was still open, and while we were hugging each other I felt embarrassed that people on the street might witness this emotional scene. Perhaps it was the five years I had spent in England with the English "stiff upper lip" that resulted in this reaction on my part. While I was hugging them, using my foot I gently closed the door behind me. Throughout the five days that I spent in Brussels I felt very inadequate in my inability to express my feelings very well.

After our reunion in the front hall of the house, we went upstairs and started to break the ice after our five-year separation. We were standing in my father's study, which, as I have mentioned before, really was the family room, when, perhaps out of habit and perhaps in order to relieve some of the tension, I took out a cigarette and lit it. I had started smoking about six months before when I had returned from Canada and was waiting around in Harrogate for my next posting. I knew of course that my parents abhorred smoking, but nevertheless I felt that I should go ahead and do what I would have normally done. I realized that this was likely to be disapproved of by my parents, but nevertheless I went ahead. When I took out my cigarette, my father said, "Oh, I see you smoke." I said, "Yes, I do now," and proceeded with lighting it. In some way I suppose it was a rather provocative behavior on my part, knowing their feelings about it, but somehow I felt it was important to establish in some concrete way my independence and my plan to go ahead with my life according to my own decisions.

During this brief stay in Brussels, I mentioned to my mother that she had told me years ago that she would give me a ring for my 21st birthday which was six weeks away. She remembered and gave me the ring—it was a woman's ring which she had inherited through her family from a Russian empress or archduchess, and this ring was too small for any of my fingers! We were both disappointed since I had treasured this anticipation throughout the war. As a temporary measure, she gave me her signet ring with the Loveday coat of arms while she arranged for a new signet ring with the de Marneffe coat of arms to be engraved. I have worn it ever since. Also in talking to my family during this visit, I began to get a clearer picture of what their life was like under the German occupation. This picture, added to, over the next several months and years is described in more detail in Appendix C.

I had long walks with Robert and Pauline. We all talked a great deal. I tried to give them an abbreviated version of what had happened to me during my absence. I didn't sleep much, because I felt that any sleep would be wasting the opportunity to talk and share information. I went with them to the Boat Club, saw our old friends, and I saw Jacques Piraux, with whom I had been in England in 1939. I felt that my parents really hadn't changed very much. They looked a little older, but their voices sounded the same. They must have been rather surprised at me because my voice had changed since I had left in 1940. When I visited my high school and went to see the headmaster I had a rather amusing exchange with him. In 1940, in early May, I was in trouble with the school and I had been told that if one more episode of lack of discipline occurred, my parents would be asked to remove me from school. When I was told this on the 9th of May, I was very concerned because I knew there was another episode in the pipeline that the headmaster would soon learn about, and that it would jeopardize my education in that school. The following day, the 10th of May, was the German invasion. School was canceled, and I actually felt that I had been saved by the Germans! This time, when I visited the headmaster in my beautiful RAF uniform, he congratulated me, was pleased to see me, and said, "I always knew that you would be very successful!"[8]

Sometime during my stay in Brussels, my father asked me who were some of the people that I had met in the air force. I told him, and also mentioned Jacques Pastur, my classmate at the RAF Instructor's School. My father looked rather pensive and said after a while, "Was his father a senator?" and I said that, yes, his father had been a senator, whereupon my father explained that he was the man who had in the middle thirties got hold of the list of the leading Freemasons of Belgium and given it to the *La Libre Belgique,* the leading Catholic newspaper of Belgium, which had printed it. One of the consequences of this publication was that a number of Freemasons during the war had been killed because of their beliefs.

My father told me that, after the liberation of Brussels and the return of the Belgian government from London, since there had been so many false identity papers circulating during the war, the government had decreed that all identity papers were now obsolete and should be exchanged for new accurate identity papers. When my father went to the Brussels City Hall to

---

[8] I had a crush on a classmate, Colette Coppée. We had exchanged "billets doux" in class which was forbidden and considered disruptive. We were caught and brought to the headmaster. When confronted, we both denied it and got away with it. But, I knew that another episode, where I had put rubber on the classroom stove a few days earlier to stink up the room, was going to come to light.

get new identity papers, the clerk behind the counter saw his name, and he said to him, "I'm so glad to see you, General de Marneffe," whereupon my father responded by saying, "Well I'm awfully glad to see you, too" and the man said, "No, no, that is not quite what I mean. I'm very glad to see you *alive*." So my father responded to that by saying, "Well, you know we've all had our very difficult times during the war, but I'm very glad to be alive, yes, thank you very much." Finally, the man said, "No, no, no, doctor, this is not quite what I mean," and he extended his hand and shook my father's hand, giving him the Freemason handshake. So my father said, "Oh, I see, well I am glad that you survived the war as well." The man explained that during the war he had gone to my parents' house to warn them that they were the next ones on the list to be assassinated. My father asked him where he had gone, and he said he had gone to 103 Avenue Louise and had kept the house under observation for three days in order to warn him, but that no one seemed to go in or out of that house. Therefore he assumed that my parents had gone into hiding. My father said, "Well, I moved out of 103 Avenue Louise in 1929 and moved to 497 Avenue Louise, where I was living throughout the war." That is apparently what saved my father's life: the assassins had the wrong address!

What used to happen was that doctors would be called in the evening after dark and told that there was a very sick child nearby and that the doctor was desperately needed. The doctor would often say that, "Well, you understand there is a curfew, I'm not supposed to be out on the street," and the people would say, "Yes, I know, doctor, but somehow can't you help this desperately sick child?" Whereupon the doctor, placing his professional and ethical principles above his own safety would decide to go. As he left his house he would very frequently be assassinated by somebody waiting for him on his doorstep. These assassinations were not committed by Germans; they were committed by Belgian Fascists who were using the war as a means of settling scores. There had been so much opposition to Freemasons—particularly from Catholics, some of whom were Fascists—that they used the war to get rid of the leading Freemasons of Belgium in this particular way.

I returned to London at the end of March and was posted to Snailwell, near Newmarket in Suffolk. Snailwell was the location of the Belgian

Training School, where young Belgians, coming from liberated Belgium, were to get their elementary flying training done. On April 10 the Belgian Elementary Flying Training School was officially opened by Air Commodore Wouters and Defense Minister Mundeleer. Three days later, while sitting in the officers mess I heard on the radio that Franklin Delano Roosevelt had died. We were lucky that he had been president during the war and supported us in England. We believed that his relationship with Churchill had been important to our survival and we knew he would be sorely missed. I wrote in my diary, "Thus goes one of the greatest Americans of all time. Our debt to him can never be paid."

An informal photo of me as a Royal Air Force officer, at Nut Tree Cottage, Bloxham, Spring 1945.

On the 17th my first pupil went solo. Life was very pleasant at Snailwell. I flew most days, depending on the weather, often three or four hours a day, instructing pupils on the Tiger Moth. On many weekends I went to Bloxham or to London. I often stayed with Norah Nicholls, my cousin in London. I attended Jackie Payne's 21st birthday party. I eventually began to fly to Bloxham on weekends, leaving the plane at the local air station.

As the weeks went by, I became more and more certain that I could never go back to Belgium permanently. I really felt that my future life would be in England. I felt a great deal of love for the country and the people of England,[9] but I also knew that this was going to be a very diffi-

[9] Even though I have lived more than fifty years in the USA and had to become an American citizen in order to practice medicine in Massachusetts, my love and admiration for England, its countryside, and institutions, has never diminished. I go to England as often as I can and I treasure my contacts with my many English relatives.

Often when visiting England we make a detour to drive through Bloxham and look lovingly at Nut Tree Cottage. In 1991 I was "caught" by the owner peeking over the stone

cult thing to accomplish, that my parents' feelings would be hurt, and that they would, in all probability, oppose my wishes.

After my visit to Brussels in March, we wrote many letters to each other. Several times a month I wrote to and received from all four members of the family many letters. We expressed our love, pride, and admiration for each other in very moving words. We were trying to make up for the past five years and getting to know each other again. I indicated in some of my letters that I was uncertain about the future and that we needed to discuss it on my next visit. My mother quickly understood that I might want to stay in England. It was a terrible blow to my parents because they had looked forward to the day I would return home. My father in fact felt that my wish to stay in England was tantamount to disowning Belgium and my family. They tried to convince me that I would be making a big mistake because: (1) According to them, medical training in Belgium was better than in England; (2) I would have certain advantages and medical school would be shorter; (3) I would make useful connections and make new friends; (4) A home life was important when studying hard; and (5) It would be less expensive. They made their arguments repeatedly, but throughout, in spite of their feelings, they made it clear that I would have to make the decision and would support me in every way they could.

On the 7th of May (which was my birthday) I was flying with a pupil when I noticed that the clouds had closed in, and, being above the clouds, I was unable to see the ground. I became very concerned that I might get lost and the weather get worse, so I decided to descend through the clouds to identify where I was and make my way back to base. It was probably a very dangerous thing to do in retrospect because I could not be sure that the land was flat and the altimeter accurate. As I broke through the clouds I suddenly saw a church spire slipping by. I was only at 200 feet and hoped that there was only one church in the village! I circled around

---

wall, and thus we met Susan and Peter Mayes, who have been warm friends ever since. In fact in 1997 we housesat in their home for 2½ weeks while they were vacationing in Greece.

It was a nostalgic treat, a walk down memory lane, as I was able to immerse myself once again in the atmosphere of the house, the school, and the village which had been my home during those momentous years almost sixty years ago.

looking for a field on which to land and eventually made a "precautionary landing." I left the pupil to guard the plane[10] while I walked to the village to discover where I was, and ran into an RAF pilot on leave. He said to me cheerfully, "Oh, good, I'm glad to see you're safe, old boy, but I was afraid that you might have been hitting the church spire and bought it." This was a very fortunate escape on my birthday. After contacting the base by telephone, I was given permission to take off again and returned to Snailwell.

The following day, May 8, was Victory in Europe Day (VE Day). The Germans had unconditionally surrendered. I went to London and participated in the enthusiastic celebrations marking the end of the war in Europe. I was one of the hundreds of thousands milling around in front of Buckingham Palace, cheering the King, the Royal Family, and Winston Churchill as they appeared on the balcony many times. London was wonderful on this occasion: all the buildings were lit up once again and the enthusiasm of the people was fantastic.

Louis Van Arenbergh, whom I knew in Medicine Hat in Canada as my first instructor, was also at Snailwell. Unfortunately, he was an alcoholic, and one night he got it into his head to chase rabbits in a Jeep across the landing field while drunk. He tipped over the Jeep and was killed.

Later on that month, I damaged my first aircraft. Decidedly May was turning out to be a most unfortunate month for me. The 14th of May was very windy, but flying had not been officially canceled, and so I decided to go flying with one of my pupils. I went up for a while and then landed. The procedure upon landing the Tiger Moth is that, when you stop, you turn to the left 45 degrees in order to see whether any planes were coming in to land behind you. Just as I did that, a gust of wind lifted my wing and the plane tipped over and we ended upside down. The poor pupil was the same one with whom I had made the precautionary landing the week before! I instructed him to release his harness carefully because, since we were upside down, he might suddenly fall to the ground and break his neck. We managed to complete the procedure without mishap. The incident did result, however, in an endorsement in my log book which stated,

---

[10] The Tiger Moth was covered in canvas, and cattle loved to lick and eat it because of the glue! So the plane had to be guarded in a field with cattle.

"being an instructor on Tiger Moth he has damaged an aircraft through taxiing with gross carelessness."

Now that the European war was over, I tried to get posted to the Far East. Although I was an instructor and I didn't believe they would need instructors in the Pacific theater, there was some discussion about recruiting pilots for gliders in the Far East to finish the war. I was not successful, however.

Around this time I received a letter from home indicating that my parents did not wish me to stay in England and wanted me back home in Brussels. I responded by saying that there were lots of things we ought to talk about and not to worry until I came home on leave once again. On one occasion I attended the Derby, an event which, in peacetime, was held at Epsom, near London, but during the war was held nearby at Newmarket. I went to the race, bet a few pounds on the favorite, and won.

I was more determined than ever at this time not to go back to Belgium permanently. I felt that I had to be independent and, although I would have loved to have been home, I knew it would have been trying for all concerned. By studying in England, I would still be able to go to Belgium frequently. I continued to try and get another trip to Belgium organized. By the end of June all my pupils had finished their course and I applied for leave. A few days later I went to London and boarded HMS *Royal Ulsterman* in Tilbury, and was given a first-class cabin. We arrived in Ostend the following day, and I proceeded on to Brussels. This time I spent three weeks in Belgium. I saw a lot of my former school friends, went to the Boat Club frequently, visited Colette Coppée, on whom I had a crush when I was 15 (and whom I was to see in the future, many times, both in the United States and in Europe). I went to visit Janine Gutt for tea and we talked about François' death.[11] I visited Lieutenant Lambion and Marcel Peters, who had helped me in France in May of 1940. This was altogether a very pleasant visit home.

I returned to Snailwell at the end of July, and one day, to my great surprise, Etienne Gutt walked into my room—it had been two years since we

[11] Janine, shortly afterward, became again a medical student at the University of Brussels. A few years later, around 1948 or 1949, while doing an internship in a hospital on the Belgian coast, she committed suicide.

had seen each other. He was a pilot in the RAF, and from then on he and I spent a great deal of time together, usually in the evening, since I was instructing during the day. We had our routine of going to the Golden Lion in Newmarket for a drink and probably a meal and spending a lot of time talking.

I continued to visit Bloxham, mostly on weekends, and I became firmer in my decision not to return to Belgium, but to study medicine in England. I wrote a long letter to my father in August inquiring about how much money he would be able to provide to continue my studies in England. There was a great deal of resistance to this decision on the part of my family. It was clear that they were very distressed that, after an absence of five years, I had decided not to go back to Belgium. My father, in particular, felt quite hurt and insulted that I was giving up Belgium, with all it meant to him, to choose a life in England. I felt bad about hurting their feelings, but I was still determined to continue on my course of action.

On the 14th of August the war in the Far East ended and Victory over Japan (VJ Day) was celebrated on the 15th. I went to London with Etienne and we had a wonderful time over the next few days. We had tea as his guest at the Royal Automobile Club, dinner at the Carlton with Patsy Dunlop, who had just returned from Canada, drinks at the Mirabelle (my old haunt), and we saw the King and Queen on the balcony of Buckingham Palace. Churchill was not there this time. The Conservative Party had been defeated in the election at the end of July, and the Labour Party was now in power. The following day Etienne and I had lunch with Patsy, and the Dunlops gave a party at the Dorchester welcoming her back to England from Canada. We rode in their car around London and eventually ended up at Dr. Dunlop's house in Hendon for milk and crackers. The following day at dawn I took the train back to Snailwell.

Now that the war was over, my mind turned more actively towards getting out of the air force and starting medical school once again. One of my major problems was going to get demobilized in England. There seemed to be a rule prohibiting the demobilization in England of a Belgian who had not been in England prior to September 1, 1939. I was afraid that if I went back to Belgium it would be very difficult to get back to England because new immigration policies had not yet been formulated.

So I went to ask my cousin, Tom Loveday, for his help. He lived near Wardington at Williamscot near Banbury and had been, until recently, vice-chancellor of the University of Bristol. He asked me who the new British home secretary was, and I told him that it was Chuter Ede. He said, "Oh, I know Ede," and he proceeded to write him a letter explaining who I was, my relationship to him, that I had come out of Belgium, that I had volunteered for the RAF, and that I wanted to be demobilized in England. He hoped that I would not be disadvantaged as a result of my service in the RAF. I subsequently learned that, as a result of this letter, the Home Office authorized me to be demobilized in England. My problem then became one of convincing the Air Force authorities to forward my formal application for demobilization to the Home Office. When I went to Air Force headquarters and requested to be demobilized in England, I was told that it was not allowed. I indicated to them, eventually, that I had reason to believe that if they forwarded my application it would be acted upon favorably. Initially, they refused to believe me until I was so insistent that they began to suspect (correctly) that I had gone outside regular Air Force channels in order to get this information. This was a violation of Air Force regulations, and I ran the risk of being reprimanded for my action. However, I shaded the truth and informed them that I personally had done nothing about it, but that some friends in government had told me that if my application was forwarded it would be favorably acted upon. On that basis the Air Force authorities did forward my application, which eventually was approved.

At the end of August, I also saw Group Captain Guillaume, one of the very senior officers of the Belgian Air Force, and requested an indefinite leave from the RAF, pending demobilization, in order to be able to resume my studies. At the same time I saw Air Commodore Wouters, who was the head of the Belgian Air Force. Wouters tried to convince me to stay in the air force and enjoy a brilliant career. He said that, as an officer and a flying instructor at 21, I was in a unique position. After the war, he said, they would send me to staff college, and there was no telling how far I could go, perhaps even Commander-in-Chief of the Belgian Air Force. I thanked them but told them I wanted to become a doctor. I am not sure they understood.

When I returned to Snailwell, I learned that my superiors would back my application for indefinite leave. For the next several weeks I continued to instruct and on weekends go to London with Etienne, stay at Norah's, go to the Mirabelle to dance, and go to the movies, including a most wonderful one, "I Live In Grosvenor's Square," with Rex Harrison and Anna Neagle.[12] In early September, Etienne and I visited Accolds, the Dunlop country house where Pauline and I had stayed in the 1930s. I also went to Bloxham with Etienne and we had lunch on one occasion at Magdalen College, Etienne's past and future Oxford college. By the middle of September, I concluded that I was leading a rather useless life at Snailwell. However, Etienne and I had our routine together: coffee in the morning, then lunch, then tea in the afternoon, and then the Golden Lion in Newmarket at night.

I received confirmation that King's College would take me back. This had not been easy because, even though there was the letter from Profes-

---

[12] Norah Nicholls was the daughter of Cary Schuster—my aunt. She was a distinguished physician, a pathologist who had been married to Marriott Nicholls, dean of St. George's Medical School in London. She was very generous to me—organized dinner parties which included me and allowed me to stay at her flat on weekend leaves.

One of the people I met at one of Norah's dinners was John Barnes, then an officer in the British Army. He was my 4th cousin once removed through the Bullock family, and we developed a friendship with him and his wife, Cynthia, over the next half century. I had met his parents while living in Birmingham in 1942. His father was the Bishop of Birmingham. Adele, his wife, was my mother's cousin. I went to tea once and she inquired about my mother of whom she was very fond. John arrived in Brussels shortly after its liberation in September 1944 and called on my parents. He was the first English relative they saw after the liberation. It meant a lot to them, and they appreciated being invited for some meals at his mess at a time when food was still in short supply.

John had a brilliant career in the Foreign Service. His last post was as British ambassador to Holland. We, with the three children, visited him and Cynthia at the embassy in The Hague in 1973 following his service as British ambassador in Tel Aviv, Israel.

After he was knighted and retired we visited them often at Hurstpierpoint in Sussex. Through them we met a younger diplomatic couple, Andrew and Sarah Burns. First we met them during their year at Harvard in 1982, then in the British embassy in Washington, D.C., as well as in Dublin, New Hampshire, and London. In 1994, we stayed with them for a week in Tel Aviv, where Andrew had become British ambassador to Israel. He then became the top British diplomat in Hong Kong after the handover to China. Andrew was knighted, and in 2000 he was posted to Ottawa, where he serves as British High Commissioner to Canada.

sor Stibbe from when I had joined the military saying that King's would take me back, there was now a different dean in charge who was not sure he needed to honor that assurance. However, I was able to convince him to do so and was delighted that King's would take me back.

Frankly, I was disappointed that I had never gone on operations. In some respects my three years in the Air Force seemed to have been a waste of time, because I had never actually achieved my ambition of being in combat. I knew, however, that it was through no fault of my own, and I had, after all, done something constructive—I had instructed many pupils in elementary flying. I took my responsibilities as a flying instructor very seriously, as had my own past instructors, with great benefits to me. I was an exacting instructor, and was not satisfied with anything less than safe, competent, and accurate flying. It was a source of great satisfaction to me to have seen all of my pupils graduate with the exception of one, who failed to make the grade.[13]

In a broader sense the past three years had been very rewarding. I had matured in the RAF. I had wonderful, enriching experiences. Although I had thought at times of going into politics or becoming a journalist or a lawyer, in the end I decided that medicine was the only profession which was worthwhile for me, even if one was not financially successful. I had also decided on the direction of the next phase of my life, i.e., to study in England. All in all, I felt that I had accomplished a lot in the past three years.

At the end of September I made my farewells to Snailwell. I said goodbye to Etienne and my pupils. We went to the Golden Lion for a final celebration, and on the 27th I left and went to Bloxham. A few days later I went to London. I still didn't have a place to live, and Dr. Dunlop, Patsy's father, kindly allowed me to stay with him in Hendon for a period of time.

---

[13] On one of my visits to Brussels a few years later, when I was in medical school, I went to a café frequented by students and I encountered one of my old pupils, who thanked me for teaching him to fly. He also told me that all of my pupils were still alive, while some others had died in various flying accidents. At the risk of sounding conceited, I thought that perhaps I had been a good role model, and that my instruction had contributed to their survival by curtailing their youthful risk-taking.

On the 1st of October I registered at King's, and two days later I started lectures. I began to make friends and met quite a number of people. Eventually, after a few weeks, I had to leave Hendon and found digs, a room in Upper Norwood, north of London. As the autumn began and I resumed my medical school studies, it looked as if it was going to be possible for me to be demobilized in England.

CHAPTER VII

MEDICAL SCHOOL

October 1945 – July 1950

In October of 1945 I threw myself energetically into my medical education, which took four and a half more years. After leaving Dr. Dunlop's house I moved into a room, my "digs," in Upper Norwood, north of London. King's College was in the Strand, and commuting between my digs and the college took forty-five minutes or more in each direction. I traveled by bus and the days were long, and during the winter it was very cold. The postwar years in England were, in many ways, worse than the war years, with food rationing still in place and the wonderful war spirit gradually disappearing. My family gradually came to terms with my decision to stay in England and continue my education there. My mother in particular expressed her understanding of my motivation, and even my father became reconciled to my decision and did everything he could to support me, including providing money for my education. Financially, I did rely upon them to provide the funds, and there is no doubt that my education in London was more expensive than it would have been in Belgium.[1] The University of Brussels would have been free, and living at home would have been less costly than renting a room.

Etienne was again at Oxford, at Magdalen College, studying law. I led an active social life, made many friends in the college, went to Bloxham when I could on the weekends, and studied hard in my room in the evening. Since I was still an officer in the Royal Air Force on indefinite leave (and drawing pay), I occasionally wore my uniform on certain spe-

[1] After a few months, financial support did come from the British government for university education—comparable to the G.I. Bill of Rights. This fortunately reduced my parent's expenses on my behalf.

cial occasions, particularly in the evening. After all the effort I had made to be demobilized in England, the moment finally came on May 13, 1946, but ironically I had to go back to Belgium for twenty-four hours to be discharged from the service! I had, after all, no trouble getting back to England!

An activity which took a great deal of my time was rowing. At King's College there was a medical student, Johnny Johnson, who had also served in the military during the war, was very keen on rowing, and very effectively organized the King's College Boat Club. I had started sculling when I was six in Brussels, and had done some single sculling in England with Etienne at Oxford and in London in 1942. But this was rowing, and I joined the crew of both the eight and four-man boats, and we proceeded to have a very successful year. We rowed at least three times a week, usually on Wednesdays, Saturdays, and Sundays, from the Thames Rowing Club on the Embankment at Putney. There was wonderful camaraderie among the members of the crew and we fit well together. In March the VIII entered the Head of the River race, a 4¼-mile course on the Thames beginning at Mortlake and ending at Putney Bridge, rowed in the reverse direction of the Oxford and Cambridge Boat Race. We did very well, starting about the fiftieth crew and ending eighth. We went to several regattas that spring and early summer, and were really very successful in the VIII and the IV, both of which I stroked. At the end of June we won at the Marlow Regatta and the next day we rowed to Henley for the Royal Regatta. We established ourselves at Henley for the next two weeks. We trained every day, usually going out once or twice a day in the VIII and the IV. The weather was beautiful, and we were putting the finishing touches to our training. Our VIII entered the Thames Challenge Cup and on the first day, Wednesday, July 3, we raced the London Rowing Club and beat them by one length. The coxless IV was entered in the Wyfold Challenge Cup, and our first heat was against the Quintin Boat Club. We had raced them earlier in the season and knew we could beat them, and so it was very disconcerting that, after the start, Quintin moved way ahead because our steering mechanism had shifted and Peter Pusey, who was steering at bow, was having a lot of trouble keeping the boat straight. We still won by 1½ lengths, but it was very nerve-wracking as the official report of the race

Having won the Wyfold Cup at the Henley Royal Regatta, the King's College (University of London) crew receives their prize. Her Royal Highness Princess Elizabeth (later Queen Elizabeth II) with Princess Margaret has presented the cup to our captain J. R. Johnson, is presenting the base of the cup to me, and will then congratulate T.H. Christie and P. Pusey, July 1946.

stated "Quintin led by a length at the quarter mile and by 1½ lengths at the half mile. King's then closed up in spite of erratic steering and led by ¾ length at the ¾ mile." The next day the VIII beat Jesus College, Cambridge, by 1½ lengths. In the semifinals on Friday, we raced Imperial College, London, which we knew to be an excellent crew, and they beat us by 2½ lengths.

We did better in the Wyfold Cup. We won our second race against Westminster Bank, by three lengths, and on Friday we beat Sabrina Club and won by two lengths. In the finals on Saturday, we beat the Thames Rowing Club by 1¼ lengths . The official report said, "Thames started at 34, King's at 36, King's led by ¾ of a length at the quarter mile and held that to the mile. Both rowed in at 36 and King's drew away." The 1946 Henley Royal Regatta was the first Royal Henley since the war, and Princess Elizabeth—later Queen Elizabeth II—and her sister Princess Margaret, presented the prizes. It was very exciting to have won a cup at Henley and to have received the base of it as the stroke of the crew from Princess Elizabeth. I have always treasured the photograph taken at that time showing me and the rest of the crew going up to the podium and receiving the cup from the princess.

After Henley, encouraged by Etienne whose Isis (Oxford) crew was doing the same, we entered an international regatta in Brussels. By that time we were tired. We had been working too hard on the river; we were stale and some of us had boils. I had one on my buttocks which had to be infiltrated with penicillin at the Westminster Hospital. There had been a lot of publicity in Belgium about our coming because my father had, in the past, been involved in some controversy about styles of rowing. It was assumed that I, his son, would row according to the "orthodox style" as opposed to the "Steve Fairbairm style," which was used by the Belgian crews. We raced against a senior crew from the University of Brussels Boat Club; these were seasoned oarsmen, and there were some other crews in the race as well. We raced in a borrowed boat, converted from a coxed four to a coxless four. In the race we did very poorly and came in last. Much was made of our defeat in the Brussels press, and people in rowing circles began asking the question, "Is this the demise of British rowing?" I think my father felt rather embarrassed at our performance, and we did also. Etienne Gutt's crew did better than we had, although they didn't win either.

Following this debacle I joined Doris Dunlop, Patsy's mother, on a trip to Cannes in the South of France. Included in the group was Ian Reid, who had been an on-again, off-again fiancé of Patsy. I had initially been asked to join the group as an escort and companion for Patsy, during a time when they had broken up. By the time of the trip, though, Ian was back in the picture, and I felt rather like an extra. I met them in Paris and we drove to Cannes and had a wonderful time. We stayed in a little hotel on one of the back streets of town. We enjoyed the beach and swimming and at night we went to the Palm Beach Casino and gambled. We saw Noel Coward and his boyfriend at a baccarat table and also the Duke and Duchess of Windsor. That's the only time I ever saw them, but they were certainly a beautiful couple.

It is surprising that we were able to take this trip to the South of France at a time when the British Treasury was very severely limiting the export of British pounds. The reason why it was possible for us to do this was that a man whom, as I understood later, was a patient of Patsy's mother, Doris Howard (as she was professionally known), had made it possible because of the businesses that he had in France for us to use local currency for our trip. This man and his wife were also in Cannes with their two children, a younger son and an older daughter, and it turned out that the attractive daughter was a very good companion for me, so that when Patsy, Ian, and I went out she completed the foursome. The four of us went dancing and enjoyed ourselves very much. This other couple was Jewish, and it turned out that they became very concerned that our relationship might turn matrimonially serious. Ian, in his humorous way, told me at one point that we ought to reassure the girl's parents that they need not worry: that my intentions were strictly dishonorable!

After our trip to the South of France we returned to London, where unfortunately my luggage was stolen from the boot of the car shortly after we arrived and while we were upstairs in the house getting a cold drink. In addition to the loss of my clothes I lost my King's College rowing blazer and the gold medal I had received as winner of the Wyfold Cup. A number of years later, I got it replaced. The thieves were arrested and I testified at their trial. All I recovered, though, was my suitcase.

For the next several months, I continued to study, although rowing interfered and I don't think I studied as well or as hard as I should have.[2] After five terms of working for the Second Examination for Medical Degrees (2nd MB), I took the exam in March of 1947 and was very fortunate to pass. I did not do well in the oral anatomy exam, but fortunately I

---

[2] Norah Nicholls wrote a poem which captured her perception of me at this time.

The Last Fling

July
This is the last fling together, dear
I am leaving the Air Force today.
Let us make the most of the weather, dear
And, for once cast all cares right away.

October
Now this is the *very* last fling, dear
Tomorrow my term will commence.
And, I must get into the swing, dear
Of medical studies intense.

December
You say that your party's unique, dear
Well, just for a *really* last fling.
For I've got an exam in a week, dear
And, I'm sure I don't know a thing.

April
Now I'm a doctor at last, dear
But, don't look for a diamond ring.
I fear you are planning too fast, dear
As I'm off for a final grand fling.

was examined partly by Professor Nichol, the chairman of the department, and partly by Dr. McKinnon, who liked me and had great respect for my rowing prowess. He was impressed by the success of our crew, and he told Professor Nichol he was sure that, if I were allowed to pass, I was the kind of person who would put his nose to the grindstone and study hard after the exam! After our victories at King's the previous year, I was asked to row for the Thames Rowing Club, and I agreed to do so. I was stroke of the Grand Challenge Cup VIII throughout the spring and early summer, winning a good number of races during that time. We went to the Marlow Regatta two weeks before the Henley Regatta. We won the first heat and lost to Jesus College, Cambridge, in the final. We were considered to be an excellent crew. In the final, Ham Ward, one of the crew and vice captain, caught his pants in the slide, which completely threw us off our rhythm, and we became very discouraged. I'm afraid that at that point I seemed to have stopped racing and, as somebody who had seen us going up to the start said afterwards, "We saw the Thames eight going up to the start and it looked like the best Thames crew we had seen in many, many years . . . but then we saw the crew rowing back during the race and they were still paddling rather than racing."

We then went to Henley. We trained very hard, lived at the Bix Rectory, and interacted a lot with each other. On the morning of our first race, Tom Sullivan, who was rowing behind me at the number seven position, felt sick as had happened in previous regattas when he was rowing for Cambridge. He was unable to race, and an excellent substitute came in (Sparrow Morris), but one who had not raced with us before. We raced a crew from Delft in Holland and were beaten by one length. The official report stated, "Thames started at 41 but Delft at 39 led by six feet at the quarter mile and drew away to a length at Fawley (which is halfway). Approaching the mile, Thames rowed at 38 but Delft held their lead." It was disappointing for us to be put out in the first heat of the Grand Challenge Cup, and the only satisfaction was that Delft reached the finals and were beaten by Jesus College, Cambridge, the crew that had beaten us at Marlow.

I spent most of the summer in Brussels, enjoying myself with the family and studying hard. Having completed the Second MB exam, I

The Thames Rowing Club Grand Challenge Cup crew, on a practice outing at Henley, July 1947. Bow, John Wilmot; 2, John Dizer; 3, Ham Ward; 4, W. Bull; 5, Hank Rushmere; 6, Peter Kirkpatrick; 7, Tom Sullivan; Stroke, Francis de Marneffe; Cox, Alan Burrough.

started my clinical work at Westminster Hospital and moved into Brabazon House, a very nice boarding house owned by Westminster Hospital for its students. It was a very convenient ten-minute walk to the hospital, and I lived there for the next three years. I made many friends at the medical school and in the house. One of my friends was Donald Knight, who was about ten years older than I, had served in the army, had written a book, and was an interesting man who eventually went into psychiatry, and whom I saw on one or two occasions at his hospital in Trenton, New Jersey. He and I, at the end of the day after studying, often went out together to one of the pubs, either locally or more often in the West End, and we became fairly regular customers at the Red Lion in Mayfair, which has remained a favorite watering hole (and dining spot) for the rest of my life.

I continued to visit Belgium whenever I could. I became very fond of another medical student at King's College Hospital, Daphne Elizabeth

Webber, whose family lived in Seven Oaks in Kent. I visited her there a few times.[3]

In 1948 I continued to attend Westminster Medical School. I did not row very much until quite late in the spring, when Thames Rowing Club asked me to stroke a "scratch" Wyfold four. I did so, and in the Henley Regatta we met in our first heat the Victoria Lake Rowing Club of South Africa, who beat us by 2¾ lengths. Victoria Lake won the final. In 1947 I had become a British subject by naturalization, a decision which was painful to my father, who felt I was rejecting my Belgian heritage. It made sense to me, though, since I was planning on spending the rest of my life in England. The 1948 Olympics were held in England and the rowing Olympics at Henley. Thames Rowing Club entered its crews in the Olympic trials and my four entered the Coxed Four Event, but we did very poorly and certainly were not chosen to represent Great Britain in the Olympic Games, although it was fun to at least have entered the Olympic Trials. Thames Rowing Club had won the Grand Challenge Cup and the Stewards (the senior four-oared race) at the Royal Regatta. Two of my former rowing mates in our 1946 Wyfold crew were in those victorious crews: Johnny Johnson was in the VIII and Tom Christie the VIII and the IV. The Olympic Committee decided that the four was relatively better than the eight, so the four represented Great Britain in the Olympics.

Early in 1948 I met Parvaneh Nasseri, a young Iranian woman who was studying in London to be a radiology technician. We met at a dance organized by the British Council, and she was a very striking and beautiful woman. We dated each other for the next year and a half and she occasionally visited me in Brussels, where she had a cousin.[4]

In the summer of 1949 I spent a lot of time in Belgium: partly to save money; partly to concentrate on studying, because by that time I had

[3] In the 1990s Daphne, now known as Dr. Elizabeth Forsythe, visited us in Cambridge when calling on the publisher of several books she authored, including one on Alzheimer's disease.

[4] Around 1963 Parvaneh, who had married Jacques Meylan, a Swiss gynecologist, and who was living in Geneva, reestablished contact with me in Cambridge while Jacques was doing a fertility fellowship at Worcester. Ever since then Bobbie and I have seen them in Switzerland and the United States frequently.

Nut Tree Cottage, Bloxham. My parents' first visit since the end of World War II. My mother is sitting between Dorothy (R) and Katherine (L), 1946.

completed most of the required course work at the hospital; and partly to be with my family. During the summer, I met Mona, an attractive Belgian woman whom I liked but who had a lover, and therefore nothing initially came of our relationship. My medical school education was drawing to an end, and I had decided to take various exams: both the examinations of the Royal College of Surgeons and the Royal College of Physicians (the so-called conjoint examinations, which occur in four parts) and the examination for a degree from the University of London, which would give me an MBBS (Bachelor of Medicine and Bachelor of Surgery, the equivalent of the American M.D.). I started taking the examinations at the end of

An informal photo of my parents, at home in Brussels, late 1940s.

1949, passed pathology in the MBBS examination, and passed the exams for the conjoint.

Over Christmas of 1949, when I was in Brussels, my relationship with Mona became more serious, and when I returned to England after my vacation, she came with me and we moved in with each other. I left Brabazon House and Mona and I looked for digs together. We had hoped she would be able to find some work in London, but this proved not to be possible. She really wasn't trained for anything, although she was well-educated; she was somewhat of a dilettante, and I found myself rather conflicted between studying hard for exams and wanting to spend time with her. As time went on, I found the relationship increasingly troublesome. I felt confused, uncertain—on the one hand we had a very passionate relationship, yet on the other hand I did not think that Mona was the person I should have a permanent relationship with or to whom I could make a major commitment.

I passed my exams successfully in May of 1950 and graduated from medical school. The question now was what to do and where. I had worked very hard, I felt rather tired, and I was uncertain about my future. I was, at that time, rather sick of life in London, yet I still did not want to go back to Belgium. I needed a breather and a change of scene. Unlike my classmates who took "house jobs" (that is, internships in a British hospital, which I could have done), I chose instead to respond to the advertisements that American hospitals were publicizing in England in their search for interns. I applied to the Elizabeth General Hospital in Elizabeth, New Jersey, for an internship, but their positions were filled and they referred my application to Muhlenberg Hospital in Plainfield, New Jersey, and that is where I elected to go. It was, of course, again distressing to my family that I was distancing myself even more from Brussels. By now I hoped they had accepted the idea that I would be making my way in life in various parts of the world, and they had, I think, become somewhat reconciled to this reality. I obtained a visitor's visa, and at the end of June I left Brussels for Rotterdam, where I boarded a freighter to take me to America.

The journey took eleven or twelve days, and during this time the only contact with the rest of the world was what we heard over the radio. Thus we learned that South Korea had been invaded by North Korea and that the United States had committed its troops to the defense of South Korea under the aegis of the United Nations. We arrived in New York late on the 3rd of July, hoping to disembark, but of course the following day was the 4th of July and a holiday, so nothing happened and we had to stay on board. The day after that, when we did disembark, I made my way from New York to Plainfield, New Jersey, and thus began my actual life as a physician.

CHAPTER VIII

POSTGRADUATE TRAINING

July 1950 – January 1953

I STARTED MY ROTATING INTERNSHIP in early July at Muhlenberg Hospital, a community hospital located in a very attractive residential area of Plainfield, New Jersey, a town half an hour from New York City by bus. The rotation involved three months each on medicine, surgery, pediatrics, and obstetrics and gynecology. I was one of four interns: a Scotsman, two Americans, and me. The Americans lived in town with their families; the Scotsman and I each had a room in the hospital, and we shared a living room with comfortable chairs and a television. The television came in very handy because after the invasion of South Korea by North Korea, there were big debates in the United Nations Security Council which were interesting to watch.

Within a few hours of arrival I was assigned to the emergency room (ER), and one of the first cases I had to treat was a skin rash which I had never seen before. Fortunately, Selena Cornwell, the head nurse in the E.R., whispered to me that it was poison ivy. Poison ivy is nonexistent in Europe, and I had never heard of it and did not know how to treat it. Fortunately, she rescued me and I was able to act as if I knew what I was doing. Shortly thereafter, I went to the medical library and read up all I could about poison ivy.

The internship was hard work since we were on duty every fourth night and it was the only hospital in the community. It was still possible, however, to have a social life, and not long after my arrival I was befriended by Selena Cornwell, a middle-aged woman, probably twenty to thirty years older than I. She was single, loved to go into New York, and go to the theater. She took me under her wing, wanted me to see the best aspects of American life, and welcomed me as a companion, someone who in later years might have been called a "walker"—in other words, someone who could escort her to restaurants and the theater, since she didn't like to do these things on her own. So on a number of occasions during my stay in Plainfield, we went into New York for dinner and the theater. In later years I introduced Selena to my aunts in England, and she went and stayed with them on a few occasions when she toured the British Isles. I think on one occasion she also went to Brussels and was shown around by my family.

I found the medical staff at the hospital very friendly and hospitable, and some of the senior physicians invited me on occasion to have dinner with them. One such occasion had a rather strange ending. One Sunday evening, a few weeks after my arrival, the chief of pediatrics, to whose service I was assigned at the time, invited me for dinner at his country club. During the dinner, one of the guests, knowing that I was British and had been trained in England, asked me what I thought of the National Health Service or "socialized medicine," as Americans liked to call it at the time. I responded by saying that, although it had its problems, I thought that, based on my experience in England and in the United States so far, it was a lot less expensive for the patients. At this point, the man got very angry, said that I had insulted the flag of the United States, and that I could start walking right now! My host, the chief pediatrician, who had been away from the table when this exchange occurred and who had left a group of very congenial people, came back to a table where the man was obviously angry at me. He was very puzzled since he didn't know what had taken place, and when he drove me back to the hospital after dinner I described to him what had happened. I thought the whole experience was very strange, and certainly I was not aware of having said anything at which anyone could have taken umbrage. But worse was to come. The following day, one of the American interns came to speak to me in the afternoon and said, "Francis, what have you done?" I didn't know what he was referring to, but he explained that while assisting the chief urologist he had heard him say, "The man should be reported to the FBI." From the context of this statement, my colleague suspected he was referring to me.

At this point, I began to feel that the situation was escalating in a ridiculous way and that I was not prepared to put up with this nonsense. I put in a call to Dr. Salvati, the physician in charge of the internship program, and requested that we meet as soon as possible. At our meeting I told him what I had heard about this conversation and the reference to the FBI and wanted to know what on earth this was about. At this point, he made a reference to the dinner at the country club and my comments about the National Health Service in England. He obviously had not been told exactly what I had said, so I proceeded to do so. I asked him whether he thought that what I had said was so terrible, and he only halfheartedly indicated that it wasn't. At this point, I proceeded to inform Dr. Salvati, who had just urged me to watch what I said publicly, that I had had no intention of doing so. I told him that I had the opportunity of doing an internship in England, but that instead I had chosen to come to the United States because I was interested in interacting with people of a different culture and different background than my own. What made the internship experience valuable to me was not only the medical training which I was receiving (and which probably would have been better in any event in a teaching hospital in England), but the opportunity to speak to other people. Therefore, if he was telling me not to do that and wished to limit my freedom of expression, I told him he should know right now that I was prepared to resign from the hospital. He realized that I was serious and proceeded to reassure me that, of course, I had the right to speak as I wished. This was the first evidence that Plainfield, and perhaps the USA as a whole, was a much more reactionary country than my image of it under Franklin Delano Roosevelt.

After a few weeks in Plainfield, I felt lonely and really missed Mona in Belgium and felt that I had made a terrible mistake in effectively breaking up with her by leaving Belgium. In an unguarded moment, I sent her a telegram asking her whether she would join me in the United States. This was really a very foolish thing to do, since I was not prepared or in a position to support her and she had, herself, no means of support in the United States. When she answered that she was prepared to come over, I got very cold feet, changed my mind, and in fact terminated the relationship at that point.

In early January of 1951, I had a few days holiday and I decided to visit Sheila and Myron Gilmore in Boston. Sheila was my cousin Margaret Whitehead's daughter and was married to Myron Gilmore, a professor of history at Harvard. They were my only relatives in the United States apart from North Whitehead and his new wife, Harriet. The Gilmores lived in Belmont and the Whiteheads in Cambridge. I stayed with them for about a week, and during that time their good friend, Maurice Pechet, organized some visits for me to the Massachusetts General Hospital, the Lahey Clinic, and to Boston City Hospital. Contacts which were to prove useful in the future.

In addition to my visits to New York with Selena, I became friendly with a number of the women lab technicians in the hospital, and we occasionally went to parties together. I became particularly fond of Carol Brokaw, a very beautiful 20- or 21-year-old woman with a great sense of humor, whose family were some of the leading citizens of Plainfield. She was engaged to a Princeton graduate who was currently serving in the navy, and this proved to be a serious obstacle to the maturing of our relationship in the direction I would have wished.

In the last few months of my internship, another episode occurred which surprised and infuriated me. One night I was on call and a black woman was admitted to the hospital in labor with her third or fourth pregnancy. In each of her previous pregnancies there had been some concern about her ability to deliver normally without a cesarean section because of the discrepancy between the size of the fetus and her pelvis. This time it also appeared that she was going to have a very difficult labor, and after I observed her for a while, I decided that the attending obstetrician on call should come and examine her. This he did, and agreed that she would probably require a cesarean section, which could only be authorized by the senior obstetrician on call. The junior called the senior at home, about one or two o'clock in the morning, and was told to give the patient some Demerol for pain. Over the next hour, I continued to observe the patient very closely and there was no progress. I called the junior attending physician again, and he came to examine the patient once more. He telephoned the senior on call once again and received the same response: give the patient more Demerol for pain. I continued to observe the patient, who by this time was showing signs of distress in terms of her pulse rate and blood pressure, and there was beginning to be some evidence that the fetus was also in distress. At this point, I called the junior attending once again and spoke very sternly to him. I told him that I was appalled by the treatment of this patient, that I could understand that since his bread and butter depended upon the goodwill of the senior man why he might not wish to antagonize him but that I had no such inhibition since I had no intention of practicing in Plainfield and that I was going to be leaving in the near future. In effect, I shamed the junior attending into making yet another phone call to the senior man and really putting pressure on him by telling him that either he should come in or he the junior would go ahead with a cesarean section. The senior man did come in, about four o'clock in the morning, took one look at the patient, did a brief examination and ordered the operating room prepared for a cesarean, which was successfully completed.

I did not plan to leave matters there and decided to report the senior obstetrician to the hospital administration. I wrote a letter in which I stated that I had been at Muhlenberg Hospital sufficiently long to realize that there were inevitably differences in the practice of medicine in different parts of the world, and that I, having been trained in England, realized that things were done rather differently in England than they were in the United States. I also indicated that I was sick of having observed needless pain and suffering being inflicted upon individuals merely because they were poor or black. (This was a reference to the fact that white women were routinely admitted to the semi-private wing of the hospital, whereas black women were always admitted to the ward.) I indicated that the administration might find it unacceptable for an intern to report a senior physician on staff, and that if that was the case I would quite understand and would immediately resign. I also indicated that if I did so, I would notify the American Medical Association of the reasons for my resignation and also notify the powers that be in England of the poor quality of care at this hospital, in the hope that no other intern would ever come from Britain to Plainfield. I submitted this letter in the morning, and within a short time my name was called over the loudspeaker and I was asked to go to the hospital administrator's office. There I found myself in an emergency meeting of the Hospital Executive Committee chaired by none other than the urologist who had thought that I should be reported to the FBI months before! I was asked what my letter was all about, and I gave a detailed description of the events of the night relative to this patient. At the end of my presentation, there was a long silence. Evidently, the members of the Executive Committee were not sure what to say and waited for the chairman of the committee to take the lead. Eventually, Dr. Cantini, the chairman, said, "Well, I don't know about you guys, but I believe that de Marneffe is right. We have no way of knowing what goes on in this hospital at night when we're not around, and we depend on people who are around to let us know what goes on. I believe that we should express our gratitude to Dr. de Marneffe for having taken this step and having told us what went on." I thereupon left the meeting, and a couple of hours later I happened to be sitting in the coffee shop with some of my colleagues when the senior obstetrician whom I had reported stormed into the coffee shop, pretended not to see me, and said to one of his colleagues, in a voice loud enough for me to hear, "I don't know what this place has come to when an intern can report a senior physician on the staff!"

As my twelve months of internship were drawing to a close, I was quite undecided about the future. I had begun to doubt whether I had made the right decision in going into medicine. I could not quite see myself listening to chests and hearts, palpating abdomens, or even delivering babies for the rest of my life. I felt that this would not be challenging enough, and I aspired to emulate one of the authors I had admired in earlier years, W. Somerset Maugham, who had also graduated from medical school in London and proceeded to write many books which I enjoyed. I developed the fantasy of hopping across the Pacific from island to island, earning my way by practicing medicine as an intern or a resident in various hospitals, and eventually becoming a writer.

With that fantasy in mind, I decided not to return to England at this time, but to explore another part of the world. My geographical knowledge of the Pacific was obviously not very good since I picked a residency in Honolulu, Hawaii, in the belief that it might be Tahiti! I picked this pediatric residency for two reasons: first, it was the most highly paid in the island; and second, I thought that it might always be useful irrespective of what my ultimate fate was in medicine.

With a heavy heart at leaving Carol behind, I left New York, flew to Los Angeles, and then on to Honolulu where, in early July, I began my residency at the Kauikeolani Children's Hospital. I had a room in the hospital; there was another assistant resident with me, a Chinese man, and a chief resident who had been trained in Cincinnati. I was very struck by the beauty of the island: the scenery, the flowers, the trees, the sky, and the people. I found that the mixture of races between the Polynesians, the Asians, the Americans, and the Europeans created a most beautiful blend. The hospital was located on the outskirts of Honolulu, but I often went to Waikiki Beach. I enjoyed swimming in the ocean, and I bought a second-hand surfboard and tried to learn how to surf.

After a while I got tired of living in the hospital and rented a room in Waikiki itself. I felt very lonely and began to feel that my fantasy of island hopping across the Pacific and of eventually writing the "immortal novel" was just that, a fantasy, and that this would not satisfy me. I decided that I needed to put my training to good use, and began to try and figure out what aspect of medicine would satisfy me. I remembered that when I was a medical student in London, I had been extremely interested in reading psychiatric textbooks. Psychiatry, it seemed to me, offered what I was looking for, namely, variety: each person would be different, with a different life story; whatever emotional problems they presented would occur in the context of a unique individual; and this would make the work fascinating and constantly interesting. As I mulled this over, I continued to lead my life as best as I could. I occasionally dated, and I found the student nurses at the hospital very attractive and entertaining. I became quite famous in the school of nursing because I was able to give them "Tonies," i.e., permanents, to their great amusement. I did a lot of reading, and learned a lot about leprosy and the life of the lepers in days gone by on Molokai. I remembered that a Belgian missionary, Father Damien, had lived on Molokai and had died there of leprosy, early in the century, in the course of his looking after lepers. I further recalled that in the mid-thirties Father Damien's body had been brought back to Belgium with great ceremony on the Belgian training ship, the *Mercator*, which landed in Antwerp, and that the King of the Belgians had attended his burial on Belgian soil. While I was in Hawaii, I wrote a paper, "Notes on America," primarily for my own entertainment and in order to pass the time, but also with the idea of sharing it with some members of my family. The paper was about my thoughts concerning America, based on the year I had spent in Plainfield.

After I became convinced that psychiatry was the only field of medicine that would appeal to me on a long-term basis, I decided that the opportunities for a career in psychiatry would be better in the United States than in Europe. I researched the annual issue of the *Journal of the American Medical Association*, where all the internships and residencies in the United States by category are listed. I selected the twenty-five residencies in psychiatry that paid the least. I had learned by then that the better the residency, the lower the salary, and I was determined to pick a residency that would give me the very best possible start in my career. I borrowed a typewriter from one of the other residents and I painfully, one letter at a time, typed twenty-five letters inquiring about residencies in psychiatry in the US. Among these letters I submitted ones to Boston City Hospital, Massachusetts General Hospital (MGH), and Yale-New Haven Hospital. Because I thought someone who was Belgian-born, with a British degree and nationality, applying for a residency from Honolulu, would not be a very attractive applicant, I wrote to Myron Gilmore and explained that I was applying for a residency at various places, including the MGH, and if he knew anybody there he might alert them that my application was coming, in the hopes that they might be willing to give my application a good look. I received a mimeographed sheet from the MGH informing me that psychiatric residencies were awarded only to those who had completed a residency in internal medicine or in neurology—neither of which I had done. Therefore, I did not forward a formal application to the MGH. I did, however, hear from a number of hospitals, including Yale-New Haven Hospital, and I was asked to fill out an extensive form, including writing an essay as to why I wanted to go into psychiatry and particularly at Yale. One day I received a telegram and thought it was from Yale. In fact, it was a telegram from Stanley Cobb, the chief of psychiatry at MGH, informing me that there was an unexpected vacancy in the residency program at MGH and to air-mail information about my training and background. I was thrilled and immediately sent him a telegram telling him that I was air-mailing information about myself but assuring him that, sight unseen, I would accept a residency at MGH if he could offer it to me. A short while later I received another telegram from Stanley Cobb informing me that he could offer me an assistant residency in psychiatry at Mass. General Hospital to begin January 1952. I was absolutely delighted at this turn of events and prepared to be in Boston in early January.

I realized that my decision to leave would be very difficult for the hospital in Honolulu, and that I was not living up to my contract. I thought the best explanation would be to invoke my mother's increasing age in Belgium and indicate to the director of residency education that her health was not good (which was true) and that I should return to Belgium because of it. I don't know whether he believed me, but he had no choice but to accept my resignation effective November 1. In my remaining time in Honolulu, waiting with great anticipation for my departure, I went to Waikiki Beach, where I swam and did some surfing. I longingly looked up at the sky in the evenings around 7:00 P.M., when many aircraft would be flying from Honolulu back to the West Coast. Eventually, I flew back to New York, went to Plainfield to visit some of my friends for a brief period, and returned to New York, where I boarded the *Queen Elizabeth* and sailed to England.

On my trip aboard the *Queen Elizabeth* an interesting episode occurred. The Cunard elevator attendant was the very same person who had supervised me and my group on the *Queen Mary* in 1943 when we made the crossing from England to New York and we were cleaning the stairway every night. I greeted him and reminded him of that time, and he kindly pretended to remember me.

In London, I went to the American embassy and applied for an immigration visa to become a permanent resident of the United States and earn my living there. Then I went to Brussels to spend the rest of the time with my family. Once again, it was a wonderful visit. I enjoyed seeing my parents and siblings and sharing with them my experiences in the United States. We did the usual things in Brussels: we went to the Boat Club, to restaurants, and I saw friends. Towards the end of December, I went back to London, picked up my visa at the American embassy, and proceeded to Southhampton to board the *Queen Elizabeth* for my return to the States.

I arrived in Boston between Christmas and New Year's. I had hoped to visit Sheila and Myron Gilmore in Belmont, because the New Year would be lonely in a completely new city, but unfortunately they were busy. My quarters were on Parkman Street, a rather dilapidated house owned by the MGH, in which the radiators were noisy and difficult to maintain at the right temperature. I was issued a white uniform, and started work on the 2nd of January. I quickly made friends with the chief resident, Peter Sifneos, and with Richmond Holder, both of whom had been brought up in Europe. The psychiatric service was in the Bulfinch Building, the original building of the MGH, erected around 1815. It was an exciting time: I studied hard and I worked hard; I read a great deal, and I was not disappointed in my choice of career. Dr. Stanley Cobb was a distinguished neuropathologist who had been psychoanalyzed, had become the chief of psychiatry in 1934 when the Department of Psychiatry was created, and had had a distinguished career at Harvard, where he was the Bullard Professor of Neuropathology. He was a kind and generous man, who invited me to his house, as did some other members of the staff, and I felt very welcomed. I had thought before my arrival that people in the department might wonder what I looked like, and whether I even spoke English, given my Belgian background, British degree, and applying from Honolulu; but it turned out that the Psychiatric Department of MGH had a long tradition of close collaboration and contact with England, and it was not at all unusual for people with British degrees to work in the MGH. I became very attached to Mass. General and to the "MGH family." I made friends with several social workers, particularly with Martha Sherwood, who was a very warm and friendly person.

During the summer, I had a week's vacation but no money to spare since my monthly take-home pay during the whole of 1952 was $57.00. My board and lodging was free, and I did not have many expenses, but I didn't have enough money to take a vacation. So I asked my parents to send me my pup tent and sleeping bag from Belgium, and I spent a week on Cape Cod, on the land on which Richmond Holder eventually built a house at Nauset Beach in Orleans. It was a very primitive holiday. I had no light; therefore I went to bed at dusk and got up at dawn. It was a lonely time, but I was visited a few times by some of the people from MGH.

As time went on, I had to think of my next residency. Peter Sifneos had done two years of residency at McLean Hospital, and with his advice I decided to apply for a residency there. I was interviewed by Dr. Paul Howard, the acting chief of staff, in the summer of 1952, and was accepted. I moved to McLean Hospital as an assistant resident in psychiatry and started work on January 2, 1953. Little did I know at that time that I would spend the rest of my professional career at McLean, where I still am almost fifty years later.

POSTSCRIPT

On my arrival at McLean Hospital, I was assigned a bedroom on the second floor of the Administration Building, where I lived until the summer of 1954. One evening, while seeing a patient in my office, I was interrupted by a call from Western Union, who read me a telegram. My mother had died in Brussels on January 30, 1953, aged 71. I knew she had been sick with pneumonia and had a bad heart, but I had understood she was getting better. A letter she wrote to me on the day she died confirmed her improvement. Her death was a great shock to me, and I was very sad. I flew to Brussels via London, where Aunt Cary kindly met me between planes. My mother's funeral was very simple: a brief ceremony at the crematorium, a meal at my parents' apartment, and burial in the family grave.

In spite of this sad beginning I enjoyed my work and life at McLean Hospital and was glad I was training to be a psychiatrist. In August of 1955 I married Nancy Edmonds and we lived in an apartment in the Botanical Garden section of Cambridge. In 1956 Nancy and I went to Europe and visited my family in Belgium and England, and also toured Switzerland, Italy, and France.

In the fall of 1956 my father died, aged 82. He had been traveling with a companion in Yugoslavia and did not feel well after swimming one evening. The next morning he dropped dead while shaving. His coffin's journey back to Brussels was eventful and distressing. My sister Pauline went to meet the coffin with a hearse at the railroad station. My father's companion was on the train, but no coffin! After a search, it was discovered after a few days on a railroad siding at the Austrian frontier. What had happened?

Around this time Prime Minister Kruschev of the USSR had been visiting Marshal Tito in Belgrade for the first time to mend fences after their break of many years before. Tight security was enforced—even interfering with the movement of the coffin! When his coffin finally arrived in Brussels, my father was cremated and buried next to my mother and his parents.

Late in 1956 Nancy and I bought a lovely Tudor shingled house with leaded-pane windows at 84 Garden Street in Cambridge. Over the next few years we welcomed English and Belgian relatives. In 1957 I became an American citizen, a requirement at that time to practice medicine in Massachusetts. This step in no way changed my love of England.

In May 1957 Peter was born, Daphne in January 1959, and Colette in April 1960. Sadly, Nancy and I divorced in 1967. In December 1969 I married Barbara Rowe Hopkins.

After many years of peregrinations in many countries, I had finally settled down. I had much to be thankful for. I had a lovely family in an interesting city and state, and a professional life which I found exciting and rewarding. It was a good life. I was a very lucky man.

Francis de Marneffe, M.D.
February 27, 2001

THE DE MARNEFFE COAT OF ARMS

HERALDIC DESCRIPTION

Ecartelé aux 1 & 4 d'argent a trois chevrons de gueules; aux 2 & 3 de gueules a l'etrier d'argent, les etrivieres du meme. Cimier: un etrier de l'ecu dans un vol d'argent chargé des chevron de l'ecu. Heaune Couronné

MOTTO

Je te surporteray toujours

APPENDIX A

How My Family Learned about My Travels in France and Arrival in England

MANY TIMES DURING the five weeks of my journey from Brussels to England in 1940, I wondered what was happening to my parents and sister who had remained in Brussels, and to my brother somewhere in the army. I also wondered when and how they would learn of my peregrinations. As mentioned earlier, I had written two postcards on the 15th and 16th of May, but had no idea whether they had received them. It was only long after the war, when my brother, Robert, gave me a copy of my mother's diary, that I was able to piece together when they learned what had happened to me.

On June 10 she learned from a friend at the Boat Club that he had seen me in Roulers on May 16, going towards Ypres, and that news was confirmed by having received my two postcards.

On July 1, my parents were visited by Andre Duprez, whom I had seen in Conches, and he told them that I had gone to Le Havre and had connected myself to some Belgian officers. Later my mother learned that I had written to Robert that I was going to Poitiers to try and contact Monsieur Gutt.

On July 10 they received news that I was leaving for England, written at the end of a letter of François Gutt to his mother. How my letters may have reached Madame Gutt is interesting. As mentioned in his memoirs, before M. Gutt left Vichy for England, an important transaction of the Ministry of Finance required him to enter the German-occupied zone of France, and permission was requested of the German military authorities for a minor official of the Ministry of Finance of Belgium and his chauffeur to cross into occupied territory to conduct some relatively minor business. Permission was granted, and the minor official of the ministry was driven by his chauffeur into the occupied zone. The chauffeur, however, was the disguised Minister Gutt himself!

I had always understood that it was on this trip into occupied France that he met his wife and gave her my letters for my family. But that is contradicted by his memoirs and biography.

In fact Gutt met his wife around the 13th of July in Vichy (see Appendix D), apparently their only meeting before he left Vichy on August 1 for his journey to England. Therefore, his trip into occupied France was a separate event and occurred after his meeting with his wife.

On July 10, my parents also received information from somebody who saw me in Poitiers on the 16th or 17th of June, and learned that I was waiting for my visa to go to England.

On July 23 a friend of my brother's arrived in Brussels and informed them that Robert was now in Paris.

On July 25 they learned that, thanks to the efforts of Mme. Gutt, who was working for the Red Cross, the Germans had agreed to release all the mobilized medical students such as Robert, and that they would be allowed to go back to university. On the 28th, when my parents returned from the Boat Club, they found Robert sitting on a bench across from the house on the Avenue Louise.

My parents learned from Robert, after his return, many details of my own adventure, including the fact that I had been in Rouen and had tried unsuccessfully to get to England through Le Havre. He had received a postal order for two pounds while in the South of France, but didn't know whether it had come from me or from England. (This was actually money sent by Aunt Dorothy to Robert.)

At the end of July, they read in the national newspaper *Le Soir* that Lieutenant Colonel Tasnier had died, and on the August 14 they got news from Mme. Tasnier telling them that she had returned to Brussels and wanted to meet with them to give them news of me.

My family learned during the month of July from Mme. Gutt (probably as a result of her meeting with her husband in Vichy around July 13) that I was now in Bloxham, and my mother said in her diary that she was able to write a letter which must now be in my hands. (I received it on August 20.) In my mother's diary is an addition written by Robert stating that I was in Conches on May 25 and that I had hooked myself up with some Belgian officers. He had received in addition a letter on June 19 from me dated June 9, in which I described having gone to Le Havre, having connected up with some Belgian officers going to Poitiers, being at the Hotel de France, and seeing M. Gutt and François. He mentioned that on June 20 he had received a registered letter from me written on June 14 telling him that the next letter to me should be sent to England.

On August 1, my mother received a letter written by Aunt Dorothy addressed to me in France and containing a certificate stating that I could stay with her in England. She found this letter in the letter box, though it had not gone through the post, and she had no idea who had slipped it through the mail slot.

On August 16 Marcel Peters, the chief scout with whom I worked for the lieutenant and the major, visited my parents, and he too described what he knew about me and of my stay with them from May 20 until June 15, which was the last time I saw them. He was very complimentary about me and said that I was a good friend—very helpful, hard-working, and cheerful.

On August 27 my mother sent a message to me in England, through the Red Cross; and on the same day she received a letter from a student at her school concerning me and containing a letter that I had written on June 11 to Lieutenant Lambion.

On August 29, my parents went to see the Lambions in Stockel, a suburb of Brussels, and their daughter then proceeded to describe many details of my adventure which they already knew: how I had connected with the officers in Rouen; how Lieutenant Colonel Tasnier had looked after me and sent me on my way to Le Havre. The Lambions described me as having been very depressed and very tired after a long bicycle trip, of my looking up the Belgian officers in the barracks in Rouen, then going on to Poitiers and looking for M. Gutt. They reported that while they were living some distance from Poitiers I went to visit them a number of times, that I had overheard a conversation between Belgian ministers concerning the forthcoming capitulation of the French Army, and that I had felt some obligation to warn them of this, and that—without actually breaking any confidences—I had managed to convey to them how serious the situation was, and that this had helped them to make a decision to leave for the South of France. They mentioned how, while I was in Poitiers, I tried everything possible to get a visa, and that M. Gutt was working very hard on my behalf to obtain this visa and that I had found François Gutt. They said some complimentary things about me: that I had a charming character and that I was supporting the morale of the others. The lieutenant said that I was a good friend, very helpful and cheerful.

On September 10 they again saw Mme. Gutt, who had come back from France, and she gave them two letters from François and Etienne Gutt containing a few words concerning me. From Etienne:

> I have received a letter from Francis de M. announcing the forthcoming arrival of François. For my holidays I had planned to bicycle to Cornwall but because of the absence of Gutt [his father] this prevented my carrying out this plan, and after a week spent with Francis (who is living with his aunt in Oxfordshire) I had been to the farm where he goes and I have learned how to ride a pony, to trot, and also to fall, and to drive a tractor. I am going to rejoin François in the near future.

And, in the letter from François:

> I have so much work that after four days I became ill and I had a terrible fever. Luckily I met Francis in Poitiers and he was very kind towards me. He was a good friend and I was very happy about it so as to avoid being reduced to the only company of ______________. When I learned that the French were going to sign an armistice I had only one idea and that is to leave with Francis and if possible with Janine and here we are now having left Bordeaux . . . . The crew of the boat has been absolutely wonderfully calm and concerned for the 1,500 refugees on board. We were received, at

> the English port, in an excellent reception center and then we were transferred to a concentration camp in London. Everybody was very kind and at last warm baths! We have seen a beautiful moon over the sea, the whole sea was like silver reflecting the moon.

On September 11 my parents had gone to visit Mme. Tasnier, who recounted her travels from Belgium into France, having left Brussels on the 10th of May, arriving in Rouen, finding me there, and offering me a bath and describing what they already knew. She described the sad circumstances under which her husband died. The Tasniers had learned of the capitulation of the Belgian Army in Rouen, and later in Bordeaux learned of the capitulation of the French. Colonel Tasnier was very depressed and sad about these events; this ate away at his health and he suddenly died.

On September 21, Mademoiselle Hamaïde, the headmistress of the school where my mother had volunteered for many years as a gym teacher, telephoned her to say that she had the opportunity of sending a letter to Portugal (which was a neutral country), and thus my mother was able to write a letter to me and one for her two sisters, which were forwarded to us in England.

On October 7 my mother learned from Mme. Gutt that "all the children are in very good health." The last entry on this topic was November 12, and it indicated that my mother, since October 7, had been sending letters through a number of different routes—letters which I eventually received. That ends the diary of my mother for 1940.

The next entry is dated July 1944, in which she reports that she has received a letter from me from Canada where I was training in the RAF and that the letter was dated in March.

APPENDIX B

Robert's 1940 Journey

IN 1999 I READ Robert's diary and discovered how many opportunities we had missed of meeting each other during these fateful weeks.

Four days after we had visited him in Ghent on May 13 his military unit boarded a train and went towards France.

He arrived at Abbeville on May 20, three days after I had gone through it, and found himself in the midst of a bombardment; the city itself was burning. They were ordered to abandon the train, and after that it was every man for himself.

Robert and a few friends found their way to Rouen and the Caserne Talandier army barracks on May 22, the very day I left Rouen for Conches with the officers. He characterized the Caserne Talandier as disgusting and a pigsty. I cannot disagree.

On the 23rd Robert made his way towards Conches (where I was at the time), but bypassed it because, as I mention in the text, it looked "too military." He and his friends made their way to Les Sables d'Olonne, where they arrived on June 2, the day after I arrived in Poitiers and found the Gutts. Their military unit was reorganized in a camp at that location, on the seacoast north of Bordeaux.

On June 15 he received two pounds from Aunt Dorothy in England, and on the 17th he sent a telegram to her inquiring about the possibility of "three places," as if he and his friends were contemplating going to England.

On June 19 Robert wrote a letter to me and to Aunts Dorothy and Cary, and on the 21st he received my letter that I had given to Roger Wattiez in Conches. On June 23, the date of the armistice between France and

Germany, Robert and the members of his unit became prisoners of the Germans and left their camp on the 24th. It seems they were under loose German supervision as they made their way north, but short of money and food.

This is the time that, through the Red Cross, my father, Mme. Gutt, and others made an attempt to get these medical students released from prisoner status and allow them to return to university. In the meantime they spent several weeks in various military barracks, under German control, with fairly light duties but short of food.

Finally, on July 18, they were freed, and Robert's objective now was to return to Brussels, but he encountered serious transportation problems. He went to Paris, stayed in some hotels, and finally arrived at home in Brussels on July 28. My parents found him sitting on a bench, in front of the house, on their return from the Boat Club.

APPENDIX C

My Family's Life under German Occupation, 1940 – 44

THROUGHOUT THE WAR I was fortunate in getting letters to and from my family. There was of course no direct mail between German-occupied Belgium and England, and therefore letters had to be sent through intermediaries in unoccupied countries. We were fortunate that we had friends in Switzerland, Portugal, and Sweden who were kind enough to either forward the actual letters, or copy them on a postcard or their own stationery. We were very grateful to Lily Österberg in Zurich, a former classmate of my mother's at the Royal Institute in Stockholm; Richard Blanc-Garin, a former classmate of Robert's then living in Lisbon; and Inger Degerman in Stockholm. On the average, I received a letter from my family every month, and often they took less than two or three weeks to reach me. They received my letters fairly regularly until 1944, when the British, in preparation for the Normandy invasion, closed off communication with neutral countries in Europe (including diplomatic bags) to insure secrecy of the dates and plans for the invasion. I later learned that my family had received no letter from me after January 1944, when I was still in Canada.

Since it was forbidden by both the British and German governments to communicate between England and German-occupied territory, one had to be very careful about what one wrote. For instance, it was vital that the German censors who read my letters not realize that they had been written in England, nor that my parents' letters were destined for England. My family would have been severely penalized, perhaps even arrested, if our forbidden communications had been discovered. The letters were often covered in colored stripes—the result of the censors' search for invisible writing. The British censors were more lenient and limited themselves to putting a notice in the envelope stating that it was illegal to communicate with enemy territory.

From their letters, I got a fairly good picture of my family's daily life. Their daily routines continued much as before the war. My parents continued their professional work. After my brother returned from German captivity at the end of July 1940, he resumed his medical school education, as did my sister Pauline. Every week they attended their gymnastic classes and went to the Boat Club to scull on the canal and swim. Both Robert and Pauline went on vacation, often camping with friends, and one winter they went skiing in France in the Jura mountains. They attended private dances and went to restaurants.

Their letters to me did not refer to the Germans or reveal much about the conditions of their lives. I had to intrepret and read between the lines. A reference to the high cost of food implied shortages and the black market. Every letter thanked me profusely for the food parcels I sent through the Red Cross, which were described as "extremely welcomed"—again, a clear reference to the food shortages of that time. Similarly, reference to an efficient stove in one room of the house suggested a shortage of coal, and so on. Most of the letters described friends they had seen, their happiness at getting my news, their daily life, an occasional vacation, and the success or failure of Pauline and Robert in their medical school exams, as well as passing along greetings and good wishes from some of my classmates whom they had seen. While I was still at school and college until the end of 1942, I could be fairly explicit about my life, but, as mentioned earlier, when I joined the Royal Air Force I had to be very careful and use euphemisms, such as referring "to the same job that my cousin Roger had done in the past," and saying that "I began to take courses in stenography." It became, as time went on, the code word we used to refer to any Air Force activities.

Three important events were, however, communicated in their letters during those years. After one year of occupation, in the summer of 1941, my family's car was seized by the Germans, and from then on they could only travel on bicycle or by public transportation. In November 1941 the

University of Brussels, where Robert and Pauline were students, was shut down for the rest of the war. The Germans wanted to have pro-German professors appointed to the faculties, and the president chose instead to close the university. This, of course, seriously complicated my brother and sister's studies: some professors and doctors, however, arranged private lectures in small groups in their homes, and also the Catholic University of Louvain generously opened its doors to students of Brussels, irrespective of their religious affiliations or lack thereof.

In 1943 I received a letter indicating that the family had been scared by the expectation that Robert and Pauline would "have to go on a long journey," but that it had been avoided because they were medical students. This was, I believed at the time, a disguised reference to the possibility of their being deported to Germany as slave laborers or perhaps to a concentration camp. A belief that I later confirmed after the war.

In July 1942, Pauline wrote in a letter that I received a month later that all the Jews in Brussels had to wear a Star of David with a J on their clothing, that they had to be home by 8:00 P.M., and that they could no longer practice medicine, law, pharmacy, or other professions. They were not allowed to sit down in the streetcars, and if they had not identified themselves as Jews they were deported to the Belgian coast, where no one else was allowed. (In retrospect, I wonder if they were not sent instead to concentration camps in Germany.) I was surprised that the German censors let part of this letter through.

Notwithstanding their letters, it was only after the liberation of Brussels in September 1944, and especially beginning with my visit in March 1945, that a clearer picture of the family's life during the war emerged.

Their primary goal was, of course, survival. They avoided, for the most part, getting in trouble with the German authorities. They did not actively participate in the Resistance. (My mother convinced herself that it was a good thing I had gone to England, because she feared that, had I remained in Belgium, I would have joined the Resistance, and probably have been arrested and possibly executed.) On one occasion, however, Pauline learned that Reichs-Marshal Hermann Goering, the head of the German Luftwaffe, was going to be in Brussels, so she bicycled to alert someone whom she knew was in radio contact with London, and the information was duly passed on. As a result, Brussels was indeed bombed, but Goering had already left.

The most serious problem, apart from possible arrest, deportation, and execution, was avoiding starvation. My family, like everyone else, depended heavily on the black market or friends. One friend who was very helpful and generous was Mme. Gutt, Etienne's mother, who stayed in Brussels throughout the war. As mentioned earlier, she and Etienne used our communication channels through Switzerland very effectively. She had a large garden and she often gave my parents some fruits and vegetables. Periodically they also bicycled into the countryside and bought some food from farmers. The challenge was to get back to their house without being arrested by the Germans, because this activity was forbidden.

As mentioned before, bicycles were a crucial means of transportation during the war and they were often stolen. In fact, my brother's bicycle was stolen, and my family tried to retrieve the bicycle that he and I had separately abandoned in France in 1940 to replace it. Taking public transportation could be very dangerous. The streetcars on the Avenue Louise where we lived were often stopped and searched by German policemen looking for armed patriots. Pauline told me that in that event one had to be very careful to secure one's pockets, to avoid another passenger slipping his gun into your pocket, thus causing you to be arrested and executed instead of him.

My family did listen to the BBC, which was of course a risk and would have had serious consequences if it had been discovered. The BBC and my letters did help them to keep up their morale and hope in their ultimate liberation. The food packages I sent through the Red Cross also helped. Other members of the family in England also sent these packages generously during the war. A variety of food was listed on the application: sardines, chocolate, and other items. I tried to vary their diet and was successful to a large extent, even though I did not have absolute control over what was in fact sent. At the end of the war I learned, to my surprise, that many of the more recent packages they had received contained only sardines. They had sardines coming out of their ears! My mother often commented in her letters that the packages had come in very handy at some of the gatherings with friends celebrating Christmas, Easter, New Year's, or birthdays.

Across the street from our house was a Gestapo headquarters in which arrested patriots were interrogated. Pauline told me how appalling it was to hear the screams of people being tortured during the night. I wonder whether that is where my classmate, Arnaud Fraiteur, was interrogated, tortured, and killed. He and two others had assassinated Paul Collin, an infamous Belgian collaborator, but in making his getaway Arnaud had to abandon his bicycle, and in Belgium bicycles were registered and had a number plate. He was tracked down and arrested. The other participants escaped thanks to Arnaud, who even under appalling torture did not reveal their identity.

The fear of arrest was constant, whether for buying on the black market, listening to the BBC, or communicating with an enemy country like England. As the war continued the Germans became more nasty. In the early part of the occupation, the German Army was most prominent, and they had a military code of conduct that was fairly correct. As the years went by, though, the SS and the Gestapo became more prominent and vindictive, as the Resistance became more active and as the Germans began to realize that they might lose the war.

I have mentioned elsewhere the fact that my parents were Freemasons, and that Belgian fascists and collaborators were assassinating members of this order. One ironic episode related to this was recounted to me by my family. The Freemasons' temples had been closed by the Germans when they occupied Brussels. However, on one occasion, they organized an exhibition in one of them for the purpose of discrediting Freemasons and others, such as the Belgian government in London. They displayed some of the Freemasons' emblems and various photographs, including those of Belgian ministers in the government in England. My parents went to the exhibition, and in fact saw many of their friends, colleagues, and fellow Freemasons, although no one acknowledged knowing anyone else. At some point during the exhibition a man started shouting, "I think this is disgusting! We are surrounded by Freemasons who have come back to their temple and to look at this exhibition!" People acted surprised and wondered who he could possibly be talking about! A few days later, Mme. Gutt came to visit my parents in a very agitated state, because in the exhibition there was a photograph of her husband, alleging that he was a Freemason. She said, "You know, Dr. and Mme. de Marneffe, that it is a total falsehood." My parents did indeed know that, because they were Freemasons, a fact she presumably did not know.

I was on the Atlantic on September 3, 1944 when I heard on the radio that Brussels had been liberated. A few days later I landed in England, and soon afterward I began sending and receiving letters from Brussels. My first letter to my family was transmitted by M. Gutt, who was about to return to Brussels with the Belgian government. Shortly after that I got a letter from my mother and from my brother describing the liberation of Brussels. Robert also confirmed that the last news of me had been received in January 1944—hence their worry. Their happiness and relief at the departure of the Germans and the arrival of British troops was almost impossible to describe. For a whole week they took to the streets, mixing with all the troops, basking in the joy of the liberation, admiring and in awe of the huge equipment—the tanks and the trucks—and inhaling the smell of English cigarettes in the street.

Gradually, normal postal service was restored between Belgium and England, and I was able to hear even more about their life during the occupation. Robert had become engaged to a fellow medical student, Claire Foulon, someone he had known for two years, and I received a long letter from my mother in response to one of mine, in which I had given her a summary of my life since leaving home in 1940. In her letter she in turn gave me the details of her life. At the risk of duplication, I have included her letter in its entirety at the end of this appendix.

The fact that I continued to be unable to go to Brussels was a great frustration to my family and to me. I could only go if I got leave from the Royal Air Force. The main problem was that there was no regular transportation from England to the Continent. Some of my friends had managed by showing up at an airfield to "hitchhike" their way out on aircraft and visit Brussels for a day or two. Otherwise, the best solution was to be a "carrier" or messenger on a diplomatic mission and carry some packages from London for one of the newly reestablished ministries in Brussels. That is what I eventually succeeded in doing in March 1945.

Though Brussels and then the whole of Belgium was liberated, the war continued to affect my family. As the concentration camps in Germany were liberated, senior medical students in Brussels were recruited to provide medical assistance to the liberated inmates. Robert and Pauline volunteered, as well as Claire Foulon, Robert's fiancée. Robert was assigned to Bergen-Belsen, and he was affected throughout his life by what he found there. He was deeply affected by the fact that inmates continued to die by the hundreds day after day, in spite of all the medical treatments provided. Their condition was irreversible. This was a profoundly demoralizing discovery for a senior medical student. Pauline was assigned and went to the Belgian Commission for Repatriation in Augsburg, Germany, before going on to the Dachau concentration camp to repatriate some inmates.

[Letter dated 16th October 1944]

Francis, my darling.

With what feelings of deep affection I read your nice long letter received this morning dated Sept 30th telling me in brief how you had spent the years since our separation. Thank you so much. I am longing to hug you in my arms and feel that you are safe. I admire the motives which made you take up aviation. I understand you. At your age I should have done likewise. We never received your letter explaining it all. At the time Papa was quite heartbroken. Roger had gone and Hilgrove.[1] He grieved as though he would never see you again. He has been the hardest hit of us all by the war. You see, he has had the responsibility of keeping food in the house, of making both ends meet, of rushing about for ration cards, etc. He has been wonderful in his self-abnegation. Robert and Pauline have not felt the war in the same way as we have, although at times they were threatened with deportation. As medical students they always managed to

[1] Hilgrove Teale was my first cousin, the brother of Roger and Meg, and was a Royal Air Force observer who was shot down over the Mediterranean during the invasion of North Africa in 1942.

escape. They managed to carry on their studies under great difficulties because the University of Brussels was closed and the professors were forbidden by the Germans to give lectures or continue to give instruction to the students. In spite of this, clandestine lectures were given. Pauline had a very hard year in 1942. In order to pass three "candidatures" [preclinical years] she had to go to the University of Louvain. It meant taking a very early train, 4 A.M., and getting back late, 9 P.M. some days. In addition to this she worked. It was very tiring, and when the period arrived for cramming for the exam she overworked and failed. After ten days rest she worked again for the second session and passed, but she was a wreck and developed first tracheitis, then asthma. The latter, though very much better as well as her general condition, is not quite cured yet. We discovered that Tippit [our cat] brought on attacks, besides dust and dewy weather, and poor Puss is banished from upstairs and his comfortable life on cushions and condemned to living in the lower regions. Pauline still has treatment for her asthma.

I will now try to tell you a little about our life and its grey monotony during the occupation, but I must say we always kept up heart and never doubted of ultimate victory. Looking back on that fateful 15th May I still see you in my mind turning the corner of the Rue Emile Claus. I still hear you saying, "Pourvu que cela ne dure pas trop longtemps." ["Let us hope it does not last too long."] How could I let you go like that? I asked myself that question many times in the following weeks before I knew you were safe with Aunt Dot, especially when we learnt that nothing had been organized and no reception prepared for the thousands of young boys who, like you, obeyed the Government's call. Papa, Pol, and I went to the "Garage" [Boat Club] that afternoon you left; in thought we followed you. "Now you would be at such and such a place, now you would be nearing Ghent, etc." we kept saying.

I have kept a little notebook in which I jotted down how we traced you. The first news was from M. Charles [Marly], who had seen and spoken to you at Roulers, then Marcel Peters brought us news, later Lt. Lambion and Mme. Tasnier. Then a letter from François Gutt to his father and shown us by his mother. Someone, unknown, also put a letter in our letter box from Tante Dot addressed to you which was to enable you to get your passport. In July we knew for certain through Etienne's mother that you were safe and with Tante Dot. Added to our anxiety for you was our worry about Robert. We thought he was on his way home when we discovered he was a prisoner at Auvours, in a huge camp. Papa moved heaven and earth to try to get him out and back here. Etienne's mother also did her best and finally he was released together with other medical students, and after staying some days in Paris, which he had managed to reach one way or the other, we found him one evening, July 28, sitting on a bench in front of our house waiting for us to come home. Thus, our minds were at rest concerning you and Robert for the time being. I liked to think of you happy in England, at an English school, doing what you had so often longed to do. I did not know then how long the separation would be, and I consoled myself because you were safe from unknown evils and by the thought that the war would be over before you were old enough to fight. Although we missed you, as time went on it was a relief that you were not here, for you would never have been able to keep inactive and calm. In 1941 and the following years the arrests made by the Germans were continual and numerous. For hiding and helping [Allied] aviators people were shot. I know of a boy who is doing hard labor in Germany for having told a wounded airman where he could get his injuries attended to. Then there was a league of young students who with other patriots assassinated Belgian traitors. The prisons were full of prisoners. Hundreds have been tortured and shot or hung. We lived in uncertainty and dread. We often saw prisoners brought to the Gestapo across the road. We saw many taken away in lorries or prison vans. The goings on there must have been dreadful. An unexpected ring at the street door might be agents of the Gestapo or military police come to investigate, and woe to those who still owned firearms, who listened to the B.B.C., who possessed a copy of the "Libre Belgique" or [other] clandestine papers. In the dead of night these often took place. Yes, I was glad you were safe from the Gestapo.

Before the Germans entered Brussels Papa took the precaution of taking down my brass shingle (from the wall of the house). I am glad he did. Thanks to this the attention of the Gestapo was never drawn to the fact that I was English. I lived all through the occupation ignored and unmolested, avoiding scrupulously all contact with the enemy. Once I was fined 100 francs for "corresponding with an enemy country via a neutral." It was for a letter I had written to you through Lily Österberg. I got Papa to go and pay it without discussion. There were many vexations. Latterly, and even at earlier periods, trams were stopped by an armed force. Everyone was turned out and the men, hands uplifted, were searched. At other times women's handbags were ransacked, identity cards examined, parcels opened. Several times bicycles were requisitioned on the roads. The last days of the occupation they were simply taken. Pedestrians were very good about warning you. They warned boys eligible for deportation too when the Germans were busy arresting people in the road.

The food problem was most acute the first two years of war. It was in 1940-41 that people got thin. We tried to live on our rations and considered it unpatriotic to have recourse to the black market. Later on we had no scruples in this matter and spent fortunes on food. The sardines and other parcels you in England sent us were a great help. They were more than nourishment, they were a moral support and a link between us and you. The hospitals at this period were full of people suffering from anemia and heart trouble from undernourishment. Many died daily. You were bound to in about three weeks time with only your rations to live on. Many people went into hospital for as long as they were allowed to stay, generally three or four days in order to get food and warmth. I cannot say that we have suffered much for want of food except during the period I am writing about. No fat of any sort, no potatoes, insufficient rations in bread, very little meat. Poor people collected the horse-chestnuts in the Avenue and ground them to make flour. I have never felt such an affection and respect for potatoes as I did for those we fetched at a risk from Meysse with our bicycles and those Robert and Pauline smuggled by boat from Humbeek. By risk I mean the risks of being caught and fined and the potatoes confiscated. By degrees we got some provisions into the house which would keep against bad days. These I saved up jealously and meted out only when absolutely necessary. A great deal was done for the poor by the Red Cross and other organizations in the way of distributing soup, dinners, biscuits, vitamins, sardines. Many people went without meat for long periods at a time. We have rarely been without, although we only had small quantities. Nearly everybody trafficked. Thanks to this the public health in 1942-43 was better than in the preceding years.

Certain newspaper articles published in England have made quite a stir in Brussels. According to them we lacked nothing and lived and fed luxuriously while the English were rationed for our sakes. It is entirely a mistake. If the English were so well received, so well fed by us on their arrival, it often entailed great sacrifice on the part of the Belgians, who saved up and deprived themselves in order to have something to offer on the great day of liberation. We are again going through a difficult period just now and have been since September, but there are signs of improvement.

There, Francis, darling, I have given you a sketch of our life during the occupation. We were fortunate in being able to keep the wireless and to carry on at the E.M.M.G. [the professional school my parents founded and ran]. The latter kept our minds off a little of the situation, and the radio was an immense moral support and encouragement. Listening in to the B.B.C. was of course forbidden—that made it still more appreciated.

I thought there was a ring of sadness in your letter, my darling. Was it disappointment at not being able to do what you had hoped? Cheer up. There is still so much to be done in the world, perhaps something more useful even for humanity than what you had hoped to do. It was so nice to know what you thought about these questions, for you know I am an idealist myself.

October 22. I began this letter, as you will see, several days ago. Yesterday John Unett [an officer I knew in Canada] joined us at the Boat Club and spent the afternoon and evening with us. He showed me your last letter to him, in which you said you were an Instructor, and I hope soon to hear more about it.

We are all very sorry about John Arthur[2] [Loveday] and Anthony [Schuster],[3] and I hope sincerely the latter is safe. Please tell Uncle Arthur

---

[2] John Arthur (Loveday), my first cousin, the son of Uncle Arthur and Aunt Mamie, was killed in the British Army in the Italian Campaign in 1944. Previously he had been taken prisoner by the Germans behind the German lines in North Africa and he and seven other officers were due to be executed. They were lined up in front of the firing squad and John

and Aunt Whisky [her sister Cary, grandmother of Anthony] how deeply we all take part and sympathize in their sorrow.

Melle Lambion came the other morning to get news of you. The Mahaux, Donvil, Chiliade, Piraux, and Mme. Collin have also been.

There are very few Canadians here in Brussels. I have not met any yet. If I do I shall remember your request and do my best. [I was so grateful for the hospitality I had found in Canada that I asked my parents to be very hospitable to Canadian troops.] Robert wants to know whether Aunt Wh. has received his letter and have you received Papa's? Robert and Mouche are engaged to be married. They told us a few days ago. I cannot say it was a surprise. They have known one another for two years and will I hope be very happy. Now I will end, otherwise my letter will not get off.

We will send our love to you and all. Tante Jeanne and Tante Maria too.

I remain as always your devoted mother.

•

---

dropped to the ground as they opened fire—the others were killed but he survived. The Germans kicked him to make sure he was dead and stole his watch. After dark, he managed to walk back to British lines.

[3] Anthony Schuster, my first cousin, grandson of Aunt Cary Schuster, as previously mentioned in the text, was first posted as missing, then confirmed killed, as a captain in the Welsh Guards in Italy, in 1944.

APPENDIX D

The Belgian Government's Dilemma: Loyalty to King or Country?

Here and there in my personal story, I have referred to political and strategic decisions of the Belgian government concerning the deteriorating military situation in Belgium and France in May and June of 1940. My own fate depended to a great extent upon the events on the battlefield, as well as on the decisions of the Belgian government. This became especially relevant when I reached Poitiers and became very close to and dependent on Monsieur Gutt and his son François. My earlier references to the Belgian government and its decisions were based on pieces of information I gleaned from occasional conversations with Monsieur Gutt, but mostly from François. But I obviously did not know the whole story.

However, it is now possible to describe in greater detail the sequence of events which determined the eventual decisions of the government. Many books have addressed the issue, but of particular interest to me have been four of them: *Souvenirs sans Retouches* ("Unedited Memories"), by Marcel Henri Jaspar, published in 1968; *Combats Inacheves* ("Incomplete Combats") by Paul Henry Spaak, published in 1969; *La Belgique aux Carrefours* ("Belgium at the Crossroads") by Camille Gutt, published in 1971; and *Camille Gutt–1940-1945: Les Finances et La Guerre* ("Finances and the War") by Jean-François Crombois published in 1999. The first three of these books were published by Fayard; the last by Quorum-Ceges.

On May 10, 1940, when Germany invaded Belgium, the King assumed direct command of the Belgian forces. This is required under the Belgian Constitution, which specifies that in addition to being the head of state, the King is also the Commander-in-Chief of the Belgian forces in the field. It did not take long, after the German invasion, for the military situation to deteriorate, and although it was not publicly announced to avoid worrying the population, it is clear from the record that the Germans were scoring military successes. As early as May 12, the King was pessimistic about the outcome of the battle because the German forces had broken through at Sedan, in France, and in subsequent days they seemed to be driving, not towards Paris, but towards Abbeville, closer to the Atlantic coast, thereby threatening to split the Allied forces into a northern and southern part, and encircle the Allied forces in the north, where the Belgian and British armies were.

Initially, on May 10, the government and the King had seen eye to eye concerning the political and the military situation. But on May 16, the ministers became very concerned about some statements the King had made. He seemed to be anticipating the surrender of the Belgian Army. In that event the ministers emphasized the importance of the King's not falling into the hands of the Germans, and remaining in free territory. The ministers were very disturbed that the King had a different notion of his responsibilities. He placed his responsibility as Commander-in-Chief of the Belgian forces on a higher plane than that of the head of state.

Thus began the profound disagreement between the King and his ministers. As the military situation deteriorated further, the ministers continued to urge upon the King the examples of King Haakon of Norway and Queen Wilhelmina of the Netherlands, who had left their homelands and established themselves in England to continue the war. Their urgings, however, proved to be of no avail, and the King issued an order of the day to the troops stating that, whatever their fate, he would share it. This was a statement designed to extract from the troops every ounce of energy and fighting spirit, and to counteract the German propaganda leaflets dropped over the Belgian troops alleging that their leaders would abandon them. The King decided, for legitimate military reasons and with timely notice to the French and British commanders, that there was no further point in the Belgian army fighting, and so, on May 28, he ordered the army to lay down its arms. Yet because he allowed himself to be taken prisoner by the Germans, Article 82 of the Belgian Constitution was invoked by the government: If the King is unable to reign, the government assumes the responsibilities of the head of state. Certain statements the King had made to the government had indicated that, after the surrender of the Belgian Army, he would probably try to form a new government in Belgium. To do so would have required, again under the constitution, the countersignature of at least one of his ministers. He had in fact asked for a blank Royal Decree from the government, which would have permitted him to form the new government. His request was unanimously denied.

The Belgian prime minister, Hubert Pierlot,was in Paris on May 27, and had meetings with French political figures, including Paul Reynaud, the French prime minister. Pierlot knew that Reynaud would make a speech on the following day, and that is how the world learned of the capitulation of the Belgian Army. The following day, Pierlot also made a speech, in which he dissociated the government from the actions of the King and released Belgians from their oath of allegiance to the King.

As the German Army continued to advance into France, by arrangement with the French authorities Poitiers was selected as the temporary seat of the Belgian government. As the hitherto unthinkable began to sink in as a likely event, namely the defeat of the French Army and capitulation of France, the Belgian government had to think about its future actions. A critical event was the speech of Paul Reynaud in June, which prepared France and the world for a military defeat. Reynaud made a desperate appeal to the United States and President Roosevelt for immediate assistance in what he called the crucial battle for Western civilization.

The Belgian government began to actively discuss its future in the light of a French defeat. Gutt and Jaspar were, from the outset, clearly and outspokenly in favor of the government going to England. Both of them believed that the defeat of France was not the end of the war, and expected England to continue to fight Germany. The British government offered at first twenty-four, then eighteen, places on a seaplane and later a destroyer to take members of the Belgian government to England. Because so many of the ministers had large families, and because they believed that to establish a government in England they had to take their large staff with them (300 of them!), the government refused the offer. The ministers decided that they should all stay together to remain the legal government of Belgium, and this sense of solidarity became their guiding principle.

It became clear on June 17 that the French government wanted an armistice, since they had sent a plenipotentiary to German headquarters. That is also the day that the Belgian ministers, François, and I moved from Poitiers to Bordeaux. The question before the government was still whether to go to England and continue the war, or whether to follow the example of the French government and give up the fight. There were some powerful opinions that supported the idea of following the French government's lead. However, Gutt and Jaspar continued to be very strong advocates for continuing the war and going to England, while Spaak, the foreign minister, and Pierlot, the prime minister, were not yet convinced.

On June 18, the Belgian government decided not to go to England but to follow the example of the French government. That is the point at which Jaspar became completely disenchanted with the decision and unilaterally decided to go to England. His colleagues were stunned when they discovered that he had abandoned the government (as François, Janine, and I were when we saw him on board our ship), and as a result the government withdrew his portfolio and he ceased to be a minister. Jaspar did not reveal this fact on his arrival in England, and he tried to raise the flag of Free Belgium à la Charles de Gaulle. Apparently he was not aware that he was no longer a minister.

The Belgian government, after a short stay in Sauveterre, went to Vichy to be near the French government, in order to deal with the two million Belgian refugees in France (fully one-quarter of the Belgian population). The French government, now under the influence of Germany, was hostile towards them, and so the Belgian government wanted to arrange their repatriation to Belgium. Gutt continued to emphasize the importance of continuing the war and going to England, and in fact had only remained behind out of solidarity with Pierlot. The whole government was profoundly depressed, as is evident from the memoirs of Spaak and Gutt. Spaak and Pierlot also admitted to having made a terrible mistake when, after the capitulation of France, they approached the King, through intermediaries, to find out whether they would be allowed to return to Belgium and whether he wished the government to return to

Brussels. By that time, the King had decided not to form a new government under German occupation. This was the result of the opinions of three distinguished constitutional jurists he had consulted. While they upheld his view that his surrender of the Belgian Army and his remaining in Belgium were not unconstitutional, his status as a German prisoner precluded his taking political action or decision as King, such as forming a new government or responding to Pierlot and Spaak's question.

Gutt was visited by his wife Claire in Vichy after a horrendous journey from Brussels, and she strongly supported his decision to go to England. But in a final desperate attempt to avoid a permanent breach between the King and his ministers, and thinking he might have a better chance than Pierlot and Spaak in convincing the King, Gutt wrote the King a long letter asking for an audience to convince him to come to England, or at least give his blessing to the government continuing the war in England. Madame Gutt, on her return to Brussels, delivered the letter to the palace. Gutt's request was turned down on the grounds that, as a prisoner, the King could make no political decisions. The King's reply was hand-delivered by his Chief of Staff to Mme. Gutt in Brussels.

The rebuff by the King forced Pierlot and Spaak finally to make the decision that the government, or as many ministers as were willing, should go to England, and act as a government-in-exile on the side of Britain for the duration of the war. All the ministers who decided not to go to England were forced to resign to avoid their being available to countersign political acts of the King. When this was done only four ministers remained: De Vleeschauwer, Pierlot, Spaak, and Gutt, who finally got his wish.

Gutt began his journey to England on August 1, 1940. He went through Spain and Portugal and thence to England, where he arrived on August 9. The understanding between Gutt, Spaak, and Pierlot was that a month after Gutt left Vichy the other two would follow. In fact, they left Vichy on August 24. They were arrested when they crossed into Spain by the Spanish authorities, who wanted to stop them from going to England. At this time, of course, Spain was under the control of General Franco, the dictator who had won the Spanish Civil War with German and Italian help. He was pro-German, although he managed throughout the war to keep Spain officially neutral and avoid being invaded by the German forces. Eventually, Spaak and Pierlot managed, with the help of people in Spain, to engineer their escape and finally they too reached England, on October 24.

Their arrival completed the Belgian government-in-exile in London. With great courage, determination, and wisdom these four ministers insured the future freedom of a sovereign Belgium by waging war on the side of Britain. As Gutt had so often reminded his colleagues, it was essential for Belgium to join Britain *before* the battle. Churchill acknowledged as much when he said to Gutt on his arrival in England in August, with shining eyes illuminating his fighting demeanor, reaching out towards victory, "My boy, you were jolly well right. You arrived in time, just before the battle. But what a battle!"[1] And indeed it was.

[1] Quoted in *La Belgique aux Carrefours,* Camille Gutt's memoirs (Fayard, 1971).

ABOUT THE AUTHOR

After graduating from medical school in London in 1950, Francis de Marneffe went to the United States for further training, expecting to eventually return to England. Once there, however, he was attracted by the professional opportunities in the Boston area, where he settled in 1952.

After training as a psychiatrist at Massachusetts General Hospital and McLean Hospital, Dr. de Marneffe worked full-time at the latter institution, and in 1962 became its General Director, a position he held until 1987. From 1986 to 1989 he was President and CEO of McLean Health Services, Inc.

From 1990 to 1994, in a post-retirement full-time job, Dr. de Marneffe served as Medical Director of Holly Hill Mental Health Services in Raleigh, North Carolina. During this time he was also on the faculties of Duke University and the University of North Carolina.

Since 1994 Dr. de Marneffe has again been based at McLean Hospital as General Director Emeritus and Senior Consulting Psychiatrist. Throughout his career he has also been on the faculty of Harvard Medical School. He serves as President of the Friends of McLean and is engaged in private practice and teaching. He swims, plays tennis, sculls in the annual Head of the Charles Regatta, and has run seven Boston Marathons.

Dr. de Marneffe has three children by his first wife, Nancy Edmonds—two daughters with PhDs in Clinical Psychology and one son with a PhD in Philosophy—and eight grandchildren. He and his wife, Barbara, travel extensively. They live mainly in Cambridge, Massachusetts, and summer in Dublin, New Hampshire.